Settler Military Politics

Series Editors: Victoria M. Basham and Sarah Bulmer

The Critical Military Studies series welcomes original thinking on the ways in which military power works within different societies and geopolitical arenas

Militaries are central to the production and dissemination of force globally but the enduring legacies of military intervention are increasingly apparent at the societal and personal bodily levels as well, demonstrating that violence and war-making function on multiple scales. At the same time, the notion that violence is as an appropriate response to wider social and political problems transcends militaries: from private security, to seemingly 'non-military' settings such as fitness training and schooling, the legitimisation and normalisation of authoritarianism and military power occurs in various sites. This series seeks original, high-quality manuscripts and edited volumes that engage with such questions of how militaries, militarism and militarisation assemble and disassemble worlds touched and shaped by violence in these multiple ways. It will showcase innovative and interdisciplinary work that engages critically with the operation and effects of military power and provokes original questions for researchers and students alike.

Available Titles:

Forthcoming:

Settler Military Politics

Militarisation and the Aesthetics of War Commemoration

FEDERICA CASO

EDINBURGH
University Press

A mamma che mi ha insegnato a combattere
A Nicola che mi ha mostrato la resilienza
A Giulia che mi aiuta a capire

Edinburgh University Press is one of the leading university presses in the UK. We publish academic books and journals in our selected subject areas across the humanities and social sciences, combining cutting-edge scholarship with high editorial and production values to produce academic works of lasting importance. For more information visit our website: edinburghuniversitypress.com

Edinburgh University Press Ltd
13 Infirmary Street
Edinburgh, EH1 1LT

First published in hardback by Edinburgh University Press 2024

Typeset in 11/13 ITC Giovanni Std by
IDSUK (DataConnection) Ltd

A CIP record for this book is available from the British Library

ISBN 978-1-3995-2546-6 (hardback)
ISBN 978-1-3995-2547-3 (paperback)
ISBN 978-1-3995-2548-0 (webready PDF)
ISBN 978-1-3995-2549-7 (epub)

CONTENTS

FIGURES

ACKNOWLEDGEMENTS

I loved writing this book despite its challenges, including a global pandemic, unemployment and relocation to a new city. I am grateful to the humans and pets who supported me in this journey and helped me find the strength and motivation to finish this project. Writing a book was a childhood dream that came true, and I am proud that this is the book that came from that dream.

I wish to acknowledge that this book was written on the stolen lands of the Turrbal, Jagera and Wurundjeri peoples. May this book assist them and First Nations Australians fight the plight of colonisation.

I thank my family for their support while I chased my dreams to the other side of the world. Being so far from them is never easy and it was particularly hard during the COVID pandemic. Their love and consistency are a real motivator to carry on when things get hard.

I am very thankful to my partner Jamie for moving to Melbourne with me and for his patience and love while I was working on this book. He is as solid as a rock and as calming as a forest. I am also grateful to our kittens, Draco and Zuzubel, for keeping things light, fun and bearable.

Deep thanks go to my PhD supervisor at the University of Queensland, Roland Bleiker. Roland saw this project begin and develop into a PhD thesis, and then morph and become what it is in this book. He taught me the elegance of intellectual kindness and the power of consistency and discipline. I am forever grateful for his wisdom and support.

My gratitude also goes to La Trobe University and colleagues in the Department of Politics, Media and Philosophy, particularly to Dirk Tomsa for helping me prioritise this project while contending with the demands of starting a new job in a new city, and to Emily

Foley for her friendship. Also, thanks to La Trobe University for funding to purchase images and tie up this project.

I wish to thank the editors of Advances in Critical Military Studies, Sarah Bulmer and Victoria Basham, and the commissioning editor Ersev Ersoy, for working with me with kindness and dedication on the production of this book.

Introduction: Settler Colonial Manoeuvres

We still know very little about the weaving of militarism, militarisation and settler colonialism. Postcolonial scholarship has advanced our knowledge and understanding of militarism and militarisation in colonial and postcolonial societies, but its insights only go so far in settler colonial contexts like Australia. Settler colonialism is a specific manifestation of colonialism whereby an imperial power expands its frontiers over Indigenous land and establishes an offshoot of imperial society. As this offshoot society becomes independent from the empire, it dispossesses Indigenous communities and replaces them with a settler society. A peculiarity of settler societies is that they lack a formal end of colonisation where power is returned to colonised Indigenous people. Instead, they are characterised by continuous efforts to normalise, shape and ultimately legitimise the settler society at the expense of Indigenous sovereignty. In this book, I tackle how militarism and militarisation contribute to the dispossession of Indigenous people and the consolidation of the settler state and society.

I began delving into this subject when I made Australia my new home and consequently became involved in the settler colonial endeavour of this country as an immigrant. I came to Australia authorised by the settler state to pursue a PhD on visual politics and militarisation in liberal societies. Back then, I knew very little about Australia, settler colonialism and Indigenous politics, and I thought that I could use Australia as a novel case study to develop my research and contribute to the literature. In fact, despite the critical mass in Australian International Relations departments, Australia remains at the periphery of International Relations. But Australia is not just another liberal society, and it soon became clear to me that this country has its own story of militarism and militarisation that intersects with the specificities of its ongoing settler colonial politics. I started taking this seriously when, in 2017, I conducted fieldwork research at the Australian War Memorial, Australia's main cultural institution of war. And this is where I wish to begin. To bring you with me into the story that led me to write this book, I reproduce three vignettes from my fieldwork.

Notes from Fieldwork

Canberra, 24 April 2017: Today is my first visit at the Australian War Memorial. I finally get to see this imposing building that collects and curates the memory and history of modern warfare in Australia, and functions as both war museum and memorial. Today I will focus on the galleries and tomorrow, I will attend Anzac Day, Australia's national war commemoration. Anzac Day takes its name from the Anzacs, the soldiers who landed in Gallipoli, modern Turkey, in 1915 as part of the Allied forces against the Ottoman Empire. The Anzacs are celebrated as national heroes for proving the valour of Australians to the international community. ANZAC is an acronym for the Australian and New Zealander Army Corps, but in Australia, it is a common word used to identify the Australian soldier, the martial national spirit and civic valour. Australian politicians often talk about the Anzac Spirit to praise the deeds of citizens and evoke national pride. I find this use of military language and heritage to steer the nation worth my attention. And I am not the only one. There is a thriving scholarship on all things Anzac, and some Australian scholars have warned about the militarisation of Australian history.

Today, my task is to become familiar with the space of the Memorial before starting the process of data collection tomorrow. I walk through the galleries of the War Memorial observing the collection and reading the vignettes. The first gallery is dedicated to the First World War. It has just been renovated for the centenary commemoration of the war. It is a modern gallery with interactive screens and evocative background sounds. There is some interesting art on the walls, including a massive painting of the Anzacs landing in Gallipoli by George Lambert. It must have taken him ages to paint it! The Second World War gallery is less conspicuous, and I make my way through it quickly. There are more swastika symbols that I was ready to digest. On my way to the gallery dedicated to contemporary conflicts and peace missions, I encounter something that I did not expect: a special exhibition on the service of Indigenous people in the Australian Defence. This exhibition is titled *For Country, For Nation*.

For Country, For Nation is engrossing. I do not know much about the service of Indigenous people in the Australian Defence, and it is great that I came across this exhibition. *For Country, For Nation* is a celebration of Indigenous military service. It is thematically curated, and the chronology is elusive. It is hard to piece together the history and politics, but the message is that Indigenous people served for the love of their country (settler Australia?), to gain an education and skills, and to prove their valour to the nation. The exhibition hints at a ban on Indigenous service but is vague and does not provide information about how Indigenous people managed to serve in spite of it. Overall, as the title of the exhibition suggests, they served for their country and for the nation. It's all hunky-dory.

But I find most surprising that Indigenous people fought for colonial Australia while it was still part of the British Empire and while the Frontier Wars of colonisation were still ongoing. The end of the Frontier Wars between British settlers and Indigenous warriors resisting colonisation is often set in the late 1930s and early 1940s, well past the First World War and well into the Second World War. What were the incentives for Indigenous people to serve in the settler military while they were still being massacred by the settlers to take over their land? I will dig more into this later tonight.

The exhibition spotlights some Indigenous soldiers. For example, there is a panel dedicated to Kate Walker (also known as Oodgeroo Noonuccal) who enlisted to pursue an education and gain employable skills. Oodgeroo Noonuccal is also one of Australia's most famous Aboriginal poets. There is the profile of William Cooper who, in 1938, led a delegation from the Australian Aborigines' League to the German Consulate in Melbourne to protest the injustice against Jewish people in Germany. The Australian Aborigines' League was primarily intended to tackle Aboriginal discrimination at home, but extended its fight for social justice to the Jewish people in Germany. As I keep walking, I find a room, almost completely empty, dedicated to Captain Reginald Saunders. On one wall there is a life-size photo of Captain Saunders posing and smiling with other soldiers. He is the only Black man in the photo. Next to this enlarged photo there is a quote by Saunders that reads:

I never fought for anybody but Australia. I always was loyal to my Country . . . I fought for the Queen of Australia – or the King of Australia – I didn't want the King or the Queen of England because I'd have just been as happy fighting against them, Australia is my

Country. I didn't owe any allegiance or loyalty to the Queen of England; they tried to bloody destroy me, and my family, my tribe, my people . . . I love my country very much and I like the people in Australia, so my loyalty was purely Australian . . .

I am not sure if it is because this quote is out of context and cut here and there, but I feel deeply puzzled about why he served in the military of the settler state that, as he said, 'tried to bloody destroy' him and his people.

As I walk through this exhibition, the message is clear: Indigenous people proudly served in the Australian military where they found a welcoming environment free from racism. I also learn that the Australian Defence has dedicated programmes to attract and retain Indigenous personnel. Admittedly, I was not expecting this institutional zeal to commemorate Indigenous military service, nor was I expecting that Indigenous people wanted to serve in the military of the settler state that stole their land or be involved in British imperial wars. Since my time in Australia, I have familiarised myself with the anti-colonial movement in Brisbane, and I generally found settler–Indigenous relations to be tense despite the rhetoric of reconciliation. *For Country, For Nation* offers food for thought and I want to do some research into the details that the exhibition left unexplored.

It is later than expected. I won't make it to the gallery on contemporary conflict today. The Memorial is about to close for the day. On my way out of the exhibition, I see a volunteer of the Memorial who is clearly waiting for me to leave. I am the last one left in the gallery. I smile at him and thank him for his patience. He must have realised my interest in Indigenous military service and that I am a foreigner because he immediately replied to me 'in this country, Aboriginal people have a long history of [military] service'. His voice is full of pride, and he talks to me with a sense of superior knowledge that a local older man can use when he speaks to a younger foreign woman who exhibits interest in local issues. In his hands, he holds two leaflets and promptly gives them to me. One has the details of the Dawn Service, the commemorative ritual that opens Anzac Day tomorrow, and the other is about the Aboriginal and Torres Strait Islander Commemoration Service. I take the leaflets and leave the Memorial.

My first visit to the Memorial has been more eventful than I anticipated, and I left with more questions than I came with. Tomorrow, I will check out the Aboriginal and Torres Strait Islander Commemoration Service.

Canberra, 25 April 2017: I get up early to go to the Dawn Service. It is raining, cold and miserable, and I should take an Uber lift rather than cycle. The driver is in the mood to talk, but I'm too sleepy to have a conversation. He tells me all the streets that are closed for the Anzac Day celebrations. I don't know Canberra, so I nod while I look at the rain. He drops me off and thanks me for attending the service. I find this gratitude a little weird but not entirely surprising coming from an older White Australian. He's clearly very proud about the Anzacs and Anzac Day and sees himself as doing a service to the community by driving people to the Memorial so early in the morning. I arrive at the Memorial at 4.15 am. It is cold, dark and wet, but the turnout is already significant. According to the estimates of the *Canberra Times*, we are expecting more than 25,000 people.[1] Most people seem White, but it is hard to tell with all these umbrellas, hats and the darkness of pre-dawn. I can definitely see people who are not White though. There are children, and some young adults, but the majority seem to be middle-age and elderly people. Despite the rain, some attendees wear their military uniform, and others have pinned their military medals onto their raincoats. From what I can see, there is gender balance. Some people hold an electric candle, the kind you can find in church. Next to me, a woman makes some remarks about the miserable weather and her friend responds that the rain and cold will help them identify with the soldiers who landed at Gallipoli in 1915.

Meanwhile, pictures of soldiers are projected on the front walls of the Memorial. This slideshow is accompanied by soldiers reading from soldiers' diaries and letters. It feels as if I am attending a religious mass *en plein-air*. At 5.15 am the sound of the didgeridoo/yidaki[2] breaks the silence and marks the official beginning of the Dawn Service. I didn't expect to hear the didgeridoo/yidaki, but this immediately reminds me about the Aboriginal and Torres Strait Islander Commemoration Service scheduled soon after the Dawn Service. I am still unsure where it will be, but I have some time between the two services to find it. Surely, we will receive directions.

The Dawn Service ends at 6 am. I have half an hour to make it to the location of the Aboriginal and Torres Strait Islander Commemoration Service. I was hoping for an announcement about the Aboriginal and Torres Strait Islander Commemoration Service and some directions at the end of the Dawn Service. But nothing, I am left to my own devices. I take my leaflet in the hope of finding some directions, but all I can see is that the location is the Aboriginal Memorial Plaque on

Mount Ainslie, which is just behind the Memorial. I regret not properly checking the location yesterday as the map on my phone points me to the nature reserve of Mt Ainslie. As I walk towards the nature reserve, I notice that everyone is walking in the opposite direction. Is this the right way? It's still drizzling. I find a volunteer and ask her if she can direct me to the Aboriginal and Torres Strait Islander Commemoration Service. She looks at me baffled and says that she doesn't know. I show her my leaflet, and without making a comment, she directs me to Mt Ainslie behind the Memorial. How come that she doesn't know about the service? Hasn't she been briefed?

I think I am close, but I am also the only person walking in this direction. Am I going in the right direction? The Aboriginal and Torres Strait Commemoration Service leaflet is sponsored by the Memorial, but where is everyone else who attended the Dawn Service going? I find another volunteer and ask him what people do after the Dawn Service and where is the Aboriginal Memorial Plaque. He says that many go for breakfast at Poppy, the Memorial's café, but I would have needed a booking. He is not sure about the location of the Aboriginal Memorial Plaque, but he knows it is on Mt Ainslie and points me there. I wonder how many people will be at the Aboriginal and Torres Strait Islander Commemorative Service. Did I misunderstand something? I double-check the date and confirm that it is on Anzac Day at 6.30 am.

Finally, I find the entry to Mt Ainslie. It is still cold and drizzling. I stare at the mud on the path to Mt Ainslie. It is not inviting. The crowd of the Dawn Service is now out of sight, and I wonder if I should venture in the forest on my own. As I have this private conversation with myself, a man with a camo jacket and an Aboriginal flag pinned to his chest walks in front of me with purposeful steps. I run after him and ask him if he is going to the Aboriginal and Torres Strait Islander Commemoration Service. He says yes but is not very talkative. I follow his fast pace in silence, trying to avoid the mud puddles. Soon we reach a few other people walking in the same direction. We all walk in silence as if going to a secret meeting.

Eventually, we reach a small crowd of people, maybe just over 100. The service is about to start and there is no time to walk around and find a good spot. I find myself next to a group of young Aboriginal men and women, some sitting on a flat rock. From where I stand, I can't see the Aboriginal Memorial Plaque. It is no longer dark, and I take a good look around. We are in the middle of the forest and people have embraced this natural location. Some sit on rocks and others lean against trees. There is nothing or no one who tells me that I shouldn't be there, and yet I feel I am in a space where I don't belong. Most of the attendees are Indigenous and so are the chaplain who leads the service and the guest speakers. This is not a service for the show. This is a service by Indigenous people, for Indigenous people.

Canberra, 25 April 2017: I am attending the last official commemorative event of Anzac Day, the Anzac March which happens on Anzac Parade, a long walk just in front of the Memorial. I walk down Anzac Parade to have a sense of the space and organisation of this part of Anzac Day. Anzac Parade is busy despite the clouds and the occasional drizzle. People are chatty and there is a much more jovial atmosphere compared to the Dawn Service this morning. Children are handing out rosemary which they tell me is a symbol of memory. Some young adults in military uniform rehearse their moves and positions.

I walk across the banners of the marching contingents that registered to attend: Army Medical Corps, Defence Nursing, Intelligence Corps, etc. Next to these, I see other banners with the names of foreign nationalities: Korea, Philippines, Turkey, India and Italy, amongst others. It is interesting that foreign nationals can march on Anzac Day too. As I keep walking, I bump into the very small Tongan contingent, four people including a young woman holding both the Australian and the Tongan flags. They wear what looks to me like a combination of traditional clothes from their culture and a modern suit.

At the end of the parade, I find a big yellow banner with a list of names and numbers. These are the dates and places where Indigenous people have been massacred by settlers. Behind the banner, there are some fifty people holding the Aboriginal and Torres Strait Island flags and more banners with the names and dates of colonial massacres. I learn that they are not part of the official Anzac Day March. They are activists from the Aboriginal Tent Embassy,[3] and their mission is to raise awareness about the Frontier Wars of colonisation that still remain excluded from the official Australian war history and national war commemoration. At the very end of this contingent there is a bigger and higher banner that reads 'LEST WE FORGET THE FRONTIER WARS'. I join the dots and realise that there is no mention of this war inside the galleries of the Memorial, not even in the special exhibition dedicated to Indigenous military service that I visited yesterday.

Another unexpected encounter. This fieldwork can't stop surprising me. The Anzac March is almost over, and I decide to join the activists of the Tent Embassy. We walk towards the Memorial, like all the other contingents did, until we meet a line of police officers. We stop. There is silence and the air is tense. I feel uneasy. I look around me and it is as if everyone knows their part in this play. There is no violence and no shouting. The activists stand in front of the police, in silence. A few of them walk forward holding wreaths. The police officers don't move, and the activists lay their wreaths at the police's feet.

I can't help to think that these wreaths in memory of the Frontier Wars laid on the feet of the police can symbolically also stand to commemorate the Indigenous people who have died at the hand of this institution.

The Puzzle

As these vignettes point out, I made a series of unexpected encounters during my fieldwork research at the Australian War Memorial and on Anzac Day in Canberra in 2017. Australia's war commemoration, Indigenous military service and commemoration, and anti-colonial resistance have stuck with me ever since, and they hijacked my interest and research leading me on the path to this book. For me, there is something deeply puzzling about the celebration of Indigenous military service by the Australian War Memorial but its continuing exclusion of the Frontier Wars, the drive among some Indigenous people to participate, celebrate and commemorate their service in the settler military, and the dynamics of anti-colonial resistance that weaponise Anzac Day to make known to the wider public the history of the Frontier Wars. I spent the remainder of my fieldwork in Canberra trying to understand more about the forces at work in Indigenous military inclusion, exclusion and resistance. And then, I spent more years on it.

The initial feeling that stayed with me was one of frustration, arising from the way the special exhibition *For Country, For Nation* seemed to shape the narrative portraying the military as a stronghold for Indigenous rights and recognition. When I first visited the exhibition, I didn't know much about Indigenous military service. But I left the exhibition with a sense that something in there was not quite right. Was it possible that while the Australian government and White settlers were waging a war against Indigenous people that involved massacres, confinement to missions and stations, and the abduction of Indigenous children, the military was an exceptional bubble of equality and fairness? And what were the incentives for Indigenous people to serve in the settler military of a government that was actively taking over their land and destroying their culture and people? The night after my visit to *For Country, For Nation*, I sat with my laptop and typed 'Indigenous military service in Australia'. Melissa Williams' documentary *Too Dark to See* (2016, no longer available) popped up and offered a more analytical and chronological picture. It confirmed that Indigenous people were barred from military service for half of the twentieth century, and introduced a more nuanced perspective about the reasons why Indigenous people decided to serve, including a stable wage, desire to travel, education and employment opportunities in White society, and to follow friends and family. I learned a bit more, but I was still puzzled by the fact that some Indigenous people enlisted despite the racist ban and at a time when they were still victims of the massacres that characterised the Frontier Wars. In conversation with Indigenous friends, leaders and experts on Indigenous politics, I decided that it was not my job to dig into the personal reasons that led individuals to enlist despite the ban. These stories are for Indigenous people to reconnect with, to heal, strengthen their communities and resurge.

This did not end my investigation and instead refined my research direction. In this book, I examine the settler colonial politics surrounding the development of Australian war commemoration. How is the Australian War Memorial and the history of Australia's war commemoration linked with the settler colonial project? What is the source of the Australian War Memorial's recent enthusiasm for commemorating Indigenous military service? Does the inclusion of Indigenous people in the military and war commemoration signify the end of settler colonialism in Australia and a break with its colonial past?

In the years after my fieldwork research, the archival and research material on Indigenous military service in Australia expanded a great deal. In the past years, there have been many initiatives and efforts to retrieve the history of Indigenous military service. The literature offers a detailed reconstruction of the history of Indigenous military service (Beaumont and Cadzow 2018), and insights into the personal stories of Indigenous serving members and their families (Cadzow and Jebb 2019). Some are sponsored by the Australian War Memorial (Grant and Bell 2018), others offer a comparative analysis of the history and experience of Indigenous people in different settler contexts (Sheffield and Riseman 2019; Poyer 2022). While acquainting myself with this emerging body of literature, I was taken aback by the limited analysis concerning the settler politics that underlie Indigenous military inclusion and commemoration. However, there are at least two reasons that can account for this conspicuous absence. First, the scholarship on Indigenous military inclusion has been mostly in the hands of historians who have focused their efforts on retrieving the history. A political and critical analysis cannot even begin if the history is not available. Secondly, as historians are writing the history of Indigenous military service, the government is strategically using it as evidence to demonstrate that the country has moved beyond its history of colonisation and that national reconciliation is bearing fruit.

And herein lies the crux of my research: does Indigenous inclusion in the military and war commemoration demonstrate that Australia is a postcolonial and post-racial society? Notably, Indigenous inclusion is celebrated as an act of national reconciliation, endorsed by both the government and the Indigenous people involved in this conversation, predominantly consisting of current or former service members and their families. And, in fact, it serves both to some degree. The Australian state looks progressive and attentive to race and Indigeneity, and Indigenous people get their family and community history and contribution to modern Australia recognised by the wider society. It is undoubtedly important to celebrate and recognise the benefits of Indigenous military inclusion, but it must be grounded in an understanding of the settler colonial dynamics that animate it. As scholars and activists remark, settler colonialism is a present reality (Moreton-Robinson 2015; Veracini 2015; Maddison 2019a; Strakosch 2019; Maddison and Nakata 2020; Birch 2021; Watego 2021), and as such, it shapes processes such as the inclusion of Indigenous people in the military and war commemoration.

Settler Military Politics

To capture the settler colonial politics surrounding war commemoration in Australia, in this book I propose the concept of *settler military politics*. My investigation of settler military politics in Australia advances the argument that military organisation and war commemoration are integral to the development of the settler state and society. The concept of settler military politics captures the manoeuvres to mobilise military organisation, war history, and war commemoration to advance and adapt settler colonialism. Overall, I argue that settler military politics produce dynamics that are essential for the formation and consolidation of the settler state and society. In my work, the concept of settler military politics emerges from the context of settler colonial Australia, but it may well apply to other settler states where the military and its corollaries have been involved in advancing settler colonialism, including New Zealand, Canada, Israel and the United States.

Settler colonialism remains an understudied phenomenon in Critical Military Studies and the military remains understudied in Settler Colonial Studies. Postcolonial scholarship on the military and war commemoration has made important contributions to understand how militarism and militarisation are implicated in colonial politics. The Pacific region is a case in point as scholars demonstrate how many of the paradisiac Pacific islands are intimately familiar with military ideologies, bases and forms of governance brought by colonial powers pushing their imperial frontiers (Teaiwa 2008a; Shigematsu and Camacho 2010; Na'puti and Frain 2023). Targeted for its strategic geopolitical position, life in the Pacific has been etched by waves of militarisation that ultimately served imperial powers and brought armed conflict to the region. Teaiwa (2008b), Rashid (2020) and Chisholm (2022) also show that imperial militarism and militarisation tend to survive through postcolonial moments and continue to shape life even after the end of colonial rule. They explain that postcolonial societies and individuals come to invest themselves in the gendered and racial logics that informed militarised colonial rule and thus, reproduce them after colonisation. This scholarship, however, deals with postcolonial contexts where colonisation officially ended, despite the legacies that it left behind. Therefore, its insights are limited in settler colonial contexts where colonisation remains active. In settler colonial societies, the gendered and racial logics that informed militarised colonial rule have adapted to liberal sensibilities such that they advance settler colonialism.

Settler colonialism is a distinct type of colonial formation characterised by a society established over unceded Indigenous land and comprising a majority of non-native people, the settlers, who have control and power over Indigenous land and people (Stasiulis and Yuval-Davis 1995; Veracini 2015). What distinguishes settler colonialism from other forms of colonialism is the permanent and sedentary nature of the colonisers who, as Wolfe says, 'come to stay' (1998: 2). Settler colonialism is not characterised by the presence of small contingents of merchants, soldiers and missionaries who govern and extract labour and resources from the colony to accrue the wealth of the metropole. Instead, it is a long-term political project aiming to establish a new society of settlers that achieves independence from the metropole at the expenses of Indigenous decolonisation. At the core of this project is the dispossession of Indigenous people and the settlers' repossession of their land. In this respect, settler colonialism destroys Indigenous life to create a settler society. The sedentary and substitutive nature of the settler society means that, once settler colonialism is engrained, there is no decolonisation that takes the form of colonisers leaving the country and returning the land to Indigenous people. At best, decolonisation can look like Indigenous resurgence that involves Indigenous agency in shaping policy and politics as well as the revival of Indigenous culture (Coulthard 2014; Veracini 2015; Maddison and Nakata 2020; Watego 2021). But ultimately, Indigenous people and culture will not return to be the main or sole authors and source of governance and power on their land.

The language of settler colonialism came to the fore of academic debates at the turn of the twenty-first century following the perceived limitation of postcolonial studies to speak about the condition of those societies where the colonisers never left. The 'post' in postcolonial studies refers to the ongoing effects of colonial rule in societies that have formally decolonised; but in some societies like Australia, colonial rule has never formally ended (Carey and Silverstein 2020). As Aboriginal scholar and writer Tony Birch (1997: 16) remarked about his people in Australia:

> . . . we live in a colonial society. Post-colonialism in this country is a job, a luxury enjoyed only by the academy.

Settler Colonial Studies developed to cast a light on the peculiarities of those colonial formations that continue to exist and have adapted to the liberal rhetoric of recognition of Indigenous people and reconciliation (Tuck and Yang 2012). Crucially, the field of Settler Colonial Studies differs from that of Indigenous studies in that the former focuses on the structures of power and oppression in settler colonial societies rather than on Indigenous agency and sovereignty which are the purview of the latter (Carey and Silverstein 2020).

In Settler Colonial Studies, the military is rarely examined. Instead, attention has been focused on the institution of the police as the main actor that carried out the work that instituted settler societies. Conversely to the police, the military has rarely been deployed against Indigenous people and, as the Australian story shows, is heralded as an institution of recognition. A sole focus on the police, however, eludes the martial and international nature of settler colonialism and frames it as domestic politics only. Settler colonialism is a matter of international relations to the extent that First Nations are subjected to foreign domination in their own country while being treated as domestic subjects and a matter of domestic politics. The inclusion of Indigenous people in the military frames Indigenous people as domestic subjects equally concerned with the defence of the country from foreign powers, and thus becomes a prop for further militarisation in the name of national security.

In this book, I use the tools of Settler Colonial Studies which have proven useful to understand the nature of the Australian state. Settler colonialism is the core engine of the Australian state which shapes nation-building (Moreton-Robinson 2015; Povinelli 2002), public policy (Strakosch 2015)(Maddison, 2019; Strakosch, 2015), and international relations (Brigg, Graham and Weber 2021; A. E. Davis 2021; Blackwell and Ballangarry 2022). Established as a British penal colony in 1788, Australia was also a social and political laboratory to produce an improved version of the British society. The settlers brought with them the British legal system, sovereignty and women to reproduce society, while the convicts provided the labour force to produce the infrastructure and the means of subsistence (Woollacott 2015). This was made possible by the settlers' declaration of Australia as *terra nullius*, uninhabited land, which, following the (European) international law of that time, authorised the occupation of the land. To be clear, the British settlers did meet the native population of what came to be known as Australia. Broome (2010), for example, reconstructs the encounter with the Eora people, the original owners of what became Sydney. This encounter was characterised by curiosity and misunderstandings on both parts. For the British, the Eora were savages without social structures and government, agriculture and trade, clothes and permanent shelters. The Eora 'wondered if the British were spirits and not human, being white, and pondered their gender as they were clothed and clean-shaven' (ibid., 30). They perceived the British settlers as invaders and savages who took over their land and resources without permission and who were unaware of the protocols for inter-tribal interactions. The settlers did not make treaties with the Eora or any other First Nation tribe. They did not start a diplomatic mission or declare war against First Nations peoples to take their land and resources. Instead, they simply declared the land theirs on the grounds that First Nations peoples did not own the land because they did not cultivate it in European style. This is the foundational moment of the Australian settler state, and the lack of treaties with First Nations peoples still today remains a bone of contention in Indigenous–settler relations. Despite efforts to promote reconciliation over the past three decades, the requests of Indigenous peoples to make treaties concerning land use and its possession and to enshrine Indigenous sovereignty in the constitution remain unmet by the Australian government.[4]

Wolfe (1994: 97) remarks that settler colonialism is not the event of taking over Indigenous land, but the structure that enables settlers' ownership of Indigenous land over time and despite changing conditions. He finds that settler colonialism is animated by what he calls 'the logics of elimination of the natives', rationalities to dispossess Indigenous people from their land that include physical extermination, confinement, miscegenation and assimilation (Wolfe 2006). Goenpul scholar Moreton-Robinson (2015) adds that settler colonialism also relies on 'the logics of White possessive', racialised discursive practices that legitimise settlers' ownership of the land. The first logic of White possessive in Australia was that Indigenous people were not sovereign owners of the land. Occupation of the land was justified on the racial discourse that framed Indigenous people as savages who did not tenure land and who could have been civilised by the British settlers. This activated a logic of elimination grounded in the belief that Indigenous people had to be civilised and become like the British or otherwise be eliminated.

Following Wolfe's theorisation of settler colonialism as a structure ultimately working to legitimise settler authority over Indigenous land, in this book, I demonstrate that war commemoration operates in the order of Moreton-Robinson's logics of White possessive. Casting a light on the military, I show that the organisation of settler defence and the ways it has been memorialised since the First World War, activate politics that consolidate the settler state and society. I map how the emergence of war commemoration in Australia amid the First World War and the visual archive of the Australian War Memorial worked to conceal colonial warfare and sanction the birth of the settler state as a political unit distinct from the British Empire; how the Australian civic spirit is intrinsically martial and, thus, how the expansion of the settler polity necessarily involves the militarisation of new subject positions, most relevant for this book, women and Indigenous people; and how the inclusion in official war commemoration without a radical rethinking that involves the inclusion of the Frontier Wars is an act of militarisation that ultimately legitimises the authority of the settler colonial state.

Settler Militarisation

In my investigation of settler military politics, I unearth the relationship between settler colonialism and militarisation, which remains understudied in the field of Critical Military Studies. In Critical Military Studies, militarisation encompasses the everyday practices by which military values, aesthetics and economies transform individuals, institutions and societies. Lutz (2002) explains that militarisation involves 'the intensification of the labour and resources allocated for military purposes', but is also a process of 'deformation of human potentials into the hierarchies of race, class, gender, and sexuality'. In other words, militarisation refers to the processes that create and reinforce hierarchies of power between groups through military organisation, war preparation, and war rhetoric and representation. As I explain in this book, militarisation so understood is a key process in the formation and consolidation of the settler colonial state.

A central argument of this book is that, in settler colonial contexts, militarisation is a technology to govern and reproduce the settler polity. I develop this argument by examining the history of military organisation, the militarisation of settler men, and the inclusion of women and Indigenous people in the Australian military and war commemoration. A notable limitation of this study is the lack of attention to migrant communities who have also been implicated in settler colonialism and militarisation. The different migrant communities in Australia and the stratification of the politics of race in the formation of the settler state create complexities that deserve a study of its own. As in many other societies, the First World War induced processes of militarisation in Australia. The deployment of White working- and middle-class men to fight in the name of the Australian nation as part of the British Empire activated racialised, gendered and imperial dynamics that consolidated the newly established White Australian nation (officially formed in 1901). Following the First World War, Australia looked more like a state with its own defence forces and national memories of war. Men took up arms out of imperial patriotism and to defend the British imperial interests, but also to prove the valour of Australian men in war. Women, Indigenous people and non-White Australians were excluded from military service not for their lack of want, but to consolidate the White patriarchal state. By the end of the war, Australia had a new national icon, the Anzac soldier, who embodied the qualities of the Australian citizen: endurance, courage, ingenuity, good humour and mateship.[5] He was also emblematically male and White.

With the Second World War came the militarisation of women. The creation of the Australian Women's Auxiliary Services in 1940, saw women involved in the war effort in auxiliary capacities. This opened space to introduce a national representation of the female contribution to war and to institute the new subjectivity of the woman at work. This challenged the masculinist stereotype of the ideal citizen, but also worked to consolidate Whiteness and the settler project. The heralding of the woman at work for war came at a time when Australia needed to modernise to keep up with liberal progress and the societal advancement of women in other liberal Western nations. It also coincided with a time when the Australian government involved selected Indigenous people in defence positions to meet the war needs and strategic requirements. The celebration of the woman at work and contributing to the defence of the nation obscured the contribution of Indigenous soldiers. It kept the national icon White while also confirming the progressive stance of the Australian state in relation to (White) women's rights.

In the past three decades we have been witnessing the militarisation of Indigenous people under the guise of efforts to raise the number of Indigenous military personnel and forefront Indigenous military service in national war commemoration. This is undoubtedly a step towards the inclusion and recognition of Indigenous people in the Australian polity, but it is also a manoeuvre to select and edit the aspects of Indigeneity and Indigenous history that suit the settler polity. In its modern form, settler colonialism in liberal societies relies on the inclusion of Indigenous people insofar as it legitimises settler authority and governance. The Indigenous soldier is the unsurpassed token of settler legitimacy which testifies to the willingness of Indigenous people to commit the ultimate sacrifice for the settler polity.

Reflecting upon my fieldwork, it became evident that there is a disparity between the willingness of the government and national institutions such as the Australian War Memorial to recognise the military service of Indigenous people and the history of the Frontier Wars. The former has been embraced and celebrated, while the latter is at best tolerated in the name of democratic contestation. This has already been recognised by Australian historian Reynolds (2013: 6), who noted that the 'Aborigines who fought for the white man are remembered with reverence. The many more who fought against him are forgotten.' The year that I attended the Anzac Day in Canberra, Indigenous veterans were leading the Anzac March. Conversely, the activists of the Aboriginal Tent Embassy were clearly not welcome by authorities as demonstrated by the line of police that stopped their march. A level of tolerance for this kind of contestation works in the interests of the settler government, which is relieved of the duty and responsibility of dealing with the history of colonial warfare. Tolerance for the activist commemoration of the Frontier Wars sends the message that the settler society is not hostile towards Indigenous people and is therefore preventing the increasing influence of supporters to the Indigenous cause. Instead of contesting the activist commemoration of the Frontier Wars, the government invests in promoting Indigenous military service as a symbol of reconciliation.

Building on Moreton-Robinson's (2015) concept of the 'White possessive', in this book, I analyse Indigenous inclusion in the military and national war commemoration as a logic that works to shift attention away from the demands to recognise and grapple with the Frontier Wars, the legacies of colonial violence and Indigenous ownership of the land. Indigenous military inclusion is most visible as a logic of White possessive when juxtaposed with an analysis of how the military and war commemoration have sustained the Australian settler colonial project. I examine this history and its continuity with the present moment. The recent inclusion of Indigenous people in military organisation and in war commemoration enables the settler state to present an image of itself as a postcolonial, post-racial state. Despite the rhetoric, however, Australia remains a settler state where Indigenous people are a political minority. In practical terms, this means that Indigenous people remain a disadvantage group in terms of health, opportunities and access to power (SCRGSP 2020). And despite the more recent efforts to include Indigenous people in key decision-making positions, Indigenous people's interests remain second to those of the settler and capitalist interests of the state.[6]

Settler Politics and the Aesthetics of War Commemoration

At the heart of my investigation into settler military politics in Australia is the official aesthetics of war commemoration guarded and curated by the Australian War Memorial. I examine the Australian

War Memorial as an institution of settler colonialism that works through aesthetic power, that is, the power of emotions evoked by visual representations and performances. The aesthetics of war commemoration curated by the Australian War Memorial keeps alive the trauma of the First World War as the foundation of the settler nation. This is recurrently updated to reflect new liberal sensibilities and geopolitical contexts such that, ultimately, the First World War remains Australia's story of origin. Thus, for example, the visualisation of Indigenous people as modern soldiers serves to invest them in the story of the First World War as the moment of national origin and at the expense of other stories of origin. Worth noting is that the Australian War Memorial excludes the Frontier Wars from its galleries even though since the middle of the twentieth century it has made it its mission to help Australians understand and commemorate *all* Australian wars. As the activists of the Aboriginal Tent Embassy who commemorate the Frontier Wars on Anzac Day remark, all Australian wars continue to exclude the Frontier Wars.

The establishment of official aesthetics of war commemoration was paramount for the consolidation of the settler state as a political unit distinct from the British Empire. As became customary in many nations during the First World War, Australia commissioned artists to represent the Australian experience of war. Initially, this was frowned upon by Britain on the ground that Australia was part of the Empire, but Australian officials succeeded in making the case that the Australian aesthetics of war commemoration was integral to that of the Empire. They argued that the Australian aesthetics of war commemoration would have memorialised the trauma of the Australian nation as part of the Empire. Nonetheless, it also gave Australia a martial myth of origin and cultivated the Australian national spirit. Although, at first, imperial and national sentiments coexisted, as the British Empire crumbled Australian nationalism became rooted in the aesthetics of war commemoration that developed after the First World War.

The magnitude of the First World War, coupled with the ambition to create the Australian War Memorial, offered an unprecedented opportunity for the settler state to erase the memory of colonial warfare. The emerging aesthetics of war commemoration grounded the narrative that the First World War was Australia's first war, thus effectively glossing over colonial warfare. As already mentioned, the lack of a war declaration by the British against Indigenous people made colonial warfare a contested terrain. The fact that colonial warfare did not respect the canons of Napoleonic warfare further complicated its legitimacy and denied its existence. Conversely, the First World War was Australia's first modern, mass, industrial war in which the federal government deployed its own national military force. Australia suffered 60,000 casualties out of a population of less than 5 million, and this local wound compounded with the global trauma. Amid this political climate and the memory boom which consolidated Western nations after the First World War (Winter 2006), the emerging Australian aesthetics of war commemoration consolidated the narrative that prior to this war Australians never experienced conflict. The Australian War Memorial accredits the First World War as Australia's baptism of fire, the moment when the Australian nation was officially born. Thus, it grounds the Australian nation in the First World War, notably a war where Indigenous people were banned from enlisting because they were not of European origin.[7]

The aesthetics of war commemoration is also a key aspect of settler military politics to the extent that it supplies visual references and performative practices to reproduce the settler state and society. The analysis in this book draws from the examination of the Australian War Memorial, the Official War Art programme from its inception in 1917 to 2022, and the commemorative services held outside the Memorial on Anzac Day that I witnessed in 2017. The Official War Art programme encompasses a vast array of visual art commissioned and acquired by the Australian War Memorial. In the following chapters, I discuss specific examples that have come to represent the settler nation and settler subjectivities, including the Anzac soldier, first introduced in the aftermath of the First World War to celebrate the militarised White founding fathers of the settler nation, the woman at work, introduced during the Second World War, and the Indigenous soldier, introduced in the early 2000s.

While I maintain that the aesthetics of war commemoration is a powerful tool of settler politics, it is not uncontested. I bring in an analysis of the performances of war commemoration drawing from my fieldwork observations in Canberra 2017. As I witnessed in Canberra when I met the activists holding the banners in memory of the Frontier Wars and attended the Aboriginal and Torres Strait Island Commemoration Service, Indigenous people are actively intervening in the aesthetics of war commemoration to shape the settler nation. I discuss the Australian aesthetics of war commemoration as a battleground where conservative nationalists, liberal progressives and anti-colonial activists pursue their political agendas. In my research on Australia's war commemoration, I have tried to pay attention to the nuances of identity politics and the subtle changes of settler colonial conditions. I found that while the settler state deploys the aesthetics of war commemoration to consolidate the settler nation and settler authority, politicised identities have used the grammar and aesthetics of war commemoration to speak back and shape the political agenda.

In this respect, I maintain that the aesthetics of war commemoration is also a site and a tool to reshape the nation and settler colonialism. Notably, given the centrality of this aesthetics in the settler national project, women and Indigenous people have sought inclusion to transform the nation from within. This is evident, for example, in the exhibition *For Country, For Nation*, where Indigenous artists camouflaged references to the Frontier Wars in their art, thus bringing the Frontier Wars into the galleries of the Australian War Memorial for the first time. These references were ignored by the Australian War Memorial, but they could not be missed by Indigenous people and other attentive audiences (Caso 2020). *For Country, For Nation*, Indigenous military inclusion and other types of interventions have created the space to talk about the continued lack of institutional commemoration of the Frontier Wars as well as to introduce, albeit only temporarily and indirectly, the Frontier Wars in the Australian War Memorial. They have also been part of the processes that are changing the conversation in Australia to bring accountability to the history and legacies of colonial violence and dispossession.

The insertion of Indigenous people and stories in Australia's national war commemoration to shape the conversation from within comes at a cost, namely, the militarisation of Indigenous people and their inclusion in the martial settler state. To quote Black American scholar and activist Audre Lorde (1983), 'the master's tool will never dismantle the master's house'. This means that Indigenous military inclusion and war commemoration can rectify the history of Indigenous exclusion from the military and the nation and bring awareness about the history of colonial violence, but cannot dismantle the unequal power relations between the settler state and First Nations peoples. Indigenous military service and Indigenous stories of war are made to be relevant only in relation to the project of settler nation-building, that is, they are valued to the extent that they bolster the legitimacy of the settler state. But what would it mean to embrace and tell Australia's unique history of war? And what would it mean to empower Indigenous soldiers to be actors of international politics rather than a token of domestic reconciliation?

While the militarisation of Indigenous people is not dismantling settler colonialism, it is enabling Indigenous agency in representing their own history of service in modern warfare and its connection and continuity with colonial warfare and pre-colonial history. This is evident, for example, in Adelaide's Aboriginal and Torres Strait Islander War Memorial which uses the Aboriginal iconography of the Dreamtime that speaks about the origin of Aboriginal culture and life. Another example is the more recent Aboriginal and Torres Strait Islander War Memorial in Brisbane, which includes the dancing Aboriginal warriors who complement the representation of Aboriginal service men and women. Beaumont (2018) notes that the revolutionary potential of these memorials lies in the ways in which they are used by Indigenous people as sites to perform traditional rituals and their own rituals of war commemoration that are not intended for settler audiences or the settler state. Drawing from the work of Winter (2006), she remarks that war commemoration is brought to life by the people who perform it. Therefore, while the memorials themselves may not have decolonising properties, they can be used as sites of resistance and resurgence.

Design of the Book

There are five substantive chapters in this book that are better read consecutively as they build upon one another. Chapter 1 introduces the theoretical framework of militarisation as governance. I define militarisation as a governing rationality predicated on the valorisation of Western-centric armed forces, and argue that in Australia militarisation works to advance settler colonial governance. The chapter traces the origin of Australia's militarisation to the early days of colonisation, colonial warfare and the organisation of Australian Defence Force at the turn of the twentieth century. Militarisation is evidenced in the ways that British generals were integral to the colonisation of Australia and the establishment of the early colonial settlements. Because of their perception of Indigenous inferiority, they did not declare a war, instead, they used deliberate violence and strategic inclusion of selected Indigenous people to dispossess and take over Indigenous land. I discuss that despite the lack of a war declaration, Australia experienced colonial warfare fought between the settlers and Indigenous people. This war was and remains unrecognised because it does not mirror the canon of Napoleonic warfare. I suggest that this is an act of militarisation that operates to erase colonial warfare and legitimate settler authority. I also propose a decolonial definition of war to see the Native Police and Indigenous resistance as manifestations of the colonial conflict. Finally, Chapter 1 discusses militarisation in relation to the organisation of the Australian Defence Force soon after Federation in 1901, when Indigenous and non-European men were excluded from military service to preserve and consolidate the nation as White. This discussion shows that race was a key discourse that enabled the operation of militarisation as settler colonial governance.

Chapter 2 continues the theorisation of militarisation as a practice of colonial governance and analyses its operation through the aesthetics of war commemoration. This examination reveals how the aesthetics of war commemoration contribute to the consolidation of settler colonial military governance and the construction of the settler nation. The chapter begins by offering a theoretical framework to appreciate the politics of war commemoration and its aesthetics. This is the framework I build on in the subsequent chapters. Then, the chapter excavates the history and settler politics of Australia's commemorative aesthetics. I introduce the story of Charles Bean, the founding father of the Australian War Memorial, and of the Australian War Art programme as the precursor of the memorial. The War Art Programme emerged at the end of the First World War to visually document and commemorate the Australian war experience. This initiative played a pivotal role in visualising Australia's unique war experience and solidified a distinct national identity separate from the British Empire. The War Art programme provided the nation with visual references about the martial identity of Australia and offered commemorative material for the institution of the Australian War Memorial. It also legitimised the suffering of the Australians and distinguished the Australian nation within the British Empire. Notably, this was not a revolution or anti-imperialism. Australia was comfortable being part of the British Empire. However, it was led by Darwinian ideas of racial evolution and a desire to demonstrate that the Australian race was not a degeneration from, but an improvement to the British Anglo-Saxon race. The aesthetics of war commemoration created a space to celebrate Australians as a nation and as a thriving White race. This vision of Australia was engraved in the Australian War Memorial when it was inaugurated in 1941. Politically, the aesthetics of war commemoration works through what I call 'militarised compassion', that is, a tactic to reproduce the settler nation through narratives and aesthetics about the suffering and sacrifice of soldiers in foreign lands. In particular, Australia's aesthetics of war commemoration promote militarised compassion towards the White soldier. Because of the exclusion of the Frontier Wars from the official aesthetics of war commemoration, militarised compassion creates a hierarchy of suffering that positions colonial suffering below the soldier's.

Chapter 3 maps the militarisation of men and masculinity as a settler governing practice from early settlement through the First and Second World wars, and up to the present day. I offer a framework to understand the valorisation of militarised masculinity as the pillar of the nation in the emerging aesthetics of war commemoration and the settler project. The militarisation of men and masculinity resulted in the figure of the Anzac soldier, who came to represent a national identity ennobled by war. This figure emerged at a time when Australia was searching for a mature representation and icon of national identity following autonomy from Britain at Federation. The First World War created an opportunity for the Anzac soldier to represent a tradition of men making the nation in war, and put the emerging Australian nation on a par with other European militarised nations. In this chapter, I also discuss the transformation of the figure of the Anzac soldier since the Second World War and the end of the British Empire. Already established as the icon and protagonist of the national myth of origin, from the end of the Second World War the figure of the Anzac soldier began to be mobilised to establish Australia's national identity separate from the British Empire and grounded in multiculturalism. This opened the space for the insertion of the Indigenous and ethnic soldiers as representations of the nation. However, as the Anzac soldier came to embrace racial diversity, it also foreclosed the space for anti-war and anti-militarism.

Chapter 4 focuses on the militarisation of women. It discusses that although this process formally started in the Second World War with the establishment of the Women's Auxiliary Services and the commissioning of the first three female war artists, women were already involved in the militarisation of Australia and its military settler politics before this. In this chapter, I discuss key figures of militarised femininity with reference to official war art, namely, the citizen-mother and the worker in the military factories of the Second World War. I argue that these were intended to govern femininity as well as to reaffirm the settler nation as a White project. In the final part of the chapter, I discuss two potentially disruptive figures, the anti-war activist and the female Aboriginal soldiers. Despite their potentially disruptive capacities, I maintain that these figures became implicated in the Australian settler colonial project.

Chapter 5 ultimately addresses the puzzle that animates this book. Upon consideration of the settler military logics that propelled modern Australia excavated in the previous chapters, in this final chapter I examine whether the inclusion of Indigenous people in the Australian Defence Force and the national aesthetics of war commemoration represents a break from settler colonialism. I begin by discussing the history of Indigenous military service which was characterised simultaneously by exclusionary practices and assimilationist logics. In 1909, non-White people, including Indigenous people, were barred from enlisting in the military to assist the consolidation of the emerging nation as White. Around 1,000 Indigenous people managed to enlist to serve in the First World War and more than 4,000 did so in the Second World War despite the racist restrictions. I analyse how their service became an opportunity to assimilate Indigenous people in White society and consider how the inclusion of Indigenous military service in the national aesthetics of war commemoration is a continuation of this politics by other means.

In Chapter 5, I also discuss how Indigenous veterans created a space to commemorate their service and the Indigenous history of war. Initially, settler institutions refused to commemorate Indigenous military service because it would have given unwanted visibility to Indigenous people. However, as the history of colonial violence became more publicly known and threatened the legitimacy of the settler state, settler institutions endorsed Indigenous military service to bolster settler legitimacy, ultimately demonstrated by the willingness of Indigenous people to serve and to die in its defence. Indigenous people used inclusion as an opportunity to emphasise the history of colonial warfare by linking the modern soldier with the traditional warrior and thus enlarged the space for truth-telling and acknowledgement of the history of violence against First Nations people. I discuss three Indigenous practices of counter-memory, namely, the representation of the Frontier Wars in the exhibition *For Country, For Nation*, the Aboriginal and Torres Strait Islander Commemoration Service, and the march for the Frontier Wars on Anzac Day. These are important practices that offer Indigenous people a space to tell their story of war and service.

In the Conclusion, I distil my discussion of settler military politics in the making of the settler martial state. Overall, this book finds that war is an essential component of settler colonialism and the development of the settler state. Gendered and racialised dynamics of exclusion and inclusion in war, war narratives and war commemoration are central to the formation of the settler state and for settler colonial governance. In a context in which war is an ever-present threat, the settler state will always have ammunition to activate the gendered and racialised dynamics of inclusion and exclusion to reproduce itself. Thus, I maintain that we need to deepen our understanding of settler military politics and the settler martial state, and that Critical Military Studies is well equipped to pursue this research.

Notes

1. The estimates after the event calculated 38,000 attendees.
2. A musical instrument of Aboriginal origins and still strongly associated with Aboriginal culture.
3. A symbol of protest and resistance that was established by Aboriginal activists in 1972 to demonstrate against the government's refusal to acknowledge Aboriginal land rights. Despite several attempts by the government to dismantle the Aboriginal Tent Embassy, it still stands as a symbol of the fight for Indigenous rights and sovereignty.
4. As I wrote this book, Australia was preparing to launch a referendum to institute the Voice to Parliament, an advisory body to parliament that would represent Indigenous Australians. This would not be a treaty-making institution and would not give First Nations peoples equal sovereignty to Australia. After a fraught and rather acrimonious campaign, the vote was held on 14 October 2023 where it was defeated: No = 60.1 per cent; Yes = 39.9 per cent. In 2018, the state of Victoria embarked on a path to make treaties with the First Nations peoples of Victoria. Other states are also considering making treaties.
5. These are the qualities that inform the Anzac Spirit. Mateship is a typical Australian word to indicate camaraderie and respect, especially between men.
6. This is at the core of the Indigenous contestation of the recent efforts to include Indigenous people in the settler state via the Voice to Parliament (Tong 2023).
7. This will be discussed in more details in Chapter 5. The 1909 amendment to the Defence Act exempted men 'not substantially of European origin' from enlisting (McDonnell and Dodson 2018).

CHAPTER 1

Settler Militarisation

Introduction

This chapter introduces the central role of discursive practices of war in the Australian settler project and canvasses militarisation as a settler colonial governing practice. Within the field of Settler Colonial Studies, the concept of militarisation is often overlooked. This oversight arises from the perception that the military plays a limited, if not insignificant, role in settler colonialism. There is also a certain degree of fuzziness surrounding the concept of militarisation which makes it difficult to deploy rigorously. It is a shape-shifting concept that travels across disciplines and between academia, public discourse and policy. As Howell (2018: 117) notes, the intuitive nature of militarisation means that it is often used but rarely defined. In this study, I define militarisation *as a governing rationality predicated on the valorisation of Western-centric armed forces and war*. Here, war is both the practice of fighting for political reasons (including war preparation) and the narratives that give meaning to the practices of war (including war commemoration) (Barkawi and Brighton 2011; Wibben 2011). In my conceptualisation, the ultimate purpose of militarisation is not war, but the governing of social relations to build a polity and project political authority. Applied to settler contexts like Australia, militarisation is a core feature of settler governance and involves practices and narratives that prop up modern warfare and the military as a means to consolidate the settler state and legitimise settler authority.

I argue that militarisation is a key process of settler-state formation and consolidation. I demonstrate this argument by examining the foundational history of war in modern Australia. Conventional wisdom maintains that the First World War I was Australia's 'baptism of fire', the moment when Australian soldiers proved the qualities of Australian nationals internationally and the Australian nation was born. In Australia, the First World War is mythologised into the Anzac Legend that serves not only as a narrative of war commemoration, but also emphasises the civic virtues of Australians. The Anzac Legend is militarising insofar as it grounds Australian national identity in war. It also has settler implications. In particular, the proclamation of the First World War as Australia's baptism of fire conceals the war that made modern Australia, namely, colonial warfare fought between the British settlers to establish their sovereignty in the new continent and Indigenous people to resist the British invasion of their old country. In Australia, this period is known as the Frontier Wars which are the very foundation of modern Australia. Without the blood spilled in these wars, there would not be Australia as we know it today.

European racial assumptions about the inferiority of Indigenous people allowed the British settlers to conduct the Frontier Wars without a war declaration. This was premised on militarism as an ideology of racial superiority (Gani 2021), and also enabled the immediate and long-term operation of settler militarisation. Immediately, the lack of a war declaration resulted in a 'secret war' of colonisation that the British fought with paramilitary organisations such as the colonial police (Richards 2008). Instead of declaring a war against Indigenous people for the conquest of their land, the British made Indigenous people subjects of the Crown. Therefore, rather than deploying the military against Indigenous people, the settlers created the Native Police that redefined Indigenous anti-colonial resistance as issues of law and order. This concealed colonial warfare and Indigenous resistance and contributed to the establishment of British sovereignty and law over Indigenous land. In the long term, the lack of a war declaration supported the idea that the British colonised Australia peacefully, thus maintaining the integrity of settler sovereignty and authority. The narrative of peaceful colonisation remained dominant until the 1980s, but institutions such as the Australian War Memorial have continued to uphold it even after by policing the definition of war to exclude colonial warfare.

Finally, this chapter highlights how race propelled Australia's militarisation at the turn of the twentieth century. As a White settler colony established on Indigenous land and in a non-White neighbourhood, Australia was vexed with racial anxiety that manifested itself in a strong attachment to the Anglo-Saxon race and a fear of abandonment from Britain. Racial anxiety played a major role in the organisation of Australia's Defence and its participation in the First World War. Australia was particularly concerned with Chinese migration and Japan's rise to power which, respectively, prompted the exclusion of non-White men from the emerging Australian Defence Force and the introduction of compulsory military training for White men. The fear of abandonment also led Australia to keep its defence under British control, which meant that when Britain joined a war, Australia did so too automatically. This was how Australia entered the First World War. Nevertheless, most Australians welcomed the war as an opportunity to either support the defence of Empire and the White race, or to prove the valour of Australia as a new nation and improved Anglo-Saxon race worthy of self-governance.

Militarisation as Colonial Governance

The concept of militarisation has gone through cycles of rise and fall and is the subject of debate in many disciplines.[1] For the purpose of my investigation into how war and the military enable settler colonialism, I characterise militarisation as a governing rationality predicated on the valorisation of Western-centric armed forces and war. It involves practices and logics that align the state, the military and society, enabling and facilitating the process of governing a society. Thus, militarisation encompasses the processes that construct, shape and rearrange social relations and identities through war, war narratives, and inclusion in military culture and power of a Western nature. Ultimately, these processes reproduce political authority and govern relations of power.

My characterisation of militarisation as a governing rationality draws from Foucault's (1991)idea of governmentality, that is, a governing rationality that operates by shaping individuals' bodies, behaviour and subjectivity. Foucault developed the concept of governmentality to describe the individualising practices of liberal governance. In liberal societies, Foucault explained, the art of governing rests less on coercive methods and more on establishing institutions and norms that imbue individuals with liberal principles and shape their sense of self. As such, liberal subjects can govern themselves by feeling invested in the system that produces them and their identity. In this respect, I understand governmentality as a governing rationality resting on the logic that subjects govern themselves by internalising an identity which gives them meaning in society.

A conceptualisation of militarisation that operates in the order of governmentality identifies the governing rationalities that achieve governance by producing disciplined and self-governing subjects through military institutions and discourses. The institution of conscription in Europe in the nineteenth century is a case in point. Conscription was more than a strategy of war; it was a militarising practice of governance that made the figuration of the modern nation-state: the citizen-soldier. Foucault (1975) identified conscription as an early expression of liberal governmentality that emerged in the eighteenth century. It was designed to discipline political subjects and produce 'docile bodies', subjects made governable through training and analysis of the body (1975: 168). Conscription was part of the political processes that targeted individual bodies to create a cohesive social body, the nation. It gave unprecedented and large-scale access to the male body to be trained, standardised and disciplined. In this respect, the military barrack was a laboratory where a 'new' man was made for the emerging nation-state. Conscription homogenised male bodies through drills and disciplinary practices, and standardised societal norms around adulthood, masculinity and marriage. It also shaped men's political identity by reconfiguring men into citizen-soldiers willing to take up arms for the protection of their political community. Ultimately, conscription welded together military and civilian discipline and became *magister patriae*, the institution that diffused the common language, a shared culture and a sense of national belonging within a territory delineated apart from other states. It was also a particularly effective governing practice to train the lower classes and rural population into political obedience and instil in them a sense of belonging and loyalty towards the central political authority (Best 1989; Drake 2002; Conversi 2008; Schneid 2009). Immersed in a military culture that revolved around the protection of the nation from other nations, conscripts went from being men loyal to no one, to becoming citizen-soldiers tasked with the defence and preservation of their nation.

Conscription and military training governed nation-states as much as empires. In recognition of the governing and disciplining properties of military training, by the twentieth century most empires had established bureaucracies to make colonial soldiers (Killingray and Omissi 1999). Raising colonial armies was a strategy of colonial governance intended to establish a relation of subordination between colonial authorities and colonised subjects and societies. Different colonial societies had different recruitment strategies, but they were all designed to position colonial soldiers under the authority of White officers (Killingray 1999: 2). Colonial armies were extensions of and supplements to the national armies of nation-empires and provided labour and resources for the defence and expansion of empires. For example, in the First World War, Britain deployed 1.5 million colonial soldiers from India, and France recruited 500,000 colonial troops from its colonies in Africa and Indochina. Most of these colonial soldiers were sent to fight in Europe to support Britain and France's national armies. Colonial soldiers were also a cost-effective strategy to guard the fringes of the empire and operate in environments inhospitable to European soldiers. Often, they were deployed locally, but outside the areas where they came from to fight against other Indigenous and local populations resisting colonisation. For example, the Dutch East India Company relied on Asian soldiers to maintain and expand its control over the east Asia region, and France deployed colonial soldiers against anti-imperial revolts in Indochina and Algeria as late as 1953 and 1960, respectively (Killingray 1999).

Notions of race and civilisation played a significant role in the militarisation of colonial subjects and the consolidation of colonial military governance. Following Orientalist logics and discourses, Europeans perceived themselves as a superior civilisation and non-European peoples as savage, violent and brutal (Said 1995). European colonisers proposed European-style military training as a way to elevate savage warriors to civilised soldiers (McKenna and Ward 2007; Streets 2017). For example, France articulated colonial military training as a gift of civilisation to Africans, and African colonial soldiers were persuaded that they had to repay their 'blood debt', 'the debt Africans owed the French for bringing civilization to their people and saving them from local and ruthless tyrants' (Ginio 2017: 6).

In the nineteenth century, the British devised the construct of 'martial race' to consolidate control over the Indian subcontinent. Martial race was derived from a pyramidal colonial hierarchy with British Whiteness at the top, followed by imperial Whiteness (e.g., White Dominions) and at the bottom, Black and Brown colonial subjects (Gilfedder 2021: 99). To increase the effectiveness of military recruitment and training as a strategy of colonial governance, the British categorised certain communities and ethnic groups as 'martial races', which denoted them as naturally endowed with warring skills, albeit of a savage quality (Streets 2017). Then, the British persuaded these groups that they could achieve warring excellence with British military technology, strategy and command. The Gurkhas from Nepal, Sikhs from Punjab and Pashtuns from the Northwest Frontier were examples of martial races that were given preferential treatment and training within the British Indian Army. They were given advantages, including promotions, representation in the higher ranks and better pay that positioned them closer to colonial power and above other colonised communities. As Barkawi (2017) explains, this was a colonial strategy of divide and rule that made possible the subjugation of the vast and diverse Indian sub-continent. The militarising construct of martial race enabled the British to maintain control over the multi-ethnic colony of India and also to retain a privileged connection with postcolonial communities in south Asia, including the Gurkhas of Nepal (Chisholm and Ketola 2020; Chisholm 2022). Entire communities came to be invested in the construct of martial race for their economic subsistence, prestige and sense of identity in ways that persist after the end of colonisation.

In fact, the waves of decolonisation of the twentieth century did not end colonial military governance. Echoing Barkawi (2015), the formal end of empires and the shift to national sovereignty did not revert imperial military structures. Today's national militaries have imperial histories that remain largely unexamined in International Relations because of the Eurocentric assumptions which link soldiering with nationalism. Colonial military elites have remained in positions of power, while military colonialists have shifted to advisory roles as outsiders, still wielding a significant degree of influence in both military and civilian affairs within the former colonies. This is documented, for instance, in the work of Ginio (2017) on the enduring ties between France and the newly independent countries of west Africa.

Postcolonial scholarship uses militarisation as a heuristic tool to understand how Western military power is derived from colonial histories and constructs such as race. In this respect, Gani (2021) discusses European militarisation as having been driven by the discourse of civilisational advancement, especially articulated as a symbol of superiority over other racialised civilisations. European militarisation embedded racial hierarchies in the European imagination whereby they considered themselves to be superior because their military technologies could shoot, kill and conquer better than other civilisations. The military civilisational hierarchies that characterised colonial encounters still reverberate today in the struggles for decolonisation and the reclamation of power after colonisation.

The postcolonial literature on the Pacific is particularly instructive on how militarisation works as postcolonial governance. Sharing similar concerns over the enduring military and imperial history in the Pacific, Teaiwa (2008a), Shigematsu and Camacho (2010) and Gonzalez (2013) speak of militarisation to identify how colonial military governance changed society at its roots and created lasting militarised identities. For example, Teaiwa (2008a; 2008b) explains that, under British colonial rule, Fiji developed a strong military culture tied to the construct of martial race. Today, this culture is mobilised to sustain a patriarchal society and divisive racial relations between native Fijians and Indo-Fijians.

Finally, there is an emerging postcolonial scholarship interested in the affective dimension of militarisation as a governing practice. For example, Rashid (2020) investigates how emotions sustsain military's hegemony in Pakistan. The anti-colonial movement foregrounded the politics of masculinity and the reclaimation of male honour through the military. Being in the military in Pakistan is perceived as a noble and selfless act, and this is sustained by a series of evocative commemorative practices and gender relations shaped by the colonial experience. Chisholm (2022) focuses her attention on the Nepalese Gurkha, a group designated as martial race by the British colonial authority. Because of the legacies of colonisation, many Nepalese men still seek to become Gurkhas in the British Army. Chisholm explains that this is motivated less by economic gains and more by affective investments and a vision of happiness distorted by colonial relations. The desire to become a Gurkha suistains power relations that not only mainitain postcolonial ties between Britain and Nepal, but also militarise life in Nepalese communities.

This literature highlights military organisation as more than military strategy; it has functioned as a practice of national, colonial and postcolonial governance. I take this to be foundational scholarship for my investigation into settler military politics and militarisation in Australia. It sheds light on the working of Australian nation-building in and after empire, and guides me to identify the racialised, gendered and affective practices of military governance that also permeate the Australian context.

Nevertheless, the idiosyncrasies of the settler colonial project prompted me to examine dynamics beyond this scholarship. For example, while colonial societies had developed bureaucracies to make colonial soldiers for colonial governance, in the settler colonial frontiers, the settlers were fighting against Indigenous people. In colonial societies, colonial soldiers were the quintessential expression of colonial power: they were disciplined subaltern workers in the service of colonial power. Conversely, in settler colonial societies, the continued existence of Indigenous people was a reminder that the settler mission was unfinished. The widespread exclusion of Indigenous people from settler militaries until the early twentieth century, and in Australia as late as the 1950s, meant that the construct of martial race was rarely deployed as a strategy of governance because it ran counter to the settler discourse that Indigenous people were either a dying race or being assimilated into settler societies.

In settler societies, the colonisers do not leave; instead, they establish a state independent from the empire that nonetheless pursues logics of Indigenous dispossession. Increasingly, these societies have come to include Indigenous people as an expression of multiculturalism and diversity, and Indigenous people are now represented in institutions such as the military as a manifestation of Indigenous–settler reconciliation. In settler societies, the construct of martial race has emerged only since the 1980s to promote Indigenous military service (Sheffield 2017). Today, Indigenous military service is sought after by settler societies because it is the ultimate expression of settler authority which demonstrates that Indigenous people are willing to commit the ultimate sacrifice for the settler nation.

Applied to settler colonial contexts, militarisation as colonial governance must capture the rationalities of martial dispossession of Indigenous land and the governing practices that legitimise the settler state and society. Therefore, it cannot be limited to an investigation of the militarisation of Indigenous people as the counterpart or mirror of colonial subjects in non-settler colonial societies. In this book, I attempt to elucidate the peculiarities of military governance in settler colonial Australia and how it works to dispossess Indigenous people from their land and consolidate a society of settlers.

Settler Colonialism and Governance

In settler societies, militarisation has its own history and manifestations because, as Veracini (2010: 5) remarks, settler colonialism is driven by a different rationality than other types of colonialism. Settler colonialism does not aim to extract resources and labour from the colony to accrue wealth to the metropole; instead, it is a political project to take control of Indigenous land and build a new society of settlers. Colonial societies are appendages and factories designed to supply resources and manpower to the imperial metropole, whereas settler colonies are pioneering land to explore the possibilities for alternative social and political formations. This means that they have different properties and modes of governance. I wish to elucidate those of settler societies drawing from the Australian experience.

The core feature of settler colonialism is the settler society, that is, a society of immigrants from a foreign country permanently established on land inhabited by Indigenous people. As Wolfe (1998: 2) puts it, settler colonialism is characterised by the permanent and sedentary nature of the colonisers who 'come to stay'. Importantly, as settlers establish their society, they replace Indigenous life and communities. Historically, settler colonialism was linked to imperialism insofar as the settlers were imperial explorers and generals looking to expand their empires to the edge of the world. These men were pioneers who established the 'frontiers', legal spaces of violence against Indigenous people designed to establish imperial possession of the land (Evans 2009). Settler pioneers brought with them imperial sovereignty, which, once established, could be transformed into nationalist sovereignty. This sovereign mutation allowed settler colonialism to survive the waves of decolonisation that have characterised the world since the aftermath of the Second World War. Instead of leaving, settlers declared the independence of the settler state from the mother country, and thus continued their project of dispossession and occupation as independent nation-states away from the spotlight and the bad press of imperialism. The link with imperialism, the cohabitation of settler and Indigenous nations, and the reliance on migration processes make settler colonialism inherently an international phenomenon which remains underexamined in International Relations.

Settler colonialism is animated by logics of possession, that is, rationalities that justify settler ownership of the land in spite of Indigenous sovereignty. Settler possession is intrinsically linked with Indigenous dispossession. These logics rely on race, and especially on the power relations instituted through the working of Whiteness. Hence, Moreton-Robinson (2015) calls these 'logics of White possessive'. Starting from the premise that during modernity – broadly identified with the European Enlightenment – Whiteness became an invisible norm of moral superiority, Moreton-Robinson expounds how Europeans established settler sovereignty on the ground that Indigenous people were primitive, uncivilised and subhuman. This is especially apparent in the case of Australia, where British settlers justified their claim to the land by asserting that it was uninhabited since, in their view, Indigenous peoples lacked a recognised government or defined land ownership. Indigenous people were perceived to live in a state of nature set in opposition to White civility. Thus, the construct of Whiteness and the attendant perception of Indigenous people's moral and civilisational inferiority were foundational to the denial of Indigenous sovereignty and the establishment of British sovereignty over Indigenous land. This racist discourse not only denied Indigenous sovereignty, but also drove measures of extermination, exclusion and discipline of the Indigenous body that reproduce settler sovereignty. Thus, Moreton-Robinson concludes that race is a means of expropriating Indigenous land as well as of regulating and defending the settler society (2015: 156).

Because of the racial foundation of settler sovereignty, settler colonialism is ultimately concerned with managing race relations. It is relevant to recall Wolfe's (2006) observation that settler colonialism is not an event but a structure and an organising system that reproduces the dispossession of Indigenous people and consolidates the new society of settlers. In his analysis, settler colonialism is animated by the 'logic of elimination of the native', a procedural and systemic way of expropriating Indigenous land to consolidate a new settler society. Initially, this logic was executed through means of physical extermination, but then relied more on practices of confinement, miscegenation and assimilation. This is because, as Wolfe (2006: 387) remarks, 'settler colonialism is inherently eliminatory but not invariably genocidal'. The logic of elimination is operationalised to manage race relations and consolidate Whiteness. For example, in Australia, the practice of physical extermination was intended to diminish the number of Indigenous bodies that were an obstacle to White sovereignty. Confinement evacuated Indigenous people from the emerging White society and subjected them to strict forms of control that prevented their interference with the consolidation of the White settler society. Miscegenation involved complicated logics of blood quantum intended to thin down and eventually eliminate the Indigenous race. And assimilation was intended to sever the family and cultural connections and encourage Indigenous people to identify with White society (Wolfe 1994). Notably, then, the logics of elimination can also manifest in practices that irreversibly alter the Indigenous sense of self by damaging and destroying people's connection to culture and land which are integral to Indigenous identity.

In its latest iteration, settler governance involves the inclusion, and at times even celebration, of Indigenous people. According to critical Indigenous scholars, including Coulthard (2014), Moreton-Robison (2015) and Simpson (2014), Indigenous recognition by the settler state is a practice that reinforces settler authority and sovereignty. Indigenous people are recognised as citizens of the settler state rather than as sovereign subjects and nations. Furthermore, these critical scholars concur that Indigenous citizenship of the settler state bolsters power dynamics that discipline and police Indigenous bodies and facilitate state intervention in Indigenous affairs. The critical investigation of Strakosch (2019: 115) shows that Australian Indigenous policy is 'the key space where the Australian state encounters Aboriginal and Torres Strait Islander polities and seeks to resolve colonial conflict in its favour'. She finds that Indigenous policy deviates attention from the power structures instituted by colonial dispossession and instead focuses on Indigenous people and their projected deficiencies as a matter of action and intervention (see also Strakosch 2015).

The settler state utilises Indigenous inclusion to prefigure a postcolonial and post-racial nation that is asserted but not manifested (Coulthard 2014). In fact, inclusion is yet to do away with structures of domination that limit Indigenous autonomy and negate Indigenous sovereignty. Maddison (2019a) explains that inclusion is mobilised to erase colonial violence and dispossession through a discourse of Indigenous–settler reconciliation. She calls this 'the colonial fantasy' to encapsulate the deluded hope of settler societies that through reconciliation, colonisers will stop being invaders and will enjoy the wealth of the nation equally and together with Indigenous people. The inclusion of Indigenous people in settler society, creates opportunities to cast colonisation as less relevant for the present (Caso 2020). As the colonial past is decoupled from the assumed postcolonial present, the decolonial future is foreclosed, and thus Indigenous people find themselves stuck in what Strakosch and Macoun (2012) call 'the vanishing endpoint of settler colonialism'. In the assumed postcolonial present, Indigenous people are treated as equal, but without an account of the disadvantaging legacy of colonial structures and deprived of the tools to achieve decolonisation (Watego 2021). Thus, when they fail to meet the expectations of equality, they are pathologised and subjected to state intervention. Strakosch and Macoun (2012) contend that this assumed equality operates as a logic of elimination which erases Indigenous alterity and conceals the power differential between colonisers and colonised that still structures settler societies (see also, Maddison and Nakata 2020).

Colonisation: Was It War?

So, how did militarisation contribute to settler colonial governance in Australia? I suggest that settler militarisation operates as a series of discursive practices that valorise modern military and warfare to rationalise the dispossession of Indigenous people from their land and the consolidation of the settler society. The first, and foundational, act of settler militarisation to consider in Australia is the lack of war declaration by the British invaders against Indigenous peoples in the early days of colonisation. The European valorisation of military warfare over other types denied colonial warfare the status of war. Colonial warfare not only established settler sovereignty, but also covered up the existence of an Indigenous population that resisted British invasion, and thus mounted the longstanding fiction that Australia was settled peacefully. As it will be examined in detail in the next section, it allowed a national myth of origin devoid of colonial violence to be established. But, first, let us examine the dynamics of colonial warfare which established settler sovereignty without a war declaration.

The lack of a war declaration is the very foundation of modern Australia. According to European international law, in the eighteenth century, European powers could gain legal sovereignty over new land in three ways: (1) by conquest, (2) by cession, and (3) by occupation of unoccupied land. Upon encountering Indigenous peoples, the British neither declared a war of conquest, nor made treaties leading to the cession of Indigenous land. Instead, they claimed the land on the ground that it was unoccupied by appealing to the legal construct of *terra nullius*, the third way to gain legal sovereignty. What led the British onto this third path was their moral and civilisational sense superiority vis-à-vis Indigenous people who had significantly different ways of organising life and society.

The claim that Indigenous land was unoccupied stemmed from the sense of superiority of the White race and civility as discussed above. It was also the product of what Gani (2021) calls 'European racial militarism'. Gani explains that racial militarism operates both as a theory of civilisational supremacy and a practice of chauvinism for the purpose of enacting colonial violence. Since the seventeenth century, Europeans established a hierarchical schema of civilisations in which they aspired to be the dominant group. This aspiration pushed Europeans to develop more sophisticated military technologies and find opportunities to test them against other populations and refine their schema of civilisations. As Gani puts it, 'rising European militarism in the 18th and 19th centuries played a central role in embedding racial hierarchies in the European imagination', and, she continues, 'that imagination was then enacted materially through imperial administration in the colonies' (2021: 551). As Europeans positioned themselves at the top of the schema of civilisation, they also universalised a narrow definition of war that reflected their own experience. They defined war as the series of battles fought by regular armies of governments of equal standing. Effectively, this disqualified other experiences of war as derivations and deviations of war (Barkawi 2016).

When the British settlers faced Indigenous people in Australia, they did not declare war because, according to them, the latter did not make opponents worthy or capable of warfare. The British saw Indigenous people as primitive, lacking clothing and shelter. Indigenous weapons did not match the power of British military technology and the British believed that Indigenous people could not mount a defence. Therefore, armed with a sense of superiority (and weapons), the British made Indigenous people British subjects with the aim of civilising them. This had two implications. First, it enabled the claim that the land was unoccupied. According to the British, Indigenous people did not have a government with which to conduct diplomacy, nor did they have the means to defend themselves, and therefore *terra nullius* was appropriate. Secondly, the absence of a war declaration and the classification of Indigenous people as British subjects disqualified Indigenous people as war opponents and made their resistance to colonisation a matter of domestic order.

Despite the lack of a war declaration, historical records show that 'conflict broke out between invading settlers and resident Aborigines within a few weeks of the foundation of Sydney and was apparent on every frontier for the next 140 years' (Reynolds 2013: 49). Colonial warfare had its own pattern characterised by the British using violence to establish the settlements, Indigenous people conducting small-scale attacks against settlers and settlements, and settlers retaliating against Indigenous people with gun violence and punitive missions. Records indicate that Indigenous people and settlers involved in colonial warfare died in ones and twos hit by a spear or firearm (Ryan 2013: 221). This was the cycle of violence that characterised colonial warfare in Australia. The number of casualties remain uncertain, ranging from 20,000 to 100,000 Aboriginal people, and from 2,000 to 3,000 settlers. While uncertain, these figures show the power imbalance that characterised the Frontier Wars.

The Frontier Wars were not a conventional war of the European type, but they were nonetheless war. Connor comments that 'traditional Aboriginal warfare must be understood in its own terms and not by definitions of "war" imposed from other cultures' (2002: 2). Just like European warfare was derived from its own society, so was Aboriginal warfare, and therefore we must investigate Aboriginal society and modes of warfare to understand the Frontier Wars. Aboriginal people lived in small autonomous tribes connected to their land. To give a sense of the diversity of Aboriginal life at the time of British invasion, there were approximately 260 distinct language groups. Each Aboriginal tribe had its own economy, culture and artefacts, but despite differences, there were similarities in the way they lived and fought. They organised in small autonomous groups and 'the aim of traditional Aboriginal warfare was to continually assert the superiority of one's groups over neighbouring groups, rather than to conquer, destroy or displace those groups' (Connor 2002: 2). As Kombumerri and Wakka Wakka scholar Mary Graham told in a public lecture in 2022, the word 'conquest' does not even exist in Aboriginal languages. The main weapons of Aboriginal people were the spear and the shield, and ambush, treachery and raids were their preferred tactics of war. This is how Aboriginal tribes faced the British invaders. They used their knowledge of the territory to study the invaders and attack them by surprise. They targeted the locations which were identified as the settler's source of food and security to weaken their opponents and persuade them to leave. But they operated autonomously rather than as one single Aboriginal group and therefore there is not one uniform tactic to speak of (Connor 2002: 21).

The nineteenth century was a particularly violent period in the Australian colonies, and despite the lack of a war declaration, it was evident to both the British settlers and Indigenous people that they were in competition and conflict with one another. Notwithstanding the lack of war declaration and the attempts of the settlers to hide colonial violence to retain the legality of *terra nullius*, historian Reynolds finds evidence of settlers using the language of war in their memoirs, communications and news reporting. For example, a dispatch from Governor Arthur to the Colonial Office in 1829 reads (Reynolds 2013: 87):

> The *species of warfare* which we are carrying on with them is of the most distressing nature; they suddenly appear, commit some act of outrage and then as suddenly vanish: if pursued it seems impossible to surround and capture them. (emphasis added)

Today, there is abundant historical research that documents colonial warfare, including the publicly available podcast series by Kooma, Murawarii and Gamilaraay radio host and activist Boe Spearim (2020), *Frontier War Stories*. The British Empire went to what is now called Australia with expansionist intents animated by economic considerations, entitlement to land and resources, and a sense of civilisational superiority. They encountered Indigenous resistance. Despite the lack of a war declaration, the British invasion resulted in the most violent period known to Aboriginal people and led to the outbreak of violence that is better characterised as warfare.

The dispossessing effects of the lack of a war declaration continue to this day. The lack of a war declaration removed the formality and legal documentation of war and enabled Australia to tell its history of colonisation as a peaceful process. For a long time until the late twentieth century, most settler Australians were unaware of the history of colonial warfare in their own country and believed that the land was settled peacefully. Until the 1980s, this was the prevalent narrative about the colonisation of Australia that children studied in school (Reynolds 1981; 2000). Importantly, this is a settler strategy because the narrative about peaceful settlement maintains the legitimacy of the settler state by concealing that it was founded on the violent dispossession of Indigenous people.

In this respect, the Australian War Memorial is an important actor of settler militarisation. At the end of the First World War, Australian official war correspondent and historiographer, Charles Bean, claimed that Australia needed a war memorial because prior to the war, Australians did not know war. He wrote:

> [W]ar *never had happened there* [in Australia]. In the 126 years, from the day when Captain Arthur Phillip's eleven ships landed their 1100 white folk in the strange silence of grass and gum trees at Sydney Cove, to that on which the same foreshore clanged with the whirl of trams and crowds in the hub of Sydney's 800,000 people – for four

generations pioneers, squatters, farmers, city folk had gone their ways
without a serious thought of being interfered with except within the
law. (Bean 1948: 54; emphasis added)

Bean's words and his vision to establish the Australian War Memorial
to commemorate Australia's baptism of fire consolidated the view
that, prior to the First World War, Australians had never experienced
the bloodbath and chaos of war but only peace and law. Effectively,
this swept colonial warfare under the carpet and removed it from the
emerging national conscience.

The Australian War Memorial has long been involved in settler militarisation to the extent that it is the primary institution that elevates
modern warfare to national myth of origin and dismisses colonial
warfare as war proper. Most notably, despite the mission of the Australian War Memorial to help Australians understand and commemorate the experience of war and the growing literature that characterises
the Frontier Wars as war, colonial warfare remains unrepresented in
the galleries of the Memorial. This exclusion is often performed by
appealing to the Australian War Memorial Act 1980 which incorporated the Memorial and established its functions. According to the Act,
the Memorial is set as an institution to commemorate Australians
who have died on, or as a result of, active service in the Defence Forces.
It also sets out to help Australians understand their military history,
which is defined as the history of: (a) 'wars and warlike operations in
which Australians have been on active service, including the events
leading up to, and the aftermath of, such wars and warlike operations';
and of (b) 'the Defence Force'. Defence Force includes 'any naval or
military force of the Crown raised in Australia before the establishment of the Commonwealth'. This very comprehensive definition of
terms and the function of the Memorial excludes Indigenous warfare
and paramilitary organisations such as the Native Police which, as
discussed later in his chapter, was a key actor of colonial warfare in
Australia.

As a way of illustrating how the Australian War Memorial Act 1980
is invoked to justify the Memorial's exclusion of the Frontier Wars
from its galleries, consider a blog from 2013 that is still available
on the Memorial's website (AWM 2014), where the blogger speaks
in defence of the exclusion of the Frontier Wars from the Memorial:

As defined in the Australian War Memorial Act 1980, the Memorial's
official role is to develop a Memorial for Australians who have died
on, or as a result of, active service, or as a result of any war or warlike

operation in which Australians have been on active service. The definition does not include internal conflicts between the Indigenous populations and the colonial powers of the day.

The blogger continues:

> The "Frontier Wars" [inverted commas in original] were a series of actions that were carried out by British colonial forces stationed in Australia, by the police, and by local settlers. It is important to note that the state police forces used Indigenous Australians to hunt down and kill other Indigenous Australians; but the Memorial has found no substantial evidence that home-grown military units, whether state colonial forces or post-Federation Australian military units, ever fought against the Indigenous population of this country.

This is a demonstration of how the Australian War Memorial has been involved in policing the definition of war to exclude colonial warfare. The author of this blog available on the Memorial's website reluctantly uses the phrase Frontier Wars, which is placed in inverted commas. He also remarks that there is no evidence of military organisation during the Frontier Wars and that violence was carried by civilians rather than the military. His is a forceful attempt to disqualify non-military and paramilitary warfare as war proper.

To be clear, this is not the personal campaign of a single blogger and it has enjoyed institutional support by the Council of the Memorial. For example, in 2013, a journalist asked the Memorial's former director Brendan Nelson (2013) about the exclusion of the Frontier Wars, to which he replied:

> [T]he Australian War Memorial is the story of Australians in war deployed on behalf of Australia overseas, not a war as it is described within Australia, in this case against colonial militia, in some cases British forces and Indigenous Australians.

This remained the official position for his term as director until 2019, although at the time of revising this book at the end of 2022, Nelson, then serving as chair of the Memorial, promised that the Frontier Wars would feature in the renovated building.[2] Nelson's position expressed in the quote above further demonstrates the operation of the Memorial to police the definition of war and distinguish between 'proper' war that involves the deployment of the military abroad and other less valid types of warfare, such as colonisation.

Here it is relevant to bring in scholarship that calls for the decolonisation of war. Barkawi, the initiator of Critical War Studies, notes that war is a universal experience, and yet, 'in social and political inquiry, war as a concept is imagined primarily in provincial terms, those of the West and its major wars' (Barkawi 2016: 199). And indeed, the settler state of Australia has greatly benefitted from the provincial definition of war and the exclusion of colonial warfare. To account for the diversity of war experiences and to decolonise warfare, Barkawi offers a critique of the main building blocks of Eurocentric warfare. He suggests that we need to move away from the idea that the state is the primary actor in war, not least because this is a relatively recent political formation. For the longest time, empires and empire-states were the main actors in international relations, but so were clans, tribes and vassal states. They too conducted war which made and shaped the international system. He also highlights that there is more to war than battle, and that many wars have relied on repressive and oppressive strategies rather than military confrontation and battle. Finally, he invites us to revisit the clear demarcation between war and peace, recognising that these concepts are arbitrary and often shaped by the narratives of the winning side (see also Sabaratnam 2023).

Imperial Military and Paramilitary Organisations in the Australian Colonies

The operation of militarisation in the development of settler Australia can further be observed by the presence of imperial military and colonial paramilitary organisations in the early stages of colonisation. This investigation is particularly compelling to dispel the belief that the military was not involved in the colonisation of Australia. It demonstrates the role that imperial military and colonial paramilitary organisations played in the militarisation and consolidation of the early stages of settler colonialism.

The military man was a prominent figure in the early settlement of Australia. Walsh (1988: 64) finds that 'Australia's development in the period between 1788–1888 owes much to the enterprise and hard work of military and naval personnel'. The first British fleet that arrived in Australia in 1788 included around 500 men from the British Navy and Marines, making up one-third of the crew. A battalion of 800 men from the British Army followed suit. They manned garrison posts and built fortifications and coastal defences in case of attack. Their primary task was to defend the British set-tlements from other European imperial powers looking to expand their possessions in the new world. However, they did not see much action in this respect, and therefore took on colonial governing roles and administrative tasks in the penal system, such as escorting chain-gangs of prisoners and officiating at the execution of convicts. They also conducted explorative missions that pushed the frontiers, developed the settlements, and contributed to the advancement of science and trade in the colonies. As Walsh (1988: 44) notes, such achievements were possible because in the penal colony, military and naval officers were men distinguished by their expertise, educa-tion and commanding presence, and they retained a monopoly in this regard until the 1850s. Furthermore, military men had substan-tial capital derived not only from their service but also from large land grants that incentivised their relocation to Australia. Therefore, the military dominated the political, judicial and economic life of the colonies. This meant not only that the settlements resembled garrison towns but also that society in the early colony had a strong military flavour.

It soon became evident that the main security threat to the col-onies did not come from other European expansionist powers, but from within the colonies themselves in the form of convict uprisings and Aboriginal attacks against settlers and settlements. The admin-istrators responded by establishing the colonial police, which was in fact a paramilitary organisation. The term paramilitary is used to describe organisations that have military-like structures, functions and training, but operate outside the regular armed forces. The colo-nial police were meant to mirror the New Police (or Metropolitan Police) in England created to respond to increasing concerns about crime and public disorder in metropolitan cities. But imperial polic-ing turned out to be different to the extent that it had less to do with the prevention and detection of crime and more with the protection of British property in the colony and the maintenance of social and racial order. Moreover, conversely to the New Police in England, colo-nial officers were armed and mounted on horses, and many had a military background that they brought into their new policing roles. The military background of colonial police officers also shaped the structure of the organisation which was strongly hierarchical and had ranks and a chain of command that resembled military units. In this respect, Anderson and Killingray (2017: 4) echo that 'colonial police were often indistinguishable from a military garrison'.

The establishment of the colonial police freed the British Imperial Forces in Australia to be relocated elsewhere. By the 1840s, the presence of the British soldiers in Australia had diminished significantly, and by 1870, the British garrison departed completely. This propelled the militarisation of Australian masculinity as discussed in Chapter 3. Connor (2002: xii) notes that following the departure of the British military, more civilians took up arms, and life in the Australian colonies became more violent as a result. By 1860, most towns had voluntary militias and rifle clubs which contributed to the spread of small firearms. Furthermore, local militias made of amateur, voluntary and part-time citizen-soldiers took up arms and tasks in support of the colonial police which often resulted in extra-judicial violence, especially against Indigenous people. Armed violence was used in lieu of justice systems and also in retaliation against Indigenous resistance to colonisation.

As part of the colonial police, in 1837, the Australian colonies established the Native Police specifically designed to deal with the 'problem of the natives'. The Native Police were paramilitary in nature and commanded by officers with a military background (Nettelbeck and Smandych 2010: 356). Officers were armed with firearms and horses, and were tasked with the enforcement of British rule, but also with the facilitation of British settlement and the expansion of the frontiers (Nettelbeck and Smandych 2010: 361; Nettelbeck and Ryan 2018: 51). The operation of the Native Police was reactive and punitive rather than preventive (Rogers 2018: 33) and involved the submission of Indigenous peoples to colonial rule, or, otherwise, their extermination (Nettelbeck and Smandych 2010: 357). It is estimated that between 1859 and 1897, the Native Police were involved in the killing of 24,000 Indigenous people (Reynolds 2013: 132).

The Native Police were not only a key actor in colonial warfare, but also an early attempt to militarise a few selected Indigenous people. It included a handful of Aboriginal men and women who served as troopers and trackers under the command of White officers. Some were recruited through coercion and intimidation (Richards 2008), while others were promised prestige and status in colonial society, colonial goods, and daily food rations and wages (Rogers 2018: 34–5). While deeply distrustful of Indigenous people, police officers recognised that Indigenous knowledge of the territory and their survival skills were an asset that helped them to do their job in the frontiers. Some Aboriginal people in the Native Police were trained to be mediators and to persuade other Aboriginal people to submit to British rule. Their inclusion in the Native Police was intended to help pacify Aboriginal people and facilitate their acceptance of British rule (Nettelbeck and Ryan 2018). The inclusion of Aboriginal troopers and trackers in the Native Police also had disciplinary purposes. As Nettelbeck and Ryan (2018: 50) explain, military training was intended to introduce and educate selected Aboriginal individuals in the ways of 'neatness, decency, and cleanliness' of civilised men, involve them in public service and make them into respectable British subjects.

Despite the training, Aboriginal troopers were not always compliant and had limited success as mediators. When the settlers realised the ineffectiveness of their strategy, the Native Police were turned into an institution to execute extra-judicial violence against Indigenous people (Nettelbeck and Ryan 2018: 50). The settlers exploited rivalries between Aboriginal people to set them against one another and incite them to kill other Indigenous people. They also deployed Aboriginal troopers far away from where they were recruited to ensure that personal connections did not interfere with orders to hunt and kill other Indigenous people (Richards 2008).

The Native Police were an effective instrument of colonial warfare, especially in the context where war was not declared and Indigenous people were under British law. The Native Police were a paramilitary organisation at the front of a war against Indigenous people which was fought in the guise of domestic law enforcement. It was also a tactic to impose British sovereignty over Indigenous people. As British sovereignty was not legitimised by treaties, the Native Police aimed to produce legitimacy by including a few selected Aboriginal people and make them the executive hand of British sovereignty over their land. The preferential treatment of the few Aboriginal people who were included in the Native Police, were compensated, dressed in colonial clothes and armed with western weapons against tribal enemies prompted feelings of resentment among First Nations people which exacerbated divisions and weakened the Indigenous resistance to colonisation. Thus, this phase of militarisation advanced settler colonialism by means of subjugation, assimilation and extermination.

In the last decade of the nineteenth century, the lethal use of force by the Native Police came under public scrutiny and the attitude towards the militarisation of Indigenous people changed in favour of a policy of exclusion. Between the mid- and late nineteenth century, the colonies established the Protection System, a legislative framework that controlled the lives of Aboriginal people and segregated them in missions under the 'protection' of White people. In 1869, 1886 and 1887, respectively, Victoria, Western Australia and Queensland passed Protection Acts to administer Indigenous people. The Protection System was a draconian regime of control that micromanaged the lives of Indigenous people and was animated by a paternalistic ideology towards inferior races and the idea that Indigenous people were a dying race. It categorised Indigenous people according to a logic of blood quantum to distinguish between those who had to be removed from society and put in missions and those who were miscegenated and ready to be assimilated. The Protection System enabled the strict control of Indigenous people under the management of White people, which included removal from their land and segregation in missions and stations, the separation of Indigenous families, and restricted access to wages and pensions (McDonnell and Dodson 2018: 35–7; Sheffield and Riseman 2019: 34). As the Protection System consolidated, the deliberate lethal violence against Indigenous people became controversial, and by the turn of the century, the Native Police were disbanded, and the Aboriginal officers redeployed as trackers in a police force that largely dropped its military nature.

Race and the Organisation of Defence

Another manifestation of settler militarisation to consider is the emergence and organisation of the Australian Defence Force. In this section, I discuss how race and racism operated as militarising discursive practices that activated Australia's organisation of defence. Ultimately, I demonstrate that the organisation of Australia's defence contributed to the settler colonial project in two ways. First, it consolidated Whiteness and the logic of White possessive. Secondly, it contributed to the development of the settler state as an autonomous political unit in international relations.

At the turn of the twentieth century, race was the glue that kept Australia close to Britain. By the mid-nineteenth century, race was a prominent political discourse in the West largely popularised by the influence of social Darwinism. In particular, race was understood as a hierarchy and structuring principle that differentiated between superior fair-skinned populations and inferior dark-skinned people (Du Bois 1925; Lake and Reynolds 2008). In this respect, it promoted conflict as much as it fostered alliances. Bell (2020) finds that the idea of the Anglo-Saxon race was a powerful political ideology that kept the Angloworld comprising Britain, its Dominions and the United States together. Accordingly, they were united not merely by economic, political and technological ties, but, above all, by deep racial connections. Bell explains that the politicisation of racial connections was source of race patriotism, that is, 'loyalty and affective signification that identifies race as a privileged site of political devotion' (2020: 251).

Race patriotism was particularly prominent in Australia where, according to Ward (2008: 243), it was more pronounced than in Canada and Britain. As a White British enclave in the Pacific, established on Aboriginal land and neighbouring Asians and Pacific Islanders, Australia felt a deep sense of racial vulnerability that animated its race patriotism. For Australia, race patriotism was more than a way to remain connected to the Anglo-Saxon race from the fringes of the world; it was also a defence strategy to ensure the protection of Britain in case of an attack from its Asian neighbours. Australia was particularly anxious about how China's migration and Japan's rising power could contaminate the White race and invade Australia (Lowe 1995: 128; Ward 2008: 240). Australia's racial anxieties became more pronounced at the prospect of becoming a separate nation from the British Empire. Therefore, at federation in 1901, Australia decided to remain tied to Britain, especially in matters of security. The British king remained the sovereign head of the Australian Defence Force, thus leaving Australia effectively without an independent defence policy. Australia gained full control of its defence policy only in 1941 and with much reluctance. In 1931, Britain issued the Westminster Statute which declared all British Dominions to be self-governing states, including in matters of defence, but the Australian parliament passed legislation requiring that the Statute be adopted by parliament to apply. That happened eleven years after, in 1942.

Australia's racial anxieties and fear of abandonment following federation are evidenced in three pieces of legislation. The first, is the 1901 Immigration Restriction Act – otherwise known as the White Australia Policy – which limited the immigration of Asians and Pacific Islanders looking for work in the Australian mines as a way of protecting the racial purity and Western civilisation of the new nation. The White Australia Policy was one of the first acts passed by Australia as a federated nation. Secondly, in 1905, Australia established Empire Day to promote loyalty towards the British Empire. This legislation came a few years after 1901 as a demonstration that Australia continued to be loyal towards the British Empire and was not losing its connection as a result of federation. Maclean (1995: 85) notes that Empire Day targeted children as an ideal opportunity to teach them about the cultural ties with Britain and the military superiority of the British Empire. The third piece of legislation is the 1909 amendment to the Defence Act which introduced compulsory military training for boys and men between the ages of twelve and twenty-six and explicitly excluded people 'not substantially of European origin or descent' (McDonnell and Dodson 2018: 39). The institution of compulsory military training in peacetime followed the European tradition of the citizen-soldier whereby military training was intended to consolidate the bond between citizens and the state, impose a common language and history, foster respect for authority, and create a sense of national belonging (Conversi 2008). The clause that excluded racialised people was designed to consolidate Whiteness by imposing racial restrictions on military service and therefore limiting the opportunities for racialised people to claim the privileges of citizenship.

Australian race patriotism contended with the emerging sense of nationalism that was also strongly influenced by racial considerations. In fact, Australia's emerging sense of national identity was propelled by a sense of racial superiority. According to social Darwinism, Australian Britons were a superior evolution of the Anglo-Saxon race that adapted to the warmer climate. Life in the colony and the warmer weather made them 'tall, strong, athletic, loyal, practical, unaffected, informal and irreverent' (White 1981: 67–72; Holbrook 2014: 9). The Australian racial evolution was demonstrated not only by improved physical qualities, but also by the ability to generate new political and industrial relations that could breed social reform, including workers' rights and female suffrage (Maclean 1995: 66–7). Australia was a social laboratory and Australian Britons understood themselves to be participants in Darwinian experimentations for the evolution of the White race. While never disloyal to the British Empire, Australian nationalism was predicated on the rejection of certain British qualities that did not fit racial evolution. For example, Australians rejected the British love for authority and the class system in favour of equalitarianism and fair go, the sophisticated manners of the British gentleman in favour of rugged manliness, and British intellectualism for a love for sports and physicality (White 1981: 76–7).

The racial considerations that animated Australia's imperial patriotism and nationalism thrust the country into the First World War. Due to Australia's defence being under British control, when Britain declared war on Germany in 1914, Australia automatically became involved as well. Some nationalists questioned the participation of Australia in this British war on the ground that it was against Australia's national interest. They saw war as an old European institution that was foreign to Australia and from which Australia should have abstained (Maclean 1995: 66). But overall, both imperialists and nationalists responded to the declaration of war with enthusiasm and mobilised racial discourses in support of Australia's involvement in it. For the imperialists, it was an honour for Australia to serve the British Empire and prevent the degeneration of the race initiated by Germany. The fact that some half a million Australians were born in England, Wales, Scotland or Ireland, and even more had British parents or grandparents fuelled the imperialist rhetoric that Australians had a duty to pay to their own blood (Beaumont 2013). The nationalists saw the war as an opportunity to reinvigorate and demonstrate the qualities of the Australian race (Gilfedder 2021). They believed that war had regenerative and purifying properties and wanted to prove to the Empire that they 'were not the degenerate spawn of convict stock, but a thriving offshoot of the mother race' (Holbrook 2014: 15; see also Beaumont 1995: 4).

As happened across the world, the First World War instigated the armament of Australia. When the war began, the Australian Defence Force was largely underdeveloped and reliant on British command. Upon federation, the colonies transferred their military forces under the control of the federal government, and the Australian Defence Force was formally instituted with the Defence Act 1903. In 1909, an amendment to this Act introduced compulsory training for men who, however, could not be conscripted for overseas service. Australia established a regular army first, followed by small naval and flying units supported and commanded, respectively, by the British Royal Navy and the Royal Flying Corps. When Britain declared war on Germany, Australia pledged all its naval vessels and sailors and 20,000 men from the Royal Army. Immediately, Australia also established a new force of recruits dubbed the Australian Imperial Force, a name designed to convey that 'Australia's destiny was intertwined with that of the Empire' (Beaumont 2008: 294). This was a voluntary force as Australia did not institute overseas conscription during the war, despite two referenda. The war boosted Australia's military capabilities and experience and Australians gained military equipment and leadership that informed Australia's defence planning vis-à-vis the rise of Japan after the First World War.

The recruitment system of the Australian Imperial Force allowed the enlistment of White men only following the legislation of the Defence Act 1909 which barred men who were 'non substantially of European origin or descent'. This was an act of settler military governance aimed at consolidating the settler nation as White. It also worked in the order of settler militarisation by attracting Indigenous people looking for opportunities into the military and pushing them to identify with White society. Despite the racial restriction, an estimated 1,000 Indigenous men enlisted. Many did so by disguising their identity while others got in towards the end of the war when Australia relaxed racial restrictions because it was struggling to meet its war needs. When Australia faced a shortage of manpower in 1917, the concept of race was revisited to allow the enlistment of so-called "half-castes", a racist term used to define Indigenous people who had one White parent and fair skin. Although each person had their own reasons for joining the military, racism and the draconian control imposed by the Protection System were structural pulling factors. Indigenous people who served regardless of the restriction and the ongoing Frontier Wars saw the military as an opportunity to escape the oppressive control of the Protection System, travel, earn a regular wage, access the privileges of White society through soldier resettlement schemes, and push for the rights of Indigenous people (Furphy 2018; Maynard 2018; McDonnell and Dodson 2018). But eligible Indigenous men wanting to enlist had to sign a statutory declaration stating that they had 'associated with White people all my life'. As Scarlett notes, this was a strategy 'to promote the enlistment of Aboriginal men who associated with white people' (2015: 168). By extension, it also encouraged Aboriginal men to identify with White society at the expense of their community, identity and sovereignty. The assimilationist implications of this approach will be examined in detail in Chapter 5. Regrettably, while some experienced social mobility and managed their money for the first time, upon their return from the war, many men could not access the entitlement of soldiers to land, and their families were restricted from accessing veteran pensions (Maynard 2007: 39; Furphy 2018).

The Second World War further contributed to the development of the Australian Defence Force. Above all, it involved the crucial settler step in 1942 to ratify the Westminster Statute of 1931 which gave Australia sovereign control over its defence policy. With this step, Australia consolidated the settler state as an autonomous political unit in international relations. The new autonomy allowed Australia to shift its defence strategy from Britain to the United States. At the start of the war, Australia felt that the British decision to rely on Singapore to defend Australia from Japan was a poor military strategy and did not align with Australia's defence needs (Ward 2008). In 1942, Japan captured Singapore and used it as a base from which to attack Australia. In the eyes of Australians, this was a crucial moment that demonstrated the inability of the British Empire to ensure the security of Australia and prompted Australia to claim control of its own defence. As an act of sovereign defence, after the war Australia entered a new security alliance with the United States and New Zealand, ANZUS, which did not include Britain. From a defence perspective, Australia was formally a sovereign state and independent actor of international politics.

The Anzac Legend as Myth of Origin

Finally, to comprehensively capture the operation of settler militarisation in Australia, it is essential to consider the contrasting dynamics between the denial of the Frontier Wars and the wholehearted endorsement of the First World War as Australia's baptism of fire, a duality that ultimately reinforces White dominance and ownership of the land. Australia's involvement in the First World War is mythologised in the Anzac Legend, a story about how the sacrifice of the Australian soldiers in foreign lands made the nation. This sacrifice consecrated the settler possession of Indigenous land, as expressed by Australian historiographer Charles Bean (1948: 1096) who wrote:

> What these men [the Anzacs] did . . . rises, as it will always rise, above the mists of ages, a monument to great-hearted men; and, for their nation, *a possession for ever.* (emphasis added)

This poetic formulation underscores how the deeds and character of the Anzacs established the legitimate and perpetual possession of the country by the settlers.

The Anzac Legend is Australia's myth of origin. Most nations have a myth of origin, and many nations choose to ground their nation in war. A myth of origin is not an invented past, but an idealised narration of events and selected memories that are accepted to represent the inception of the nation. The scholarship on nationalism finds that a myth of origin grounds a nation's sense of identity and is fundamental for its reproduction, generation after generation (Anderson 1983). A myth of origin gives nationals a shared story to relate to one another, feel connected and foster a sense of belonging to an 'imagined community'. War is particularly fitting because it offers stories about heroism and tragedy, leaders and milestone events. It also offers highly emotional tales that can be passed on to future generations.

Australian children are introduced to the Anzac Legend as Australia's myth of origin in school where they learn a romantic story about how Australian soldiers made Australia when they landed at Gallipoli, in Turkey, on 25 April 1915 (Lake 2010a; Bailey and Brawley 2018; Holbrook 2018). The Anzac Legend is a mythologised narration of the bravery and sacrifice of Australian soldiers that contains highly emotional tones and a strong focus on personal stories. A quantitative study finds that 90 per cent of Australians associate the Anzac Legend with Australian national identity, with little variation by socio-demographic factors (Donoghue and Tranter 2015). Anecdotally, I keep going back to a friend's comment about the fact that in school, young Australians spend much time on the First World War, and no time on the Australian electoral system. The Anzac Legend is guarded by the Australian War Memorial and propagated also by other institutions such as the Department of Veterans Affairs (DVA) which sponsors educational resources. A most remarkable resource is the Anzac Portal, a Wikipedia-type website rich in archival material from the Australian War Memorial and which has been extensively consulted to produce this book.

Just as a myth of origin establishes the beginning of the nation in a particular moment, it also conceals other foundational histories. The Anzac Legend as Australia's myth of origin begets important critical questions. Holbrook (2014: 8) asks 'Why do so many Australians believe that their nation was born on a battlefield in Turkey on 25 April 1915, rather than in Melbourne on 1 January 1901 when six colonies became one Commonwealth?' Reynolds adds:

> If the Anzacs made the nation what does this say about the first hundred years of settlement? Was it all merely preparatory, just a prelude? Was there nothing that happened within the Australian colonies before 1915 that had the importance of the Anzac landing? (Reynolds 2010: 37)

These are important questions that highlight the arbitrariness of the Anzac Legend as Australia's myth of origin. Indeed, the Fist World War was a traumatic event for Australia and the world but, as Reynolds (2010: 38) insists, why has it been chosen as Australia's myth of origin, especially considering that Australia has several stories of progress and success such as early female suffrage, workers' rights and the welfare system?

An answer can be found in the investigation of Australia's anxious nationalism. Settler nations are particularly plagued by anxious nationalism because they are younger, and their history is complicated by less than flattering stories of migration, colonial violence and occupation. They also have imperial histories that they need to shake off to assert autonomy as nation-states. In this respect, settler societies are invested in having a strong myth of origin that can ground their people's sense of identity and belonging to the new place (Holbrook 2014).

The Anzac Legend aptly provides a narrative of national origin that is devoid of colonisation. It speaks about young enduring men who bravely sacrificed their life in foreign lands for the value of freedom. It insists on Australians as courageous and freedom-loving young men who cannot possibly be the British settlers who took the land and freedom of First Nations people. This is a myth about Australians as a new people and who are not the British colonisers. The insistence of Australians as a new people is a settler tactic to erase their connection with colonial violence and claim indigenous belonging to the country (Curthoys 2009: 11).

Furthermore, the Anzac Legend also served to manage the relation with imperial Britain and eventually emphasise Australian nationalism and autonomy. The Legend emerged soon after the First World War when the Australians fought alongside the British and in the name of the British Empire. Without betraying imperial belonging, it told the story of Australia as a modern embattled nation of its own and spoke of Australians as a people and how they distinguished themselves in battle and as a nation (Holbrook 2014). The Anzac Legend emerged at a time when nationalism was asserting itself as a major driver and organiser of international relations, and thus it gave Australians a sense of national identity, as well as national and international legitimacy. As the British Empire disintegrated, the Anzac Legend offered solid foundations to assert Australia's nationalism separate from the Empire. Between the 1960s and 1990s, the Anzac Legend was mobilised to recraft Australian national identity away from the British Empire and in the direction of multiculturalism, Australia's new policy since the late 1970s. The story was stripped of its militarist and imperialist connotations and narrated as a sentimental story of young Australians who bravely fought for their nation and greatly suffered because of the war (Holbrook 2018: 55). Ever since, the British Empire is rarely mentioned and, and its place has been taken by stories of women, ethnic soldiers and, more recently, Indigenous soldiers. While this may be taken as a sign of progress, Bongiorno (2014) explains that a multicultural Anzac Legend sustains a composite society united in its reverence for war and the military, and where questioning war and the military is considered to be un-Australian. This can help explain the limited critical engagement with Australia's war history despite the enormous war history literature. Being un-Australian is a poignant accusation in a settler society made of immigrants like Australia because nationalism relies on civic values, of which militarism is one. The accusation of being un-Australian can strip someone of national belonging with little recourse and appeal to blood ties.

The Anzac Legend grounds Australia's national identity in modern warfare. In recognition of the importance of modern warfare for the Australian nation, Inglis (1998: 343; see also Inglis 2016) describes the Anzac Legend as Australia's civic religion, that is, a body of precepts and rituals that offer a moral compass for citizens and the nation. The Anzac Legend gave rise to the Anzac Spirit which defines good citizenship derived from the qualities that the Anzac soldiers demonstrated in war. Australians have something that can be described as a reverence for war and the military not only because they believe that their nation was born from the ashes of modern warfare, but also because their civic identity is enmeshed and modelled upon the soldier. The civil–military nature of the Anzac Spirit is evident when considering that it does not describe soldiers only, but also the civilians who demonstrate heroism and sacrifice for the nation. Beaumont (2014: 344) notes that the Anzac is not the soldier who kills for Australia, but anyone 'who dies for his country'. In this civilian outfit, the Anzac Spirit applies to police officers who fight crime, fire fighters against bushfires and, more recently, nurses serving the nation in the Covid pandemic.

This is relevant because it shows that the Anzac Legend is more than a myth of origin, but also Australia's militarist ideology. Eastwood (2018: 48) suggests that militarism reproduces subjects attached to war and the military, including their discursive operation as settler tactics. The Anzac Legend as Australia's militarist ideology may not produce a warmongering rhetoric but reproduces political subjects and a polity invested in the ideological apparatus that sustains the racist and settler foundations of Australia. The ideological apparatus of the Anzac Legend ingrains within Australians a sense of national identity derived from war and the military, consequently positioning these topics beyond scrutiny and critical investigation. It grounds the nation in the idea that White settlers made Australia their own through sacrifice, hard work and love of freedom, and anyone who dares to question or dispute this is simply invited to leave.

As the Anzac Legend is a core defining Australian identity and civic value, it can be invoked by politicians to celebrate citizenship (Beaumont 2014), justify Australia's military involvement (McDonald 2010), normalise military spending (Medcalf 2022), and steer Australians in political directions (Bromfield 2017). The personal and professional backlash that comes from scrutinising military history and speaking up against Australia's militarism is well documented. For example, the historians and authors of the book *What's Wrong with Anzac: The Militarisation of Australian History* (Lake et al. 2010) have spoken candidly about the threats and abuse that they received while conducting and disseminating their research on Australia's military mythology. The public response to scrutiny and critical investigation was even more vitriolic when it came from women of colour Yumi Stynes and Yassmin Abdel-Magied, who, respectively, criticised the Australian military and the cult of war commemoration in 2012 and in 2017. They animated the hatred of White nationalists who demanded that these women went 'back to where they came from' despite both being Australian citizens. Their critical position with regard to the Anzac Legend and the military made them un-Australian, a quality further confirmed by their skin colour.

Notes

1. The interdisciplinary nature of militarisation can be gauged in the book edited by González, Gusterson and Houtman (2019), *Militarization: A Reader*. For a time, the concept of militarisation was popular among political analysts and historians who debated the outbreak of the two world wars (Gillis 1989), the arms race and military tensions in the Cold War (Luckham 1984; Mann 1987; Shaw 1988), and military dictatorships in the Third World (Wolpin 1981; Ross 1987). With the end of the Cold War, the term lost its popularity mostly due to the belief that militarism and militarisation were giving way to democratisation and liberalism. Instead of militarism and militarisation, scholars preferred to discuss security, human security and securitisation (Bernazzoli and Flint 2009; Stavrianakis and Selby 2013). But while mainstream scholarship was losing interest in the concept of militarisation, critical feminist scholars were finding a fertile ground for their investigations. A key scholar in this area is Cynthia

Enloe (1983; 1993; 2000). Since the 1980s, her work has driven the critical feminist research agenda on militarism and militarisation with questions about the militarisation of women's life. Her research also sparked an intellectual curiosity about manifestations of militarisation in unconventional spaces, such as domestic life, personal feelings and the life of non-uniformed individuals (e.g., see Moon 1997; Cowen and Gilbert 2008; Dowler 2012; Åhäll 2016; Basham 2016). As a result of this, there is a rich feminist scholarship on militarisation. Recently, the feminist scholarship on militarisation has come under criticism in the work of Howell (2018), who argues that feminist conceptions of militarisation tend to subsume questions of race, class and disability under the category of gender. Howell stated that we should 'forget militarisation' on the ground that the concept is politically unhelpful and analytically weak. Instead of militarisation, Howell offers the concept of 'martial politics'. Several scholars have responded to Howell's provocation (MacKenzie et al. 2019), including Millar (2021) who attempted to draw a line between martial politics and colonisation.

2. At the end of 2022, the Memorial was assigned A$500 million for renovation to be finished by 2028.

CHAPTER 2

The Settler Politics of War Commemoration

Introduction

This chapter continues the theorisation of settler militarisation as a practice of colonial governance and examines its operation through the political aesthetics of war commemoration. It demonstrates how war commemorative aesthetics contribute to settler colonial military governance and settler nation-building. I investigate the settler politics of war commemoration by examining the historical development of the Australian War Memorial and its commemorative aesthetics in preparation for a detailed examination of selected pieces and events in the following chapters. As already noted, the Memorial is Australia's main cultural institution of war with a mission to assist Australians in remembering, interpreting and understanding the Australian experience of war and its enduring impact on Australian society. This is an ambitious mission that spans across the realms of commemoration and history, seamlessly merging them. The Memorial is simultaneously a war Memorial and museum, as well as the temple of the Anzac Legend, where the national myth of origin is kept alive and adapted to changing socio-political circumstances. Nicoll (2001: 12) describes the Memorial as an ambitious project that collapses memory and history, reality and theatricality, the individual and the collective, the sacred and the secular. When I visited the Memorial for the first time in 2017, its aesthetic power was immediately evident. The Memorial is an imposing building that hosts a large collection of objects, documents and art chronicling the Australian war experience since just before federation. It purports to resolve the tension between history and memory by recounting the history of war as the story of the men and women who gave their lives to make the nation.

Its aesthetics create a semi-religious atmosphere that projects the cult of the soldier as martyr, a figuration of settler colonialism that operates to conceal colonial warfare and produce feelings of attachment to settler society and rightful belonging on Indigenous land.

The argument pursued in this chapter is that, since the end of the First World War, war commemorative aesthetics have been the solid foundation of Australia's settler national identity. As explained in the previous chapter, Australia's settler nature makes its nationalism inherently unstable and anxious, always at risk of being challenged by the existence of Indigenous people who survive dispossession. Commemorative aesthetics create attachments and visual references to the First World War as the birth of the nation. They ground the settler nation in a moment that is identified as the legitimate starting point of modern Australia and conceal the Frontier Wars. As the guardian and curator of the national commemorative aesthetics, the Australian War Memorial has substantial cultural power to define the nation's identity. According to a former director of the Australian War Memorial, Steve Gower (2019: 1), the Memorial is one of the main, if not the most important, Australian cultural institution due to its unique role as the first institution to narrate Australia's history as that of an independent nation. The Memorial was envisioned during a critical period when Australia was striving to forge a distinct national identity separate from Britain, and the emerging Australian aesthetics of war commemoration played a significant role in supporting that nationalist endeavour. Australia's nationalism, however, is inextricably linked to settler colonialism and the settler dispossession of Indigenous land. The emerging commemorative aesthetics in the aftermath of the First World War consolidated Whiteness through the exclusive representation of White male soldiers and contributed to the displacement of Indigenous people by evoking settler feelings of attachment and entitlement to Indigenous land.

I also examine the Australian War Art programme which was established towards the end of the First World War to record and commemorate the Australian war experience through artistic representations. This initiative led to the establishment of the Australian War Memorial as a national institution that commemorated the Australian experience of war within the British Empire. The art produced under the Australian War Art programme visualised for posterity the war that became known as Australia's baptism of fire. It also identified and depicted the experience of Australians at war as unique and distinct from the British and the other British Dominions.

In this respect, commemorative war art played an important role in calibrating the distance from the British Empire and consolidating a sense of national identity. Finally, I discuss the history of Anzac Day to contextualise the practices of war commemoration happening at the Australian War Memorial on 25 April. The institutionalisation of Anzac Day formalised the Anzac Legend as the tradition that grounds the Australian nation in modern warfare. On Anzac Day, the rituals of war commemoration reproduce the legend and, with it, the settler myth of origin.

The Politics of War Commemoration and Nation-Building

To build the argument that war commemorative aesthetics are a pillar of settler national identity, we must first establish the politics of war commemoration. In a humanistic vein, war commemoration can be understood as an expression of the human need to grieve and create meaning out traumatic and destructive experiences. According to Winter (2006), war commemoration is the product of individuals and social groups coming together to remember and work through the traumas of war. He emphasises that, ultimately, war commemoration is shaped by people, and criticises what he sees as overly political analyses that centre the state as the main actor. However, war commemoration is personal as much as it is political, and the state plays a key role in war commemoration. Leaning on the latter side of the debate, I make two points about the politics of war commemoration that are relevant for my discussion.

First, war commemoration is an instrument of nation-building. War memory is a powerful tool to generate nations as 'imagined political communities' held together by shared memories and feelings (Anderson 1983). Nations can be understood in the words of Hutchison (2016) as 'affective communities', that is, as groups of individuals held together by shared emotional understandings of tragedy. War commemoration is crucial to maintain the nation as an affective community, for it brings together individuals around a shared understanding of the experience of war. It creates a language to speak about the individual and collective traumas of war, thus giving meaning to an experience that, by definition, destructs meaning. In creating a communicable and meaningful experience out of trauma, war commemoration produces an arsenal of meanings that bond individuals together, and nations use to describe themselves and others. As a practice of nation-building, war commemoration shapes the nation's identity. It offers a unified narrative about past hardship and collective accomplishments; it inspires patriotism by spotlighting the sacrifice of soldiers for the nation; and it strengthens community bonds by channelling individual feelings towards the nation.

In recognition of this, states have exhibited a strong interest in taking charge of war memory and creating official accounts and a state-sanctioned collective memory of war. This is demonstrated by the innumerable state-sponsored war memorials and commemorative practices around the world (see, for example, Bell 2006). According to Edkins (2003), the very existence of the state is predicated on its ability to control the narrative of war and create a collective memory that unifies the nation. This stems not only from the fact that nations are affective communities, but also from the need to control certain memories and experiences of war that can become a threat to the existence of the state. Notably, when soldiers experience war trauma, it can lead to feelings of betrayal from the state. This, in turn, poses a risk to the state's legitimacy and authority to recruit and deploy citizens into war. War commemoration pre-empts this by elevating the sacrifice of soldiers and creating an official account of war on which soldiers can reflect their personal experiences of war and feel like national heroes.

To the extent that states mobilise it to secure legitimacy and authority and create a unified national identity, war commemoration can be understood as a practice of militarisation ultimately intended to govern society, as discussed in the previous chapter. State-led commemoration flourished in the aftermath of the First World War because of the need to justify the carnage of industrial warfare. The unprecedented death toll of the war, brought by mass conscription and new war technologies, coupled with its imperial nature, represented a challenge to the state's ability to protect its citizens. To confront this potential threat to state legitimacy, after the war, state authorities that had the power to conscript citizens during the war, took charge to write the obituaries of dead soldiers, fitting them into heroic stories of nationalism (Edkins 2003). This served to manage impoverished and traumatised societies and to justify the loss of lives and livelihoods in war for the birth, re-birth or protection of the nation.

State-sponsored war commemoration constructs a collective memory of war that draws from the experiences and memories of soldiers and the commemorative rituals and aesthetics that spontaneously develop in a society after war. To create a collective memory, states scrutinise veterans' memories and commemorative practices and selectively incorporate them into nationalistic collective memories, omitting the negative ones while adopting and promoting the positive and politically advantageous ones. Veterans' war experiences are transformed into what Mosse (1990: 7) calls 'the myth of the war experience', displacing the loss of meaning in the face of war and recasting trauma as a significant and sacred event of political rebirth. This process grafts soldiers' memories of war into a collective memory that can leave soldiers unable to see their own personal experience of war in the dominant narrative. States also selectively take on practices and aesthetics of war commemoration developed spontaneously by social groups to mourn and remember. In the hands of the state, the complex experiences of war, characterised by human suffering, destruction and trauma, are moulded into a linear narrative that depicts the state as the fulcrum of political rebirth. As war memories come under the purview of the state, private grief becomes overlaid with official rituals of commemoration and overshadowed by narratives of national service and duty (Edkins 2003).

The second point is that war commemoration is adaptive. According to Ashplant, Dawson and Roper (2000: 16), the politics of war commemoration emerge from 'the struggles of different groups to give public articulation to, and hence gain recognition for, certain memories and narratives'. Some of these groups pre-exist the experience of war, whereas others are brought into existence by a shared experience of war; however, both view war commemoration as a way to assert their existence and seek recognition. Social groups articulate their war memories within existing discourses, adding to, or contesting them. The state is a major player in these politics of war commemoration, not least because it purports to be the ultimate agent of public recognition. Thus, social actors ultimately seek recognition of their war memory and experience through the endorsement of the state. Therefore, they tend to invoke and find expression in the discourse of national identity that contributes to nation-building as discussed earlier. Social groups have different levels of power, and therefore ability, to insert their war memories into the dominant discourse. Those more closely aligned with the centre of state power have an easier way to express their war memory than marginalised groups. As Ashplant, Dawson and Roper put it 'the weaker and more marginalized have less access to the agencies of either state or civil society, and less capacity to influence prevailing narratives or project their own narratives into wider arenas' (2000: 21). The racial and gendered discourses that elevate the White man as the legitimate national soldier who fights for the protection of the state have enabled the dominance of White men in Western war commemoration, whereas women and people of colour have had more difficulties inserting their war memories and experiences in the mainstream public discourse.

State institutions such as war museums and memorials play a crucial role in managing and adapting collective memories. They endorse politically usable individual and group war memories and crystallise them into collective memories of the nation. Conversely, they work to repress memories that pose a risk to the dominant nationalist discourse and national unity. State institutions also operate to accommodate "risky" memories in the dominant nationalist discourse when they threaten national unity. In fact, marginalised groups may strive to assert their war experience in opposition or contestation of the dominant nationalist discourse, and instead of repressing them, state institutions may work to include them. They tend to do so when a society is deeply divided, and the memories of marginalised groups gain momentum in a section of society as counter-memories (Ashplant, Dawson and Roper 2000: 27). The inclusion of counter-memory in the official collective memory involves a degree of adaptation such that they can fit in the dominant discourse. However, this not only adapts the war memories but also transforms and domesticates the marginalised group, as the narrative surrounding its war memories – and from which the group derived its sense of self – changes. In this respect, national narratives have great assimilative power. This is particularly the case when inclusion comes at the expense of the articulation of difference and political change.

The Political Aesthetics of War Commemoration

Aesthetics play an essential role in the politics of nation-building of war commemoration. Baker (2021: 9) aptly describes aesthetics as 'the creative and representational practices with which artists and other creators engage the senses and emotions to convey human imagination and experience'. The aesthetics of war commemoration identify those practices and objects that convey the experience of war by engaging human senses and emotions, including memorials, artistic and literary expressions, and rituals of remembrance. Aesthetic practices are well positioned to overcome the challenges posed by war to represent and speak about trauma (Hutchison 2016).

They are unique instruments to make sense of war at the individual and collective levels, and to pass on the memory of war to future generations, such that humanity does not commit the same mistakes. The imperative to remember is tied to the necessity to create and shape meanings, especially when traumatic events such as war wipe away life as previously known. Thus, the aesthetics of war commemoration create an opportunity to script a new reality anchored in the past by appealing to human senses and emotions. This I call 'the political aesthetics of war commemoration'.

The political aesthetics of war commemoration emphatically put politics in aesthetics. To appreciate how, we can recall Rancière's (2004) discussion about the politics of aesthetics. According to Rancière, aesthetics pertain to the 'distribution of the sensible', or a system of perception that frames intelligibility, that is, what can be seen and spoken about and by whom. As he puts it:

> Aesthetics can be understood in a Kantian sense – re-examined perhaps by Foucault – as a system of *a priori* forms determining what presents itself to sense experience. It is a delimitation of spaces and times, of the visible and the invisible, of speech and noise, that simultaneously determines the place and stakes of politics as a form of experience. Politics revolves around what is seen and what can be said about it, around who has the ability to see and the talent to speak, around the properties of spaces and the possibilities of time. (Rancière 2004: 8)

For Rancière, the political debate is shaped by the aesthetic experiences that we have and do not have, what we see and how we feel. Accordingly, the aesthetics of war commemoration frame perceptions about war and channel emotions in the direction that is relevant to the present.

Aesthetics are essential to the politics of war commemoration because remembering war necessarily involves the participation of people. In this respect, I concur with Winter (2006) that individuals and social groups are an essential part of the war commemoration equation. States deploy the aesthetics of war commemoration to engage people and involve them in the rituals that pass on memory and make it meaningful at the collective level. In this respect, the aesthetics of war commemoration operate in two ways. First, they provide a framework through which individuals can understand and remember conflict. They provide an indication about the subjects of memory, the topic and even the feelings that we are supposed to feel when remembering war. Secondly, the aesthetics of war commemoration offer sites for identification that encourage individuals to perform acts of remembrance. They evoke feelings towards the subjects of commemoration that make people engage and come back year after year. It is important to note that while being affective sites, the aesthetics of war commemoration still need a narrative to activate its affective power and evoke feelings, especially when the subject of commemoration is located further back in the past.

The political aesthetics of war commemoration rest primarily on the affective dynamics of power involving remembering and forgetting and how they inform collective identities. That is, the aesthetics of war commemoration represent certain war experiences and memories at the expense of others that do not get represented. By being included in the aesthetics of war commemoration, certain war memories not only get passed on, but they also prompt emotional attachments from the people who engage with their aesthetics. For example, by the end of the First World War, the main subject of the aesthetics of war commemoration changed from the battle to the soldier. This 'opened up the possibility that soldiers themselves were victims of war, whether they were on the winning or the losing side' (Winter 2017: 3). This aesthetics of commemoration created affective attachments towards the soldier-victim who was not only an individual who suffered, but also the symbol of the sacrifice of the nation. His suffering came to signify the trauma experienced by the nation, the loss of life and the injury to the social fabric. He also represented political loyalty and the resilience of the political community. And thus, his war trauma became the foundation of the political community that re-emerged after the war. He became a martyr of the nation and, still to this day, he evokes feelings of attachment to the nation as a cause worth dying for. In other words, he was a propeller of the nation as an affective community. Notably, the aesthetics of the soldier-martyr after the First World War was totalising and excluded the war experiences of women and people of colour. This obscured the suffering of these subjects, but also foreclosed their presence and participation in the narratives and affects that reproduce the nation.

In this context, the political aesthetics of war commemoration following the First World War played a crucial role in reinforcing Whiteness and nationalism, even as empires still existed. Not only were the main actors of the First World War empire-states, but also race was a significant organisational force which determined who could fight and where. Nevertheless, the aesthetics of war commemoration largely forsook colonial soldiers fighting for the empire in favour of White men fighting for their nation. The exclusion of colonial soldiers from the aesthetics of war commemoration promoted nationalist narratives of racial purity and made the White soldier the symbol of national pride. As the contributions to Wellings and Sumartojo's (2021) edited book on commemorating race and empire show, the lack of representation of race and empire in war memory after the First World War explains the predominant Whiteness of contemporary war commemoration. This demonstrates how political aesthetics of war commemoration shape world politics and have long-term effects.

As already noted, war commemoration is not static and immutable, and adaptation is a core feature of the politics of war commemoration. Aesthetics play an important role in adapting war commemoration, and certain aesthetics of war commemoration are adopted to facilitate the transformation of war commemoration and the nation that it reflects and reproduces. Aesthetic interventions of counter-memory by marginalised communities can create new commemorative practices and narratives that challenge and confront the dominant discourse. They can also become sites of activism that question national identity and unity. When aesthetics interventions gain momentum and popular support, state institutions and agencies can decide to include them into the mainstream and adapt them as discussed above. This allows not only control of the narrative of war memory, but also of the affective attachments developed towards the subject of the memory intervention.

These two sections offer a framework to begin to understand Australia's politics and aesthetics of war commemoration. In the next sections, I will apply this framework to map the development of Australia's aesthetics and politics of war commemoration. I will highlight how the aesthetics of war commemoration enabled Australia to differentiate itself from Britain and assert its national autonomy and identity. However, Australia's nationalism is strictly intertwined with settler colonialism. The development of Australia's national identity goes hand in hand with the displacement of Indigenous people from their land and forgetting the history that led to it. War commemoration and its political aesthetics assisted this process as discussed below.

Australia's War Commemoration at the Crossroads between Nation and Empire

In Australia, the emergence of war commemoration is linked with the development of the Australian national identity and the consolidation of the settler nation-state as a political unit autonomous from (yet still connected to) the British Empire. At the end of the First World War, war commemoration gave White settlers a narrative about who they are as a nation and how they legitimately belong to Indigenous land. Thus, it effectively worked as a logic of dispossession. As seen in Chapter 1, the separation of the colony from the empire is an essential part of Indigenous dispossession and settler colonial governance. The independence of the colony allows settlers to pursue Indigenous dispossession through settler nationalism and to claim belonging to Indigenous land. Australia entered the First World War as a British Dominion animated by imperial patriotism, but by the end of the war, Australians had consolidated a stronger sense of national identity, aided in large part by the establishment of war commemoration that centred the Australian national experience.

Prior to the First World War, war commemoration in Australia had primarily an imperial nature. For example, the memorial built in Melbourne in 1889 commemorating the imperial expedition in Sudan (1885), made no mention of the Australian contingent, and instead commemorated imperial soldiers (Damousi 2008: 291). The commemoration of the South African Wars (1899–1902) included references to the new nation, but imperial patriotism was the central theme (ibid. 293). As a settler colony, Australia was long troubled by the lack of a sense of self and its reliance on imperial identity, but since federation in 1901, Australia had been looking for an identity to ground the nation (White 1988). The First World War offered such an opportunity and war commemoration assisted the consolidation of a narrative about who Australians are. However, as will become evident in the discussion, nationalism did not displace imperial belonging and did not cut ties with the British Empire. Instead, Australia's war commemoration at the end of the First World War assisted the country to manage its proximity with the Empire and the racial discourse to the advantage of settler colonialism.

The development of national war commemoration in Australia was enabled by the drive of some individuals who pursued nationalism for personal aspirations, most notably Charles Bean, the founding father of the Australian War Memorial. Bean was a key architect of Australia's nationalism, but was not disloyal or against the British Empire. Quite the opposite, he is described as 'in love with Britain and Empire' (Inglis, quoted in Gilfedder 2021: 99). Like most Australians at this time, Bean straddled a dual loyalty towards the British Empire and the Australian nation. However, he identified Australian nationalism as a site of personal opportunities. Individuals like Bean were crucial to the development of colonial nationalism in the age of empires. In his influential study on nationalism, Anderson (1983: ch. 7) discussed how, as more people were able to travel between the colonies and the imperial metropole, some started imagining new national vernaculars that differentiated the people of the colonies from those of the metropole. They also saw personal opportunities to be gained from affirming those new national vernaculars, including publishable material that would appeal and easily sell to a targeted audience, as well as positions of power and prestige in the new world. Often, these individuals were or became entwined with the colonial state and took on positions that allowed them to promote colonial nationalism at the state level.

Bean was one of those individuals who, in his travels between the imperial metropole and the colony, realised that he could have capitalised on the differences between imperial and colonial subjects. Bean was born in the Australian colony of New South Wales in 1879 and moved to England at the age of ten. He attended Clifton, a school rich in British imperial tradition. He returned to Australia in 1904, just three years after the federation of the Australian colonies and the official declaration of the Australian nation. Upon his return, he sought to capitalise on the new Australian national identity and wrote a book about his impressions of Australians as a man returning from Britain. While critical of some British characteristics, Bean was not an anti-imperialist. He was loyal to the Empire but was also influenced by racial Darwinism that was popular at that time. His nationalism was informed by the idea that Australians were an evolution of the British race adapted to the harsh environment of the new continent. Of course, for Bean, Australians were only those people who descended from the British and not Indigenous people or the Asian and Pacific immigrants who worked in the mines and plantations. He was also interested in Australian masculinity and had little to say about Australian women. In his book, he emphatically described Australian men as a best version of the British man and celebrated the 'bushman', the iconic image of the Australian man living in the country (we will return to this figure in Chapter 3). He could not find a publisher for his book but managed to publish it as a series of essays in a newspaper. Bean persevered, and in 1907, published an article noting the qualities of the Australian man as improvements from the Briton's. He wrote that the Australian 'is a tall, spare man, clean and wiry with a certain refined ascetic strength . . . [He is a] Briton reborn' (Bean, quoted in Holbrook 2014: 43). In

1908, Bean became a journalist and used his work to celebrate the Australian (male) national type and promote Australian nationalism as an imperial asset. His first assignment was to report on the British Royal Navy in Australian ports, which he used to advocate for the establishment of an Australian navy to support British naval power in the antipodes. In 1909, he was assigned the coverage of the Australian wool industry which he praised 'for creating some of the outstanding national types' (quoted in Inglis 1979). He further consolidated a romantic image of the Australian man and race in two books, *On the Wool Tracks* (1910) and *The Dreadnought of the Darling* (1911), in which he distinguished the Australian bushman from the British gentleman.

At the drums of war, Bean saw greater opportunity to distil and emphasise the Australian national type and capitalise on Australia's nationalism. When the war started, Bean envisioned himself as becoming Australian official war correspondent and, even more ambitiously, as Australia's official war historiographer. Neither of these positions existed at the start of the war. In September 1914, Bean participated in a ballot held by the Australian Journalists Association to become Australia's war correspondent and won the position. This, however, lacked the endorsement of the London War Office and was not an official imperial position. In fact, the position of official dominion war reporter that Bean dreamed about did not exist. The lack of endorsement from the London War Office meant that Bean could not send official dispatches about the actions undertaken by Australians, including the Gallipoli mission which became the birth of the Australian nation. The scoop of the Anzacs landing in Gallipoli was instead broken by Ellis Ashmead-Bartlett, the Empire's official war correspondent. Ashmead-Bartlett sowed the seed of the Anzac Legend, later cultivated by Bean.

While unable to be the man who informed Australians about their first military action as nationals, Bean learned an invaluable lesson from Ashmead-Bartlett's reporting of the Anzacs landing in Gallipoli, namely, the power of myth-making. Bean was a reporter who valued accuracy and adherence to facts, a quality that attracted the antipathy of the Australian soldiers when he described their rowdiness in his dispatches from Egypt earlier in the year. Conversely, Ashmead-Bartlett gained popularity among the soldiers for his dispatch about the Anzacs landing in Gallipoli, which was a bombastic description of the valour of the Anzac soldiers and a mythological narration of their 'test' of war (Kent 1985). About Ashmead-Bartlett's dispatch,

Bean commented that there were some inaccuracies, but betraying his value of accuracy, continued that they 'scarcely mattered when weighed against the spirit of the event which Bartlett had captured so vividly' (quoted in Fewster 1982: 20). He later used myth-making in his project to memorialise the Australian experience of war and create the Anzac Legend.

Despite the obstacles that Bean encountered in Gallipoli to be Australia's official war correspondent, he used his time in the peninsula to distil and shape colonial manhood and the 'Australian type'. With a view to develop the historiography of Australians at war, he observed and described the Australian soldiers in great detail and remarked the differences with the British soldiers (Stanley 2017: 25; Hutchison 2018: 7). He described the Australian soldiers as exceptionally tall, boisterous and brave men, natural soldiers with a distaste for authority and a strong sense of equalitarianism, endlessly resourceful and loyal to their mates. Inevitably because of the composition of the Australian Imperial Force,[1] Bean was in fact observing and describing British migrants, often of Scottish and Irish origin, and as Connor (2016: 121) comments, these British migrants 'became unwitting examples of Bean's distinct Australian character and Anzac legend'. At this point, Bean was more interested in crafting a mythological narrative of Australia's nationalism than adherence to truth. Moreover, as British settlers in Australia, there was little that distinguished British migrants from Australians, apart from a birth certificate.

Notably, Bean described Australian men in Gallipoli as natural soldiers and deployed the colonial discourse of martial race in reverse to boast the Australian race. As noted in the previous chapter, martial race was a colonial construct to govern Black and Brown colonial subjects and make them fight under the command of White officers. The discourse of martial race relied on a broader schema which designated the British race as the superior martial race demonstrated by their ability to conquer other inferior races (Gilfedder 2021: 96). As White Anglo-Saxons, Australians were both an extension and a modification of the British race, and there were two views of their role in the martial race schema. On the one hand, Australians were considered to have the same status as the British race by virtue of being its extension. On the other hand, they were lesser than the British race because they were distant from the source of race and civilisation (Gilfedder 2021: 99). Bean's description of Australians as natural soldiers was a way to elevate the Australian race through military prowess derived from the connection with the Anglo-Saxon race, while separating it from the British race through martial manhood shaped by the harsh life in the colony. The importance of designating Australians as a martial race was to put them on par with the British race and assert their ability to be masters of their own destiny.

After Gallipoli, Bean travelled with the Australian Imperial Forces to the Western Front, where he conceived the idea of memorialising the Australian experience of war. He was influenced by his witnessing of the violence that unfolded in 1916 and 1917, and especially by the battle of Pozières, a place that he described as 'a ridge more densely sown with Australian sacrifice than any other place on earth' (Hutchison 2018: 24). The carnage of Pozières claimed 23,000 Australian lives, not all of whose remains could be repatriated. This inspired Bean about the need to memorialise those who died far away. In mid-1916, Bean visited the Canadian War Record Office that was established in London with the approval of the London War Office earlier that year. There, he realised the nation-building properties of war memory. Just like Australia, Canada was a British Dominion with dual loyalty towards the empire and the nation, striving to write its national history within the British Empire. Bean believed that what was granted to Canadians would not be denied to the Australians, and after Pozières he encouraged the Australian soldiers to collect war souvenirs for memorialisation. Bean insisted that the souvenirs were called 'relics' to underscore their sacred aura and generative properties (Inglis 1998: 335). He then contacted the Australian Ministry of Defence to suggest that the relics (including trophies, souvenirs and photos) collected by the soldiers at Pozières were returned to Australia and displayed in a war exhibition to commemorate the soldiers who had died.

In March 1917, the nationalist project of Australia and Canada to collect war relics was trumped by imperial aspirations, when Britain established the Imperial War Museum. This was intended to produce a collection of war memorabilia from all fronts and covering the whole of the British Empire, including the Dominions and India (Hutchison 2018: 28). Bean took this as an opportunity to formalise the Australian War Record Section as part of the Imperial War Museum. However, he was disappointed that the Australian War Record Section was in London and that the Imperial War Museum had the first call on all war memorabilia of the Empire, including the Dominions. For Bean and his Canadian counterpart, Beaverbrook, the Dominions' War Record Offices were a nationalist project, whereas for London they were part of a larger imperial project to showcase the vastness of the Empire and adorn its fringes with imperial war trophies. Bean and Beaverbrook worried that the Imperial War Museum would have subsumed the Dominions' experiences of war into that of empire with little space for national expression.

To face this predicament, Bean sought ways to differentiate the Australian project from the imperial. Initially, he thought about establishing an Australian War Museum as a national subsidiary of the Imperial War Museum in Australia, and, in 1919, submitted a proposal to the Australian government. However, Bean's proposal was not met with the enthusiasm that he expected. Australians had little experience with battle warfare and war commemoration as a political instrument of nation-building. The government was reluctant to display the war to a largely traumatised nation which had suffered large numbers of deaths in battle (Gower 2019: 20). By the end of the war, the initial enthusiasm for the war had disappeared, and Australia was deeply divided and impoverished. The post-war decline in the standard of living would have made it difficult to justify public spending for a war museum, and the government seemed to just want to move on from war. Moreover, there were concerns that an Australian war museum would have had too much competition from the Imperial War Museum, and the government did not want to interfere with the imperial project by being seen as claiming the Australian memorabilia from the Empire (Hutchison 2018: 144–5). Despite the challenges, in 1921, Bean sent 25,000 relics from the Australian War Record Section in London to Australia to prepare a temporary exhibition in Melbourne intended to test the Australian appetite for a war museum. The temporary exhibition opened in 1922 and it was a success. It attracted an estimated 750,000 visitors, and the governor of Victoria, Lord Stradbroke, spoke of it as a 'Mecca for Australians' (Gower 2019: 21).

The success of the temporary exhibition in Melbourne emboldened Bean to pursue his project to establish an Australian war museum. Bean envisioned an Australian war museum not as a competitor, but as being complementary to the Imperial War Museum. He wanted it to be a memorial to the Australian Imperial Forces and a space which consecrated the Australian experience of war as a nation within the empire. Therefore, he realised that an Australian war museum should instead be the Australian War Memorial. Initially, the idea of a national war memorial was met with resistance from grassroots movements insofar as it would have taken funding for commemoration away from them. Eventually, in 1925, Bean's idea was supported and endorsed by the newly elected government of Stanley Bruce, and the national memorial was instituted by decree with the Australian War Memorial Act. This Act effectively put the state in charge of war commemoration. As a trusted man of vision, Bean was assigned the task of developing the project, backed by the state's endorsement.

Bean's work to differentiate the Australian man from the British and record the Australian experience of war has significantly impacted how Australians have understood the First World War and how they see themselves as a nation. This influence is primarily attributed to the creation of an Australian myth of origin as laid out in Bean's official war historiography. Bean was appointed official war historiographer in 1919 and completed the project twenty-tree years later. He wrote about the men who landed in Gallipoli and fought in the First World War as the founding fathers of the nation who 'tested' the national type in war and impressed the qualities of the Australian man and soldier onto the nation. The national type described by Bean was emphatically a man and a White Anglo-Saxon. He had imperial ancestors, but he was an Australian national. He was a better version of the White Anglo-Saxon, and he finally proved his manhood in war. The importance of recounting his deeds in war was attributed to the fact that the First World War was Australia's first war ever, a narrative that worked to erase colonial conflict. By mythologising White male achievements in a war far from home, the work of Bean to commemorate the White Australian soldier in the First World War advanced the idea that the sacrifice of Australian soldiers in Gallipoli and Europe conferred settlers the right to belong on Indigenous land and pursue a settler project to reproduce the new nation.

The Australian Aesthetics of War Commemoration

The development of the Australian aesthetics of war commemoration was foundational for the establishment of an Australian war memorial and the consolidation of Australian nationalism. The Australian aesthetics of war commemoration emerged in Gallipoli when Bean was living with and observing the Anzacs. He recognised the power of aesthetics upon noticing that soldiers were drawing and writing about their war experience. He realised that the soldier's first-hand account of the war was the most powerful expression of the national type and therefore decided to enlist it towards his project to define the Australian man and distinguish him from the British. Towards the end of the Gallipoli campaign, Bean encouraged Australian soldiers to submit their writings, poems, cartoons and drawings to be collected in a book to send back home to Australia. Published under the title of *Anzac Book*, Bean's collection was a first-hand account of Australians at war and an influential representation of the Australian national type. As it provided personal accounts of the war, in Australia, the *Anzac Book* sparked an emotional connection with soldiers and became an instant bestseller. It allowed Australians to gain insight into the realities of war and be proud of how Australian soldiers faced war hardship. The book also had commemorative functions and honoured the soldiers who lost their lives in Gallipoli.

The *Anzac Book* was an embryotic form of commemorative aesthetics that found its full expression in the War Art Scheme intended to commission Australian artists to represent and interpret the Australian experience of war. For context, during the First World War, states commonly commissioned war artists to produce propaganda and control the war narrative. Germany had developed a strong and sophisticated propaganda machine that relied on posters and films. In recognition of the effectiveness of Germany's visual propaganda, in 1916, Britain established a pictorial section of the War Office to develop visual propaganda and instituted the British Official War Art Scheme (Brandon 2007: 40). Russia and Austria also had an official war art programme. Brandon (2007: 49) contends that official war art schemes also function to reduce the number of artists who could publicly challenge official views of the war.

In Australia, however, the War Art Scheme was less animated by propaganda aims and was more a politically motivated commemorative tool (Hutchison 2018: 57). It was officially established in 1917 when Bean gained permission to create the Australian War Record Section as part of the Imperial War Museum. However, another man propelled its emergence, Will Dyson. Like Bean, Dyson saw personal opportunities in the promotion of Australia's nationalism. He was born in the Australian colony of Victoria, but when the war started he was living and working as a cartoonist in England, which made him eligible for conscription in the British Army. Dyson was a talented cartoonist and was known for his satire and witty commentary on British politics. He was also a socialist and had little sympathy for the Empire. When he was called to arms, Dyson did not want to join the Imperial British Army, and instead wrote to the Australian High Commissioner to propose his service to illustrate the feelings and character of the

Australian troops in France. Inspired by other national experiences, Dyson wanted to be Australia's national war artist. The record is inconclusive about whether he was animated by nationalism or was trying to avoid conscription (Hutchison 2018: 34); regardless, he went to the war front as an artist rather than a soldier.

Under the patronage of the Australian military and political authorities, Dyson went to France and produced some of the most compassioned representations of the Australian experience of war. Although the Australian High Commissioner was enthusiastic and granted Dyson honorary status to be a war artist in France, this appointment was fraught with imperial tensions. Just as happened with Bean's position as war reporter, the London War Office rejected Dyson's appointment as war artist. The British Official War Art Scheme covered the whole of the Empire, and there was already an imperial official war artist in France. This was particularly frustrating for the Australian High Commission because the London War Office granted permission to Richard Jack to paint for the Canadians. There is little evidence to explain why Jack was given permission and Dyson was not. Hutchison speculates that Jack, being a well-known British artist associated with the Royal Academy, may have been favoured, whereas Dyson being 'an antipodean caricaturist with strong socialist politics' may have faced greater scrutiny (2018: 37). The Canadians had a similar project to use war art to craft and promote the Canadian national identity. But conversely to the Australian War Art scheme, the Canadian scheme commissioned many British artists in the name of aesthetic beauty (Brandon 2007: 40). Bean commented on the appointment of British-born artists in the Canadian War Art Scheme, expressing his view that the Canadians took the wrong approach, as it contradicted their nationalist aspirations (Hutchinson 2015). For Bean, the Australian War Art scheme was intended for Australian artists to paint Australian soldiers for Australian and international publics.

Bean met Dyson in France and he admired the artist's honest and intimate representation of the Australian soldiers. Regardless of his admiration, Bean recognised that Dyson was not the right man to bring the Australian aesthetics of war commemoration and Australia's national identity to the next level of recognition. Despite his talent as an artist and his entrepreneurial push to become Australia's war artist and establish the Australian war art collection, Dyson was not a member of any artistic club. He was a cartoonist and held political leftist and anti-imperial views. His art was not fine art, it was too personal and too politically controversial to elevate Australia's aesthetics of war commemoration and lead a nationalist project that remained loyal to the Empire. Bean was persuaded by the artists that he met in Europe that the Australian War Art scheme needed to be associated with the finest Australian artists from the Royal Academy and other prestigious artistic circles. Consequently, many of the artists commissioned by the Australian War Art scheme came from the Heidelberg School. This was not only a prestigious artistic movement, but also, before the war, it came to symbolise Australian national identity through the representation of the landscape (Travers 2017: 25). The Heidelberg School established the Australian landscape as the artistic representation of nationalism and as the feature that sets Australia apart from Britain. The sun, the trees and the blue skies of Australia were the antithesis of the British cities and grey skies and were therefore markers of difference with Britain and a symbol of Australian national identity.

Bean envisioned that to elevate the nation, the art produced under the War Art Scheme had to be not only fine art, but also a historical record with commemorative functions. He wanted war artists to be eyewitnesses of war. Therefore, artists commissioned under the Australian War Art scheme were sent to the front with a military rank, a wage and a commission of a minimum of twenty-five sketches to develop into canvas paintings upon their return from the war. They were given a good degree of artistic freedom and could paint what they wanted if it represented what they saw with their own eyes. Despite the artistic freedom, the emphasis on capturing first-hand the war in action had the implication of excluding the experience of war on the home front and the female perspective (Speck 2004). Furthermore, while artists were free to represent what they saw in war, the canvases that they produced were ultimately approved and rejected by Bean, who, as Hutchison (2015: 28) puts it, was not only agent of memory but also its arbiter.

The aesthetics of the Australian War Art scheme of the First World War focused on the White male soldier in battle and produced a pictorial record of the nation's baptism of fire. Conversely to Britain and other nations in Europe where artists introduced modernism and avant-garde to represent the human deformation of industrial warfare, Australian artists produced classical and romantic representations of battle with recognisable features of Australian nationalism, most notably the landscape. Bean himself discouraged Australian official war artists from using modernism on the ground that it could not serve commemorative purposes. Modernist art was renowned for the deformed human forms that conveyed physical dismemberment and mental derangement, and Bean was concerned that veterans could not or did not want to identify with those representations (Nicoll 2001: 40). Furthermore, modernism was about the individual experience of the destructive power of war, which clashed with Bean's idea about the generative properties of the war that baptised the Australian nation into existence. War was to be represented as a collective experience that made the nation, and battle art articulated Australian nationalism through the aesthetic of tragic heroism. It enabled the retention of the landscape as the primary signifier of Australian national identity, and gave Australians who did not fight the impression of knowing how Australian soldiers fought.

The battle aesthetics of the war art collection of the First World War came under the harsh scrutiny of art critics. Not only did it exclude modernism at a time when this style was becoming prominent in Europe, but it also conspicuously lacked the female perspective. In the Second World War, the War Art Scheme responded by commissioning women and modernist artists. The Second World War art collection looks remarkably different from that of the First World War, with a broader range of themes, artistic styles and medium. Social realism is the prevalent style, but surrealism and impressionism also found a way in. The soldier shares the spotlight with the worker, including the female worker (analysed in Chapter 4). There are representations of battle in modernist style, such as those of Ivor Hele who depicted human bodies intertwined with machines and tanks (see Chapter 3). The inclusion of modernism did not come without concerns. For example, the work of Hele was deemed to be too confronting for permanent exhibitions and therefore was put in touring exhibitions. There was also a concern that the tired soldier protagonist of social realism could have damaged the semiotic power of the Anzac soldier protagonist of the First World War collection, and therefore challenge the image of national identity that the War Art Scheme was so carefully crafting.

After the Second World War, the War Art Scheme was significantly resized reflecting the national exhaustion with war. Forty-two artists were commissioned during the Second World War, whereas only two were appointed for the Korean War, two more for Vietnam, and no one was officially commissioned for the First Gulf War. By the 1980s, critics questioned the ideological load of the collection since the First World War, and its artistic value was deemed to be dubious and full of 'bad art' (Nicoll 2001: 8). Following this realisation, the Australian War Memorial started acquiring and commissioning more modernist and critical art, but the new addition only rendered more visible the ideological value of the art commissioned under the Official War Scheme until then. Nonetheless, the new addition gave the collection more breath and the battle paintings were reclassified as historical records and documentary material rather than as fine art, a move that ultimately contributed to the blending together of memory and history (Nicoll 2001: 14). Today, the war art collection looks very different from what it used to be. Since the Australian military intervention in East Timor in 1999, artists commissioned by the War Art Scheme have greater freedom of expression and can be interpreters of war rather than recorders (Green, Brown and Cattapan 2015).

While the Australian aesthetics of war commemoration have developed significantly since the First World War, having included women and different ways of seeing the war, race and the Indigenous perspective have been conspicuously absent. There were virtually no representations of people of colour and Indigenous people until 2012, when the first Aboriginal artist, Tony Albert, was commissioned. Albert was commissioned to represent the North-West Mobile Force (NORFORCE), an Army unit which operates domestically and comprises of around 60 per cent Indigenous people. Reflecting a growing national sentiment about Indigenous inclusion, in 2016, Alick Tipoti became the second Indigenous official war artist and the first Torres Strait Islander to be commissioned in the War Art Scheme. He represented the 51st Far North Queensland Regiment, another army unit with a large representation of Indigenous soldiers. In 2017, Megan Cope became the first female Aboriginal official war artist and was attached to the Australian military contingents in the United Arab Emirates. The commission of these three artists reflects a growing interest in including Indigenous people in defence as discussed in Chapter 5. In 2022, the art of the latter two artists was only starting to appear on the Memorial's website, and we are yet to see how it will be integrated into the galleries of the Memorial after refurbishment in 2028.

A notable absence in the Australian aesthetics of war commemoration at the Australian War Memorial is colonial conflict. This ought to be understood in the context in which Bean identified the First World War to be Australia's first war and colonisation was dismissed and excluded from the definition of conflict, as discussed in Chapter 1. The lack of representation of the colonial conflict is emphatically juxtaposed against the rich and detailed representation of the First World

War as Australia's baptism of fire which erases colonial violence as the foundation of modern Australia. As Lydon (2018) shows, there were several visual representations of the Australian colonial conflict which circulated throughout the Empire for different reasons. However, in Australia, these came to largely be ignored and side-lined to avoid recounting the history of the Frontier Wars. The flourishing of the Australian aesthetics of war commemoration centred around the First World War made them further irrelevant and inconspicuous.

The Political Aesthetics of the Australian War Memorial

The war art collection produced under the War Art Scheme of the First World War was the foundation of the Australian nationalist aesthetics of war commemoration, but it was the institution of the Australian War Memorial that consolidated the political aesthetics of nation-building. In fact, the war art produced under the War Art Scheme has been collected and curated in exhibitions held at the Australian War Memorial. Above all, the Memorial itself is a potent political aesthetics of war commemoration. Bean envisioned the Memorial to be more than a depository of war relics. He wanted it to be a sacred place that not only united the nation for mourning the losses of war, but would also define and shape Australia's identity.

To reflect its symbolic power, the Memorial was established in Canberra, Australia's capital since 1909, and was positioned at the base of Mt Ainslie, facing Parliament House. The Memorial was established by decree in 1925, but the building was not inaugurated until 1941. The construction of the building involved grappling with the conflicting push of nationalism and the pull of imperial ties. For example, in the construction phase, there was a proposal to bring to the Memorial an unknown Australian soldier from Europe. After the First World War, the idea of honouring an unidentified soldier who symbolised all the fallen soldiers and represented the sacrifices made in war gained popularity and spread to various countries, including Australia. Bean and his collaborators were concerned that, in the imperial context, the unknown soldier brought to the Australian War Memorial could have been a British soldier and his tomb could become a symbol of the British Empire in Australia rather than a nationalist symbol in the British Empire (Inglis 1998: 340). For this reason, the idea of the unknown soldier was discarded. Contending imperialism and nationalism, the Memorial was inaugurated in 1941 with both the British anthem 'God Save the King', and the Australia anthem 'Advance Australia Fair'. Notably, it was inaugurated on Armistice Day, 11 November, which is Britain and Europe's most significant day of war commemoration, rather than on Anzac Day, which is Australia's most significant day of war commemoration. At that time, Australia celebrated both dates for war memory, whereby the former was for imperial war commemoration and the latter for national war commemoration. The inauguration of the Memorial on 11 November accentuated the imperial nature of national commemoration.

Despite the imperial pull, the Australian War Memorial was born as a temple to the new nation. The building contains the relics from the martial origin of Australia and the art that elevates the Australian experience of war to baptism of the nation. The architecture itself is worth mentioning for its symbolic nationalist properties. In fact, the design of the building strategically enshrines the most Australian characteristics. The building is in the Australian capital of Canberra, and being at the base of Mt Ainslie, it is surrounded by iconic Australian flora and fauna: oak, wattle and gum trees, and magpies, whip birds and kangaroos. The Australian flora and fauna are also represented in the adorning architecture of the Memorial. Notably, along the walls of the cloister containing the Roll of Honour, one can observe twenty-six sandstone gargoyles by sculptor William Leslie Bowles representing uniquely Australian fauna: the kangaroo, the koala, the emu, the bush turkey, the carpet snake, etc. Controversially, there are also two gargoyles representing a male and a female Aboriginal face. In a most generous and perhaps naive interpretation offered by a staff member when I visited the Memorial, these two faces represent the first inhabitants of the land and commemorate them as such. Another interpretation is that when the Memorial was designed and built, Aboriginal people were considered subhuman and closer to animals, and during the Frontier Wars, they were hunted like animals and their heads used as trophies (Nicoll 2001: 175). The heads of Aboriginal people as trophies adorning the Memorial also sends a message of the settlers' victory and conquest of Indigenous land. Until very recently, these two gargoyles were the only reference to Aboriginal people in the Memorial, a fact which speaks volumes about the institutional efforts to exclude Indigenous people from the construction of the nation (for details, see Chapter 5).

The Hall of Memory is also worth a mention insofar as it is a temple to the Australian citizen-soldier. It was conceived to be the holiest place of the Memorial dedicated to soldiers and their qualities in war, as endorsed by the Australian nation. The budget for the Hall of Memory was allocated in 1936 and it was meant to cover stained-glass windows representing the heroes of the First World War. In 1939, the Second World War began, and in 1945, it was decided that the Hall of Memory should also include the heroes of the new war. The Hall of Memory was inaugurated in 1956. The stained-glass windows are dedicated to the soldiers of the First World War. They are divided into fifteen panels, each of which represents a war hero wearing the uniform and military equipment of the First World War and typifying a civic–military quality. There are three sets of qualities – personal, social and fighting – that characterise Australian nationals not only as soldiers but also as civilians. Of the fifteen figures, only one is female. She is a nurse and embodies the quality of devotion. The wall mosaics are dedicated to the soldiers of the Second World War. There are four human figures representing the defence services in the war: the Australian Army, the Royal Australian Navy, the Royal Australian Airforce, and the Women's Services. The last human figure is a woman.

The presence of two female figures in the Hall of Memory shows an awareness of women in war, a topic which will be discussed in detail in Chapter 4. However, the female figure was contested, and it was forbidden from being at the centre of the Hall of Memory. Prominent sculptor Leslie Bowles (who sculpted the Memorial's gargoyles) was commissioned to create a figure appropriate for the centre of the Hall of Memory. He proposed 'a female figure, raised beyond a sarcophagus, symbolising Australia proudly and courageously giving her all in the cause of freedom and honour' (Inglis 1987: 48). Female figures are common in the war commemorative canon as they represent sacrifice and mourning. Bowles' proposal, however, never came to fruition because the Memorial committee deemed the female figure to be inappropriate as the centre piece of a temple dedicated to the citizen-soldier, who was archetypically male.

There were also concerns that the female figure would have recalled republican freedom in the spirit of the American statue of Liberty and Marianne, the symbol of the French republic, and Australia did not want to send anti-imperial messages (Inglis 1987). Instead of the female figure, the Hall of Memory housed the bronze statue of a serviceman almost 3 m tall that emphasised the ontogenetic qualities of Australian men (see Lake 1992 and Chapter 3, below). The statue represents a proud, bare-chested soldier wearing the trousers of the army uniform. The male soldier stands on a pedestal that contributes to the monumental height of the statue. Standing in front of this statue, the first thing that hits the eyes of the viewer is the heavy boots of the soldier. To see the face, one must look up, thus prompting a pose of reverence towards the soldier. But the soldier does not return the viewer's gaze. Inglis (1985: 120) explains that the soldier's theatrical pose of defiance symbolises Australia's pride in giving its men for the causes of freedom and honour. He also comments that this statue sends a clear message that 'this memorial [the Australian War Memorial] belongs to men at war' (Inglis 1987: 49). The sculptor, Raymond Ewers, stated that he conceived the figure as an avatar of 'young Australia in an attitude of Remembrance, Hope for the Future, Achievement' (Inglis 1985: 122). This statute was later moved to the Australian War Memorial's Garden of Remembrance, where I saw it (see Figure 2.1), and replaced with a less militaristic symbol of the four pillars of creation: water, earth, air and fire.

Notably, all the human figures in the Hall of Memory are White, a quality that fades into the background unless one interrogates the ethnic composition of the Australian Imperial Force. As discussed in the previous chapter, the 1909 amendment to the Defence Act

Figure 2.1 Statue of the Serviceman that was housed in the Hall of Memory in 1959. The statue is now in the Garden of Remembrance of the Australian War Memorial. Photograph taken by the author in 2022. © The author.

exempted men not substantially of European origin from enlisting. Nonetheless, records indicate that around 1,000 Aboriginal and 500 Chinese Australian men served in the First World War. Other European nationalities were also represented, including Russians and Italians, both nationalities that according to the racial ideology of that time were considered inferior to the Anglo-Saxon race.

The conspicuous absence of the Aboriginal soldier in this pantheon of national icons came under public scrutiny in the early 1990s, when the Australian government started to retrieve the history of Indigenous people in the Australian Defence Force to promote national reconciliation (see Chapter 5). To rectify racial exclusion, seventy years after the original proposal, in 1993, the Hall came to host the tomb of the Australian unknown soldier. In the eulogy by Prime Minister Paul Keating delivered at the inauguration, he remarked that the unknown soldier has no race and sought to frame Australia as a united, multicultural and postcolonial nation (Nicoll 2001: 29). Given the complete collapse of the British Empire by this time, there was no danger that the unknown soldier could represent the empire. Instead, in a flip of history, the unknown soldier came to represent the multicultural nation, including Aboriginal service people.

Despite rhetorical efforts to make the unknown soldier represent diversity and national unity, there remains an unresolved tension, namely, the lack of representation of the Aboriginal warrior who fought against the colonisers. Birripi woman, actor and director, Syron (2015) notes that the unknown soldier is an empty mirror of the forgotten warrior of the Frontier Wars. The unknown soldier buried in the Hall of Memory simply cannot represent the Frontier warrior, and therefore cannot resolve the colonial past, because the former enacts the politics to forget the latter. The unknown soldier represents the nation because he or she wears the uniform of the modern military soldier who made the nation in Gallipoli. But, as already discussed in Chapter 1, the book-marking of Gallipoli as the moment that made the nation enacts a settler military politics to erase the colonial violence that founded modern Australia. Because the unknown soldier cannot stand as representing the Frontier warrior, it cannot enact national reconciliation and truly stand for diversity as Keating wanted. As Reynolds (2013: 237) puts it, 'We will know that we are all members of the same nation when a shrine in memory of the fallen warriors is placed side by side with the tomb of the unknown soldier.'

Nevertheless, the attempt to make the unknown soldier represent gender and racial diversity points to the remarkable ability of the Australian War Memorial to reflect socio-political changes and help Australian society to adapt. In particular, the use of the tomb of the unknown soldier to promote multiculturalism highlights the significant role that aesthetics of war commemoration play in shaping national identity. I have witnessed this first-hand since starting my research into the inclusion of Indigenous people in Australia's war commemoration. When I visited the Memorial for the first time in 2017, there was no mention of Indigenous military service in the permanent collection. There was only a vague reference to Indigenous soldiers through the tomb of the unknown soldier and, for the very first time, a temporary exhibition dedicated to Indigenous military service titled *For Country, For Nation* (see Chapter 5). Since that time, references to Indigenous military service have increased and some of the artworks collected in *For Country, For Nation* were still at the Memorial when I visited last in November 2022. At the time of writing in 2023, the Memorial is undergoing major refurbishment and the board has promised that on completion in 2028, Indigenous military service will be fully integrated. The political implication of this inclusion will be discussed in Chapter 5. For the moment, it is important to note that this inclusion aims to reflect a growing societal push to recognise Indigenous people in the Australian nation.

Anzac Day as Civic Religion

The final aspect of the Australian political aesthetics of war commemoration that I wish to discuss in this chapter is Anzac Day. Celebrated on 25 April in honour of the Anzacs landing at Gallipoli in 1915, Anzac Day is a key commemorative aesthetic and plays a crucial role in the transmission of the Anzac Legend. As a public holiday, on Anzac Day children do not go to school and business is restricted. For many Australians, Anzac Day is more than a public holiday; it is a sacred day. The sacredness of Anzac Day is also reflected in the restrictions on the sale and consumption of alcohol by the Australian states. Anzac Day is characterised by a ritualistic format which involves two events: a service at dawn which is the time when the Anzacs landed in Gallipoli called the Dawn Service, and a parade of soldiers and veterans marching to the city's war memorial saluting the crowds, called Anzac Parade or March. Every major Australian city holds these two commemorative events and almost every town holds at least one or a similar ritual. Anzac Day is enveloped in a sacred aura of religiosity and commentators have described it as the only day in the Australian calendar that bears any kind of holiness (McKenna 2010: 128; Inglis 2016: 19). It is important to understand the devotion and respect that Anzac Day compels. The religious tone of Anzac Day makes it a powerful aesthetic of settler nation-building.

The association of Anzac Day with religion and spirituality can be traced back to its inception. Anzac Day emerged in 1916 as a day of public celebration for the sacrifice of soldiers as well as of mourning for the loss of soldiers' lives. Falling in April, in 1916, Anzac Day coincided with Easter which overlaid the Christian rhetoric of death and resurrection onto the commemoration of Anzacs (Beaumont 1990: 163). Protestant and Catholics, however, had a different relationship with the war, and therefore, with Anzac Day. Protestants were closer to the British Empire and saw the war as an act of high Christian virtue, whereas Catholics were less supportive of the Empire and endorsed the anti-conscription campaign (Beaumont 1990: 164). Therefore, the former used Anzac Day at Easter to praise the sacrifice of soldiers for the Empire, and the latter distanced themselves from it. This division was not just religious, but social, and there was concern that it could have affected recruitment. In Brisbane, the chairman of the State Recruiting Committee prompted a meeting of politicians, prominent businessmen and clergymen to overcome the division and promote the institution of a commemorative committee (Gammage 2016: 249). This was presided over Canon David Garland of the Church of England and of Anglo-Catholic conviction (Moses: 2015: 29). Canon Garland offered a middle-ground between the Protestants and the Catholics. He campaigned for the government to establish Anzac Day as a national day, and simultaneously worked to drop the celebratory tone of the day promoted by the Protestants in favour of an approach purely intended to commemorate the dead accorded by the Catholics. Furthermore, he promoted the sacrifice of soldiers as a unifying theme and bolted it at the centre of Australia's ritual of war commemoration.

The infusion of Anzac Day with religion had political implications. First, a unified religious front promoted national unity in grief. This allowed most Australians to endorse Anzac Day as a public ritual of mourning and to consecrate memorials to the dead. Importantly, these became sites of rituals that enabled Anzac Day to reproduce itself and the nation in time. Secondly, the overcoming of religious division through a unified inter-faith approach allowed the Hughes government in charge during the war to use the Anzac Day and the religious rhetoric to promote recruitment. As Beaumont (1990: 169) recounts, in places like Sydney, recruiting agents used Anzac Day to speak to young men and persuade women to send their sons to war. In London, Anzac Day was used to mask the defeat at Gallipoli and keep morale and recruitment high. Beaumont continues to explain that the wounded and dead soldiers were mobilised to evoke sympathy and obligation, and ultimately to promote the patriotic cause. The religious tone was also used to involve children in supporting the war and to inculcate in them the official version of the war. In fact, for the purpose of commemoration, children 'were fed a constant diet of literature glorifying the heroism of Australian forces and extolling the virtues of the British Empire' (Beaumont (1990: 166). Finally, the religious tone of Anzac Day under state directives served to discipline the soldiers, especially when they disturbed public order because of mental illness and dissatisfaction with the conditions on coming home. Organisations in charge of supporting returning soldiers had at their disposal a religious rhetoric of compassion to offer solace and calm down agitated men and their families.

One such organisation was the Returned Service League (RSL) which became prominent in the execution of repatriation schemes. The RSL was a conservative institution and pressure group led by military and former military people. As the RSL advanced soldiers' rights, it also gained political influence and inserted itself into the organisation of Anzac Day. In the 1950s, the RSL took over Anzac Day from the church as demonstrated, for example, by the resolution passed in New South Wales in 1955 that removed all denominational content from Anzac Day services and precluded clergy from leading them (Inglis 2016: 18). The aim of the RSL was to replace the worship of God with reverence for the soldiers. Thus, the RSL substituted the religious theme of soldiers' sacrifice with that of the soldier as national hero and used rituals of war commemoration to promote a patriotic and militarist rhetoric. The theme of the soldier national hero appealed to alienated ex-servicemen and channelled their frustrations and war trauma, but it also elevated the 'returned soldier to a privileged position in Australian society at the expense of other groups' (Beaumont 1990: 172).

Upon observing the ways that the RSL took over the church and handled Anzac Day, Inglis argued that, by the 1960s, Anzac Day had become a substitute for religion, a ceremony devised by 'people who were unable to get comfort from traditional Christian affirmations about what happens after death' (Inglis 2016: 19). This was a time when Christianity had started to lose its relevance in Australian society and was unable to enjoin the nation and provide comfort for the loss of life. The RSL took over Anzac Day and changed the rhetoric but did not change the aesthetics. This is evident, for example, in Inglis' description of an RSL gathering for Anzac Day where the room was darkened apart from an illuminated cross, and the chairman invited the participants to repeat altogether 'Lest we forget', just like a religious congregation would say 'Amen' (ibid.). This led him to the realisation that the RSL did not make Anzac Day secular, instead it transformed it into Australia's civic religion as a body of precepts and rituals that serve as a moral compass for citizens (Inglis 1998: 343).

The transformation of Anzac Day into a civic religion enabled it to survive the Vietnam War, a conflict which was internationally controversial and polarising of Australian society. This was the first conflict in the history of Australia when Australians were conscripted for overseas service. The introduction of conscription made the war even more unpopular among young Australians, who were also influenced by the international anti-war movement and hippie culture. They rejected Anzac Day as a glorification of war, a characterisation that also reflected the RSL's leadership and its nationalist and militarist rhetoric intended to support the Australian war efforts. This polarisation made Anzac Day a target for anti-war and feminist demonstrations (see Chapter 4) and was detrimental to attendance. This was also a time when most of the veterans of the First World War were passing away and therefore Anzac Day was losing relevance.

By the late 1970s, Anzac Day seemed to be on its last legs. But at the turn of the century, it went through a revival when politicians discovered Anzac Day as civic religion and its ability to enjoin and direct the nation. Prime Minister Bob Hawke was the first politician to recognise the affective power of Anzac Day for political purposes and used it to distance Australia from Britain and craft a post-imperial and multicultural Australian national identity (Holbrook 2016). Initially, the government was wary about associating too closely with Anzac Day given its unpopularity and association with the RSL's militarism and imperialism in the previous decade. But Holbrook (2016: 221) explains that by that point, the popular film *Gallipoli* by Peter Weir released in 1981 had done a great deal to reframe Gallipoli and the Anzac Legend away from militarism and imperialism and shape it around the suffering of young innocent Australian men. Prime Minister Hawke riffed on this, and in a speech in 1986, described the Anzacs in Gallipoli as innocent victims commanded by British generals and caught in a war not of their own making (Bongiorno 2017). The takeover by politicians and the change of theme from the soldier as hero promoted by the RSL the decade before, to the soldier as victim enabled the revival of Anzac Day. The discourse of the soldier as victim emerged amid international preoccupations with Vietnam veterans suffering from post-traumatic stress disorders (see Chapter 3). Prime Minister Hawke banked on the international recognition of post-traumatic disorder among Vietnam veterans to graft the Vietnam War onto the Anzac Legend, and, in 1987, he appealed to the rhetoric of the soldier as victim of war to authorise the Welcome Home Parade for the Australian Vietnam veterans and rehabilitate them as 'missed' national heroes (Bromfield 2017).

At the centre of post-Vietnam War Anzac Day as civic religion is the figure of the soldier-martyr, and the congregation venerates the veteran, dead or alive but broken. The martyr symbolises suffering for a just cause (Winter 2017: 125), and attached to the soldier, represents the supreme martial sacrifice for the nation. As today most Australians are divorced from the lived experience of war, the soldier-martyr is a token of veneration through which they can connect with self-sacrifice for the nation and express sentimental nationalism (McKenna and Ward 2007). Moved by devotion for the soldier-martyr, on Anzac Day, some Australians go on pilgrimages to historical sites of battle (Scates 2006) or to the Australian War Memorial in Canberra. Former Prime Minister Tony Abbott took the next step and infused his Anzac Day speeches with a Christian rhetoric likening the Anzacs to Christian saints (Bongiorno 2017: 118).

When I attended Anzac Day services at the Australian War Memorial in 2017, the sacred and religious tone was very evident, especially in the Dawn Service. The service resembled an open-air mass with the theme of soldiers' sacrifice. It was led by a military chaplain from the Stone of Remembrance, an altar-like table that is common in religious architecture. I arrived before the service and found soldiers and veterans reading from other soldiers' diaries and letters in what reminded me of the reading of the gospel in church. During the service, the chaplain invited us to sing the hymns and speak together the words 'Lest We Forget'.

It is important to note the religious aesthetics of the Dawn Service because it sanctifies the soldier and positions war beyond scrutiny. When I attended the Dawn Service, the figure of the suffering soldier occupied centre stage. Large-scale images of soldiers were projected onto the walls of the memorial (see Figure 2.2). They created the visual effect of the soldier as martyr, that is, the soldier who died for a just cause (see Chapter 3). The images were devoid of the violence of war and represented the soldiers in mundane activities that emphasised their innocence and invited a sense of contemplation for their life that was lost too soon. The large images dwarfed the service participants, and the vertical position compelled us to look up in a gesture of reverence. By positioning soldiers' suffering as the pillar of war commemoration, the Dawn Service invites unity in compassion. This form of unity is also achieved through the collective singing of the hymns. As Frame (2016c: 199) notes, signing the hymns is designed to create a communal experience which bonds a group of people together in the act of transforming the 'I' into a 'we'. He continues that the invitation to sing the hymns is a solicitation to make the words of the hymns one's own. The lyrics of the hymns used in the Dawn Service speak of the tragedy of war and invoke a benevolent God who cannot end war but can forgive human mistakes and offer spiritual comfort from the tragedy of war. They also convey the idea

Figure 2.2 Large-scale images of Australian soldiers projected onto the walls of the Australian War Memorial during the Dawn Service. Photograph taken by the author in 2017. © The author.

that brave and selfless soldiers fight just wars in the name of God, and in the hope that there will be no more wars. They evoke a sense of unity in tragedy, and of compassion and solidarity towards soldiers who fight for a just cause and whose wrongdoings are ultimately judged and forgiven by God. In my experience of the Dawn Service, I found that the religious aesthetics invited feelings of uncritical compassion for the soldier-martyr.

Militarised Compassion and Settler Nation-Building

At the heart of the aesthetics of war commemoration as a strategy of settler nation-building is the emotion of compassion. Compassion is a powerful emotion that works by putting one in relation with the suffering of someone else by instilling a desire to ameliorate their situation (Welland 2015: 115). It is premised on the power differential and distance between a suffering subject and a privileged spectator of that suffering (Berlant 2004: 4; Sontag 2004; Dauphinee 2007). Compassion works politically when it prompts a desire to address the suffering of others. However, this desire cannot always be translated into action, in which case secondary reactions that are self-referential are induced. These include the need to disengage from the subject of suffering and a moral position that is a declaration of one's own virtue.

The aesthetics of war commemoration can evoke what I call 'militarised compassion', that is, an emotional connection with the soldiers that ultimately leads to a supportive stance for war as a way of ameliorating their suffering. Militarised compassion can be activated by aesthetics representing and alluding to the soldier as victim and the suffering soldier. These aesthetics evoke a sense of reverence for the sacrifice of the soldier in the name of the political community and a desire to repay a debt of honour to the soldier. In the context in which most citizens do not serve in war, the most immediate way to repay the debt of honour to the soldier is to support the troops. As Millar (2022) contends, the rhetoric of support for the troops in post-conscription societies is an attempt to supplant military service as a prerequisite for being a 'good citizen'. In this respect, militarised compassion is a potent emotion that reproduces the nation as an affective community à la Hutchison (2016), revolving around gratitude as a public response to the sacrifice of soldiers. The ritualistic nature of the aesthetics of war commemoration sustains the reproduction of the nation as an affective community held together by militarised compassion.

In the context of Australia, militarised compassion functions to perpetuate the settler nation by elevating the suffering of soldiers as the foundation of the nation. Curthoys (1999) explains that suffering has long been an important aspect of the Australian national identity, even before the First World War. Suffering was a prominent theme in stories about the pioneers in Australia. For example, they spoke about the suffering of British convicts who endured forced labour to build the new settler society, and of the explorers who muddled through an inhospitable land. Curthoys also discusses Australian stories of suffering as having profound consequences for race relations. Notably, the suffering of White British settlers struggling to resettle in Australia justified or erased their acts of violence and dispossession against Indigenous people. The First World War introduce the theme of military suffering, and a new story in the Australian context. This type of suffering was a particularly useful tool in the quest to craft an Australian national identity because of its widespread and national nature. Virtually everyone in Australia experienced suffering because of the war. Race relations are relevant here too. Due (2008) remarks that war commemoration can be read as a continuation of the tradition of White suffering as a logic of Indigenous dispossession whereby the suffering of White men in uniform fighting for *their* country in faraway lands legitimises their belonging and ownership of the country.

Militarised compassion evoked by the aesthetics of war commemoration bestows generative power and primacy to military suffering at the expenses of other types of suffering, most notably the suffering of Indigenous people endured during the Frontier Wars and because of the structures of settler colonialism. It creates a hierarchy of suffering between uniformed subjects – read White soldiers – and the non-uniformed subject – read Aboriginal anti-colonial warriors. The Australian aesthetics of war commemoration described in this chapter consolidates military suffering as the pillar of the nation. At the same time, it omits and erases colonial warfare as the moment that made modern Australia. The consolidation of ritualised practices of war commemoration organised by the church and supported by the state after the First World War strengthened a popular emotional attachment to the trauma of the war and the narrative that it made the nation. As the aesthetics of war commemoration grew stronger, there was less and less political space to represent and remember the conflict against Indigenous people that enabled the settlement of the colony and society.

Set against the exclusion of the Frontier Wars, the buttressing of soldiers' suffering as foundational for national identity enacts the dispossession of Indigenous people. It legitimises White belonging on the basis that White people built the nation with selfless sacrifice and suffering. The exclusion of the Frontier Wars denies that the suffering of the Indigenous warriors who fought against the colonisers and of the communities which endured colonial violence is also foundational for modern Australia. The exclusion of the Frontier Wars from the official aesthetics and rituals of war memory operates a distinction between those whose suffering counts and those whose suffering does not. The recent inclusion of Indigenous soldiers in state-sponsored war commemoration has adapted the narrative that the Australian nation rests on the sacrifice and suffering of those men and women who fought and died in foreign lands. While originally it was only White suffering that counted, now Indigenous suffering counts too. What remains unchanged, however, is that only suffering endured in foreign lands and at foreign hands is foundational for the nation.

The centring of the soldier-martyr in the aesthetics of war commemoration is also particularly effective in advancing settler colonialism. It is hardly a coincidence that the public endorsement of the soldier as victim and the figuration of the soldier-martyr emerged in the 1980s when Indigenous voices for rights and justice intensified and the Australian public started to become increasingly aware of the history of colonial violence upon which Australia is built (Moreton-Robinson 2015: 42). Politicians and nationalists were particularly concerned that the Indigenous movement and the growing public awareness about colonial violence could have fragmented the nation and undermined the celebration of the bicentennial of modern Australia in 1988. Amid contestations about the celebration of the bicentennial on Australia Day, politicians identified military history and Anzac Day as less controversial and more politically usable to promote national unity (McKenna 2010). At that time, Anzac Day had already been stripped of its militaristic connotation and the subject of the Anzac Legend was the soldier–martyr who evoked militarised compassion. Enveloped in militarised compassion, Anzac Day was shielded from criticism and attack.

The revived interest in military history also created an opportunity to present the nation as gender progressive and postcolonial. In fact, this was a time when women were integrated in the military and war commemoration, and the figure of the Indigenous soldier came to the fore through emerging historical research. Within this progressive context, the suffering of the soldier was made to be representative of gender and racial diversity as well as the glue of the nation. As it will be discussed in Chapters 4 and 5, the inclusion of women and Indigenous people in the aesthetics of war commemoration reflected the need to update the settler nation in the face of political challenges. Women were introduced at the end of the Second World War to police gender at a time when women stepped outside their traditional roles to help Australia meet its war needs. They were also introduced at a time when Indigenous soldiers became more visible in the Australian Defence Forces and when the Australian government created Indigenous-only battalions to patrol the north. Thus, the introduction of women in the aesthetics of war commemoration diverted attention away from questions of race and towards more manageable questions of gender. The more recent inclusion of Indigenous people in the aesthetics of war commemoration comes at a time when the settler state of Australia is implementing a politics of Indigenous recognition to resolve the colonial conflict in its favour. On a symbolic level, inclusion in the Anzac Legend and the aesthetics of war commemoration signifies acceptance and inclusion in the nation, but this inclusion is on settler terms as long as the Frontier Wars remain unacknowledged and unaccounted for.

Note

1. Connor (2016: 113) finds that British migrants enlisted in the Australian Imperial Force 'in numbers out of proportion to their percentage of the Australian population'. According to the 1914 census, 27 per cent of the men enlisted in the Australian Imperial Force were born overseas, the majority of which in Britain.

CHAPTER 3

Crafting the Anzac Soldier as National Hero

Introduction

Following from Chapter 2, this and Chapter 4 examine the gendered representations of settler war commemoration. Here, I analyse the construction of the Anzac soldier and its function in the Australian settler colonial project. The figure of the Anzac soldier emerged in the First World War, and ever since it has been a key definer of national identity and paradigm of good citizenship. As the protagonist of the Anzac Legend, the Anzac soldier sanctioned the Australian nation with his sacrifice and suffering in faraway lands and embodied the civic qualities of the Australian national. Despite recent efforts to include women and racial minorities in the Anzac Legend, the archetypal Anzac soldier is male and White of British descent. Because of the exclusion of women from active service and the lack of recognition of people of colour who contributed to Australia's war efforts during the First World War, the politics of war commemoration solidified Whiteness and masculinity as foundational elements of the emerging settler nation.

I argue that the commemorative figure of the Anzac soldier is a militarising representation that disciplined settler masculinity and governs citizenship. I trace the progressive militarisation of settler masculinity from the Frontier conflict to today's multiculturalism. In the Frontier conflict, settler masculinity was derived from imperial violence and colonial warfare and was therefore martial. The martial nature of frontier masculinity was essential to establish the early colonial settlements, but was also a liability for the development of the new settler society. It was too closely associated with Britishness to produce a new nation and too recalcitrant and lawless to legitimise colonial self-governance and state authority. Military wars provided opportunities to reform frontier martial masculinity through military discipline and battle. The First World War served as the catalyst for a significant transformation, giving rise to the portrayal of the Anzac soldier as a symbol of Australian militarised masculinity and settler nationalism. This soldier epitomised disciplined conduct, employing violence solely against deserving adversaries, while also embodying the distinct qualities of the emerging Australian nation, setting it apart from its British origins. In this respect, the Anzac soldier is more than a reformed frontier masculinity; he is the father of the settler nation. With this analysis, the chapter highlights the ontogenetic properties of militarised masculinity in the settler colonial context.

This chapter also maps the transition of the Anzac soldier from national hero who made the nation to victim of war who needs to be protected and supported. As discussed in the previous chapter, the recognition of post-traumatic stress disorder in the 1980s created a political space to frame the soldier as victim of war, and thus to demand support and compassion for the soldier regardless of who they are and what they did in war. Reflecting on the construction of the soldier as victim, I apply the concept of militarised compassion and discuss its function in settler military politics. The chapter ends with a discussion of the politics of multiculturalism and the ethnic soldier.

Militarised Masculinity and Settler Nationhood

In the Western tradition, the practice of war and the cultivation of militarised masculinity hold significant roles in the process of nation-building. Tilly (1992) provides evidence of the pivotal role of warfare in the establishment of robust Western state bureaucracies. Similarly, Mann (1993) discusses how war and military organisation contributed to the rise of centralised nation-states. Feminist scholarship identifies the war–nation-state relationship as a multifaceted triad that includes masculinity. This perspective emphasises that the capacity to wage war and reproduce the nation-state is inherently tied to the process of militarising masculinity and men (e.g., Peterson 1992; Yuval-Davis 1997). According to Elshtain (1987), the militarisation of masculinity relies on the 'Just Warrior' tradition which dignifies men through war and the gendered logic of protection. Just Warriors are depicted as courageous men who deploy controlled and morally justified violence in defence of their homeland, families and women. This portrayal underscores how masculinity becomes a platform for generating political violence, effectively serving as a means to engage in the process of constructing nation-states.

Following the Western tradition, the Australian nation came into being as a result of the practice of war and the cultivation of militarised masculinity. While the nation was formally established through the federation of the colonies in 1901, it was the landing at Gallipoli that came to be known as the birth of the nation. The importance of war as a practice of nation-building is further remarked by the fact that there is no public holiday commemorating the federation of the Australian colonies, whereas Anzac Day continues to be commemorated as a national day. The importance of war for Australia's nation-building was captured by the media in the years after the landing at Gallipoli. For example, in 1916, the *Brisbane Courier* declared that Gallipoli was where 'Australia had her birth and her baptism in the blood of her sons' and 'had leapt from the cradle of her nationhood into the front rank of the bravest of the brave' (quoted in Lake 1992: 309). In April 1918, the *Sydney Morning Herald* echoed this sentiment by stating that in Australia, the First World War 'means the birth of a nation' (quoted in Lake 1992: 311). Notably, Gallipoli was identified as the birth of the nation, even though Australians participated as imperial soldiers and the Gallipoli mission failed in its military objective to capture the Turkish peninsula, resulting in the retreat of the Anzacs and the Allied forces. Nevertheless, what elevated Gallipoli to this status was the Australian soldiers' embodiment of military values.

The origin of the Australian nation is traced to Gallipoli because of the belief that it was there that the crucible of war first put Australian masculinity to the test. Lake explains that for Australia as for other nations, 'the test of nationhood was a test of manhood' (1992: 310). Gallipoli was hailed as 'the supreme test of courage and endurance of Australia's masculinity' (Shute 1995: 3). Media commentators understood that Gallipoli was a military defeat, yet they spotlighted the soldiers' sacrifice as the paramount trial of masculinity and nationhood. In 1922, a *Sydney Morning Herald* commentator reflected: 'But was [Gallipoli] a failure to Australia? It has made us a nation . . . If the nation is to be born, if the nation is to live, someone must die for it' (quoted in Lake 1992: 309). This commentator referred to the soldiers' sacrifice for the nation's birth. Importantly, the Anzacs did not perish to defend the Australian nation; Australia's participation in the First World War was due to Britain's involvement, and Australians were defending imperial interests. Commentators like the one just quoted were leveraging the European tradition that constructed men as protectors of a feminised political community and according to which dying in war is the ultimate proof of masculinity as well as nationalism. The narration of the nation's birth became centred around men in war and militarised masculinity. As an illustration, in 1916, the *Brisbane Courier* wrote:

> Gallipoli would stand as a symbol of great deeds greatly wrought, a place where the courage, strength and endurance of our southern manhood was put to a supreme test and did not fail. (quoted in Lake 1992: 309)

The veneration of the Anzacs' masculinity and their manly attributes as the embodiment of nationhood was also a core theme in Bean's commemorative and historiographical endeavours, thus solidifying its place within the Anzac Legend (Lake and Damousi 1995). Bean's glorification of the soldier shifted attention away from Gallipoli as a military defeat and ennobled the sacrifice and achievements of soldiers as fathers of the nation. Shute (1995: 38) adds that this veneration served to encourage men to fight in the imperialist war machine, but on a symbolic level, it also marked the triumph of masculinity over femininity in the making of the nation. It erased the pivotal history of Australian women's suffrage and consolidated the patriarchal nature of the new settler Australian state by establishing a nationalist discourse premised on the citizen-soldier as the model Australian citizen. This is important because, as will be discussed in detail Chapter 4, some empowered women were pushing to extend political and economic rights to Aboriginal and Asian women, thereby challenging the Whiteness of the emerging nation (Lake 1999a). The suffrage of Australian women was granted with the underlying belief that they carried the responsibility of perpetuating the nation as predominantly White. However, it became evident that some were transgressing their roles as mothers of the White race. The transgression of politicised women was met with the assertion of the seminal power of militarised masculinity over femininity to produce the nation (Lake 1992).

The heralding of masculinity as a proof of nationhood must be understood within the imperial context and the pursuit of national legitimacy. At the turn of the twentieth century, Australia grappled with the curse of settler societies, namely, anxious nationalism. Born as a penal colony and closely tied to Britain as an imperial Dominion, the identity of Australia was a persistent subject of apprehension. Struggling to conform with the established norms of nationalism that evolved in eighteenth- and nineteenth-century Europe, settler societies such as Australia often resorted to drawing from the history of their mother country to ground their nation within a traditional framework (Holbrook 2014: 8–9). In *Inventing Australia*, White (1981) documents the many iterations of Australian identity, including the worst prison on Earth and the workers' paradise. Australia's identity was strictly tied to the British metropole. It was part of the so-called 'new world' together with the Americas, but unlike most of the Americas, Australia was not independent from the European empires. Australia did not have a revolution of independence and was comfortable being part of the British Empire. Lacking a tradition of independence and national revolution, Australia was often represented as a child of Britain. Australia was imagined as a young boy in Dickensian pantaloons and frills or as a good and obedient boy scout. At other times, Australia was represented as a young female shepherd, who nevertheless had nothing to share with the young, combative and republican female figures such as Columbia, representing the United States, and Marianne, representing France after their respective wars of independence (White 1981: ch. 7).

In the early twentieth century, Australia was yearning for a mature figure of national representation that did not forsake imperial ties. The war offered such an opportunity. The Anzac soldier emerged as an ideal symbol of national maturity. He embodied the manly character of the nation, and at the same time his uniform and mission upheld loyalty to the Empire. The soldier graduated Australia from its youthful identity and metamorphosed the nation from a young female entity into a mature male one. Lake's analysis also finds instances where the media's commentary transformed Australia's gender depiction from female, as seen in phrases like 'her birth' and 'her nationhood', to male. This transformation is exemplified in an article from the *Brisbane Courier* in 1922, stating: 'the day when the nation had reached *her* majority, and stepped out of childhood into *manhood*' (Lake 1992: 310; emphasis added).

The idealised figure of the Anzac soldier was first established by the British official war reporter Ellis Ashmead-Bartlett, who broke the scoop of the Anzacs in Gallipoli. In his dispatch, Ashmead-Bartlett described the Anzac soldiers using bombastic language that emphasised their confidence, courage and physical qualities. He wrote:

> The Australians who were about to go into action for the first time in trying circumstances were cheerful, quiet, and confident. There

was no sign of nerves nor of excitement . . . Though many were shot to bits without the hope of recovery, their cheers resounded . . . They were happy because they knew that they had been tried for the first time and had not been found wanting (quoted in Fewster 1982: 19–20).

Ashmead-Bartlett further commented that 'the physique of the men is remarkable' and called them a 'race of athlete' (quoted in Fewster 1982: 18). Examining Ashmead-Bartlett's war diary, Gilfedder (2021: 102) finds that the reporter wanted to dispel the fear of racial degeneration and was therefore more interested in salvaging the British race than in crafting the Australian nation. Gilfedder elaborates on how the processes of industrialisation and urbanisation in Britain gave rise to apprehensions regarding the moral and physical decline of the British race. Likewise, medical professionals with an interest in eugenics formulated theories about the potential pathological risks associated with Anglo-Saxons residing in tropical colonies. For Ashmead-Bartlett, Gallipoli was a 'test' of fitness of the Anglo-Saxon race. In fact, he characterised the Australians as 'colonials' and not as nationals. They were an extension of the Anglo-Saxon race undertaking a racial test of fitness, which they passed. As Ashmead-Bartlett commented, 'These raw colonial troops in these desperate hours proved worthy to fight side by side with the [British] heroes of Mons, the Aisne, Ypres and Neuve Chapelle' (quoted in Holbrook 2016: 165).

As discussed in Chapter 2, Ashmead-Bartlett's representation of the Anzac soldier was then taken up by Bean to pursue a nationalist agenda. Bean endorsed Ashmead-Bartlett's characterisation of the Anzacs despite the historical inaccuracies and created the Anzac Legend. However, Bean saw race differently than his British counterpart for whom Australian prowess was derived from their Anglo-Saxon race. Bean subscribed to an environmental account of race whereby the Australian race was shaped by its environment. For him, the Anzac soldier was not the continuation of the British soldier, but a Briton reborn and shaped by the harsh conditions of Australia. In his descriptions, Australian soldiers were tall and suntanned and representative of a healthy, strong race forged in the struggle against the wilderness of the new world (Gilfedder 2021: 103–4). Bean's contribution to the ennoblement of the Australian man propelled persistent references to the Anzac soldier as a national hero and noble man as discussed below.

Ultimately, Bean's portrayal and commemoration of the Anzac soldier as national hero had important implications for the advancement of settler colonialism. The Anzac soldier represented the Anglo-Saxon race reborn in the colony, consequently lending credibility to the Australian nation due to its population being comprised of a robust and vigorous racial group with a sense of national identity. According to Bean, the prowess of Australian soldiers in war was a measure of the nation's worthiness, positioning it on equal footing with Britain and other European nations. Embodying and fighting in the name of White British civilisation, the Anzac soldier represented a civilised masculinity that used violence only for moral purposes such as fighting German militarism and the preservation of civilisation. This elevated Australian settler masculinity, which prior to the First World War had only fought against Indigenous populations perceived as uncivilised and unworthy adversaries. The establishment of an Australian militarised masculinity erased the violence of colonial warfare by popularising the belief that prior to the First World War Australians did not know war. In this light, the figure of the Anzac soldier stands as a cornerstone of settler nationalism not only crafting an icon of Australian nationalism, but also veiling the martial violence of the Frontier Wars.

Masculinity in the Settler Frontier

Australia's militarised masculinity has its roots in the imperial and colonial dynamics that took shape during the early stages of settlement. This follows Connell's (2005) ideas that masculinities are defined in the continuities and discontinuities of socio-historical contexts. Therefore, understanding Australia's militarised masculinity and its involvement in settler military politics necessitates an exploration of the roots and evolution of Australian settler masculinity. This exploration should extend back to the establishment of the settler frontier, unravelling the intricate links with imperialism, settler colonialism and race relations. Australian settler masculinity emerged and developed in the Australian frontier and within the matrix of empire–colony relations, the penal system and frontier violence. It capitalised on its association with the British Empire to assert racial superiority and dominance over Aboriginal people, while simultaneously operating in a subordinate role to British masculinity. The militarisation of Australian settler masculinity resolved this tension in favour of settler nationalism.

Most settlers in Australia in the late eighteenth century and early nineteenth century were British men and they carried with them imperial masculinity as a weapon of colonisation. Imperialism and the industrial revolution gave British men a sense of superiority reflected both in their civilisational status and masculinity. The ideal notion of masculinity comprised qualities necessary for business entrepreneurship, military triumph and successful colonisation, including independence, fortitude, courage, daring, resourcefulness and paternalistic duty (Wilson 2004: 18). Abroad, the white skin was their signifier of power that immediately positioned British men as superior in relation to Brown and Black people and their civilisations (Hall 2004). In Australia, as in other colonial settings, the perceived superiority of White male settlers gave them a sense of entitlement to Aboriginal women, who were often raped and bartered as strategies of colonisation (Hall 2004; Woollacott 2010: 313). This further entrenched conflictual dynamics with Aboriginal people, as well as the idea in the minds of settlers that Aboriginal men were inferior to them because they were unable to defend their women and have marital relationships as defined by White civility.

Imperial masculinity in Australia was strong and was primarily embodied by military men. As already noted in Chapter 1, military men held prominence during the early stages of settlement until 1830s, when more free settlers relocated to Australia. Five hundred men from the British Navy landed in Australia with the first fleet, and 800 men from the British Army followed suit to provide garrison duties. British soldiers also arrived in Australia from their tours in India. Sick and injured soldiers and officials were sent to New South Wales to recover, and often ended up staying (Woollacott 2015: 13). Wright (2011) further explains that the military presence in Australia was the product of the militarisation of Britain in the late eighteenth century. The British Army expanded sixfold in the face of the wars against revolutionary France and the Napoleonic French Empire, and soldiers came to dominate British society and the middle class. After the British defeat of Napoleon at Waterloo in 1815, there was little employment for British officers. Nevertheless, Britain wanted to maintain military readiness and a standing army and offered soldiers continued employment at half-pay. It soon became evident that half-pay was not enough to maintain themselves and their families, and soldiers started becoming restless, thus posing a challenge to social order. To face this, the government introduced veteran companies for service in the Australian penal colony of New South Wales where soldiers were involved in the penal system to transport, guard and officiate the punishment of convicts.

British officers in the colonies were more than penal functionaries; their skills, discipline and authority made them suitable settler governors and administrators (Wright 2011: ch. 6). Stanley (1988: 67) finds that, together with the church, until the 1830s, the British Army was the main institution upon which colonial authority rested. Military men did not, however, rule with the fist only; they took on roles as politicians, frontier explorers, tradesmen, men of arts and science, as well as policemen against bushrangers[1] and Aboriginals (Walsh 1988). Thus, military officers and soldiers wielded substantial influence over the governance and social organisation of the colonies. Early Australian settler society and frontier masculinity were imprinted by military values, and particularly 'discipline, inequality, deference, and brutality' (Evans and Thorpe 1998: 19).

The cultivation of British military masculinity in the colony was intertwined with settler colonialism. In 1826, the British government instituted land grants for military men which allowed them to become landowners in the colony. This was effectively a system of land grab predicated on military masculinity. The British government had two main incentives for instituting the land grants for soldiers and officers. First, it allowed the conversion of the soldier's half-pay into a form of remuneration that would keep soldiers satisfied and stop them from revolting. Secondly, it not only encouraged soldiers to relocate to Australia as a means of distancing them from British society, but also aimed to establish a robust presence that could dissuade the French from making any attempts to seize Australia (Wright 2011: 25). On their part, British soldiers saw land grants in the colony as an opportunity to rise from the ranks and become gentlemen and landowners (ibid., ch. 2). Woollacott (2015: 36) conjectures that the prospect of financial security and land ownership could explain settlers' and military men's preparedness to enact brutal violence against Indigenous people who were protecting their own land from invasion.

Violence and brutality defined the initial phase of the Australian colonies, profoundly shaping Australian settler masculinity. These behaviours were not solely directed towards Indigenous populations but were also frequently inflicted upon convicts. Comprising almost exclusively men, convicts arrived on ships and were assigned to tasks such as construction and agriculture to develop the colony's infrastructure. Controlled by strict discipline and subject to harsh punishments, convicts played a crucial role in the colonisation of

Australia. Evans and Thorpe (1998) discuss that in the penal system, settler men formed a class system divided along two lines, commanding military men and convicted criminals, with not much in between. This class system was animated by a gendered organisational logic where the commanding masculinity held a privileged position, deriving its status from the subjugation and emasculation of convicts. Evans and Thorpe highlight flogging as a crucial gendered practice that reproduced the class system involving commanding men and convicts. Flogging was ordered by military officers and enforced by military guards (Stanley 1988: 66). It was a violent practice, but it was not a randomised or spontaneous event of the kind of beatings and male fights. It was a carefully orchestrated and ritualised practice to administer pain in a controlled way, often under the supervision of surgeons. Intended to impose 'a sense of submission, surrender, and vulnerability – traits associated conventionally with feminised behaviour' (Evans and Thorpe 1998: 24), flogging was a way of establishing hegemonic masculinity.

The quest for hegemonic masculinity of commanding military men must also be understood in the broader imperial context. As Evans and Thorpe comment, a central feature of commanding men's hegemonic masculinity was 'the desperate desire . . . to prove they are not girls' (1998: 19). Military men in the colonies lost their sense of hegemonic masculinity which they derived from fighting in war. Being involved in imperial conquest was a way of regaining their sense of masculine triumph, but hegemonic masculinity relies on the continuous disavowal of the feminine (Connell 2005). Flogging and the emasculation of convicts, as well as violence and retaliation against Aboriginal people was a ritualised reproduction of their hegemonic masculinity. Furthermore, flogging and other punitive actions also had a society-building function. They were intended to discipline convicts to a point where they could be freed and turned into yeomen, middle-ranking servants in the new estates of military men. Having yeomen further improved the status of British military men, especially those of lower ranks, who in the colonies had the opportunity to enter the class of gentry through land grants and the possession of estate servants (Woollacott 2015: 7). In this respect, the assertion of hegemonic masculinity by commanding military men worked to produce a colonial social order and class system.

The violence and lawlessness that characterised the early colonial period distanced Australian settler masculinity from its British counterpart. In Britain, the conception of manhood included attributes such as rationality, prudence and self-control, whereas in Australia, settler masculinity privileged physical strength, survival, hunting, shooting skills and being prepared to kill (Woollacott 2009). Despite the influence of British masculinity on Australian settlers, their masculinity was ultimately defined by the violent reality of colonial life. In fact, violence was the primary definer of life in the Australian colonies, including violence against convicts, the frontier violence against First Nation people, and assaults by bandits and bushrangers. In this environment, physical strength and survival skills were paramount. Australian settler men also had a different relationship with family and women in comparison with British men. In Britain, the qualities of manliness were defined in relation to the family and men's ability to protect women and children. These were less prominent in colonial Australia, mostly because of the lack of women and family units. Some military men and free settlers relocated with their families, but nevertheless, until the late nineteenth century, there were significantly less women than men. Male convicts outnumbered female convicts. Free migrants tended to move on their own or with male friends, and only few women relocated as free settlers because there were not many jobs for them in the mines and cattle stations of the colonies except as prostitutes. This gender imbalance shaped settler masculinity to privilege independence and the company of other men, especially in rural areas.

The development of settler masculinity also revolved around the pursuit of unrestrained freedom and lawlessness. The free migrants who moved to Australia in the early nineteenth century were independent men attracted by the wilderness of the colony or men escaping family commitments and looking for freedom (Woollacott 2006). The pursuit of unrestrained freedom in the Australian colony was a source of concern in the imperial metropole, especially when viewed in light of the potential for universal male enfranchisement. Men's violent behaviour in the colony and their quest for unchecked freedom, particularly from family commitments, raised questions about whether men in Australia were civilised enough to be enfranchised. The White male settlers from the cities responded by engaging in a discourse extolling the virtues of free settlers. This discourse played a pivotal role, serving not only to secure the enfranchisement of colonialists in Australia but also to eventually attain colonial autonomy and self-governance (Woollacott 2015). In this discourse, colonial violence was either omitted and concealed or justified on moral principles and the duty to spread civilisation. Violence against convicts was known to the British metropole, and settlers argued that it was necessary to establish the social order, and also that it was matter of the past. Violence against First Nations people was less known and of interest to the British metropole and Australian settlers often omitted it. When mentioned, it was characterised as an unfortunate circumstance of the moral mission to bring civilisation to the savages and establish the settler society. Thus, the free White settlers portrayed themselves as moral yet embattled, in an attempt to make settler violence coexist with definitions of civility. This was also rendered possible by their concealing of the violence against women and children, and their insistence that colonial violence targeted men only (Lake 2020).

Throughout the nineteenth century, Australian settler masculinity was further defined in relation to labour within the imperial–colonial matrix. As industry flourished in the colonies, Australia emerged as a land of opportunity and a haven for the working class, drawing an increasing influx of British free immigrants (White 1981: ch. 3). Often coming from the lowest classes, British free immigrants were eager to work and find economic opportunities that were foreclosed to them in the static and hierarchical class system of Britain. They created the image of the industrious, moral and economically productive White man who escaped the unjust working conditions and class system of Britain and enriched himself through his labour in the colony. This figure was a new man, and his masculinity was defined not only by his productivity, but also in opposition to the British middle-class gentleman characterised as an effeminate intellectual with no strength and virility.

The image of the Australian settler working man also drew from race relations within the colony. He was defined by his White race as master of non-White labourers. By the mid-nineteenth century, various schemes brought workers from India, China and the Pacific Islands to Australia. Many Chinese came with the gold rush and with British merchants. Some Indians were convicts, while others came as servants with the British aristocracy and the British Indian Army. Pacific Islanders worked in the whaling industry and sugar cane plantations (Woollacott 2015: 78–9). And then, of course, there were Aboriginal labourers whose work for settlers coexisted with the settler massacre of Aboriginal communities. Settlers often claimed personal relationships of friendship with Aboriginal people who were exploited and paid with rations instead of a wage or given wages lower than Indian and Chinese workers (Woollacott 2015: 86–7). White workers entered into relations of domination with all of these non-White workers who were often unpaid or underpaid and exploited. Woollacott (2013) documents the exploitative working conditions of non-White labourers and finds that they were codified in the legal system and labour relations that favoured Anglo-Saxons. The racial hierarchies of labour were an economic model that provided cheap labour to build the colonial society as much as a moral ordering that sanctioned the moral superiority of White men who pacified, dignified and civilised non-White workers. Within this racialised moral order of labour, the abilities of the non-White workers were attributed to the White master and his authority, discipline and wisdom. Racial hierarchies such as these constructed the image of a virtuous Australian White man. Nonetheless, because of the importance of the working man as an icon of Australian identity, the presence of non-White workers was perceived as a threat. Therefore, some of the first acts of federation were to restrict the ability of non-White workers to work or to come to Australia. For example, in 1901, the Pacific Islands Labourers Act ordered the deportation of some Pacific workers and the Immigration Restriction Act prevented non-White workers from coming into Australia. As Lake (2003) explains, this racist exclusion was predicated on the desire to preserve the supremacy of White working men who built Australian civilisation as White and of British descent.

Sport was another key definer of Australian settler masculinity throughout the nineteenth century. The British Army introduced cricket in the colony in the 1820s and in the 1830s it was popular among the gentlemen of Sydney (Stanley 1988: 67). The physicality of the colonial sportsman was contrasted to effeminate British intellectualism, and therefore he was readily associated with the improvement of the British racial stock (Adair, Nauright and Phillips 1998: 55). Sporting matches between Australians and Britons were frequently seen as an assessment of the health and vitality of the Anglo-Saxon race (ibid., 57). In fact, both sets of sportsmen were representatives of the Anglo-Saxon race, but the Australian sportsman embodied the vision of the improvement and future of the race. Following social Darwinism, the public debate about Australia's ability to improve the Anglo-Saxon race was divided between those who believed that the climate and social circumstances in Australia would produce a stronger, manlier Anglo-Saxon race, and those who conversely believed that the warm weather of the new continent would enfeeble the physical and mental abilities of the race. In this context, sport 'was considered to be something of a litmus test for the state of colonial society' (ibid., 57). Furthermore, lacking a history of war, in Australia, sport was a valid alternative way of elevating Australian settler masculinity. In fact, sport was often compared with war in the ways that men proved their manliness vis-à-vis worthy enemies (Mangan 2012). The importance of sport and its substitutive function for war is also evident in the fact that when Bean wrote the official historiography of Australia at war, he made plentiful references to sport.

The last archetype of Australian settler masculinity that developed in the nineteenth century is the bushman, a man who choose to live outside the urban centres in the countryside. The origin of the bushman can be traced to the bushrangers, convicts who escaped the penal system and found refuge in the bush. These escaped convicts were often of Irish and Scottish descent. When the rural pastoralist economy developed, the bushman, became the solitary worker of the countryside. In the second half of the nineteenth century, the bushman became the epitome of Australian hegemonic masculinity because of his complete disavowal of femininity (Moore 1998). In fact, there were very few women in the countryside and no women in the bushman's social environment. He became the symbolic representation of Australian mateship and homo-social bonding. His masculinity was not derived from the imperial ties but from the Australian environment. He embodied the strength and pragmatism necessary to survive in the harsh environment of inland Australia, including the bonds with other men. He was also characterised by a disdain for authority and the only law he liked to follow was the law of nature. It is interesting to note here how, in the imperial–colonial matrix, the bushman reversed the gendered axiom that associated women with nature and men with culture. The bushman was at one with nature and his masculinity was derived from that connection. Positioned within settler colonialism, the identification of the bushman with nature was a mechanism of White possessive whereby Indigenous land was appropriated by the settler man through the logical connection between his masculinity and the land.

At the turn of the twentieth century, the bushman became the icon of the Australian national type. This was mostly thanks to the work of the nationalist bohemians of Australian urban centres who captured the rugged masculinity of the bushman as the symbol of Australian national identity. His figure distanced the Australian man from the sophisticated, intellectual and classist masculinity of the British gentleman. Murrie (1998) discusses the figure of the bushman as being largely inflated by the urban bohemians who were looking for opportunities to capitalise on an Australian icon but also had no experience with the countryside. For them, the bushman was a fantasy of unrestrained freedom in the colony: unrestrained by family, the bushman was a man free to drink, swear and engage in licentious behaviour with prostitutes and Aboriginal women. This was not just a fantasy of the urban bohemian, but also a political move that embraced rugged masculinity at a time when the Australian feminist movement became more prominent and male violence was restricted by law (Murrie 1998: 70–1).

From this picture of Australian settler masculinity in the nineteenth century painted so far, we can gather that it was largely characterised by violence and was connected, albeit in competition, with British imperial masculinity. Australian settler masculinity had begun to chisel an Australian sense of identity, but its violent nature hindered the sanctioning of Australian masculinity on a par with British and European masculinity. Australian settler masculinity served to assert White belonging and to dispossess Indigenous people, nonetheless it was too uncontrolled and immature to represent the new nation. The First World War offered Australian nationalists an opportunity to burnish Australian settler masculinity by dignifying his violence through military war and elevating the Australian military man to a symbol of nationalism, civility and modernity. The remainder of this chapter maps the militarisation of settler masculinity. At first, this process occurred naturally when Australia entered the First World War. However, it was soon orchestrated and managed by the architects of nationalism, and most notably by Charles Bean through war commemoration, to create a national icon that represented the new nation of Australia. For Bean, war was the baptism of fire of Australian men and Australian national identity. Bean's vision to create an infrastructure and a tradition to commemorate the Australian soldiers was instrumental in consolidating the image of Anzac masculinity that was positioned at the centre of the Anzac Legend and Australian national identity.

The Digger

The militarisation of Australian settler masculinity begun in the First World War and culminated with the emergence of the iconic Anzac soldier. However, between the settler masculinities discussed above and the Anzac soldier there was an intermediary, the figure of the digger. The term digger originally identified the miners of the Australian goldfields, but in the First World War it was applied to the Australian soldier of the Australian Imperial Forces allegedly because of the association between Australia and the gold mines (Seal 2004: 19). Digger was used colloquially by both Australian soldiers to address one another, and foreign soldiers to identify Australian soldiers (Dennis et al. 2009). Seal (2004: 19–21) finds the word digger first used in soldiers' letters, poems and trench magazines, and concludes that the digger tradition and the image of the digger were primarily articulated in the informal, private and oral culture of the soldiers. As an image articulated by the soldiers, the digger was unpolished and raw. The spontaneous and authentic nature of the image of the digger stands in opposition to the carefully curated figure of the Anzac soldier that was invented as part of the institutionalisation of war memory. On this premise, Seal (2004: 4) contends that although both the digger and the Anzac refer to the Australian soldier, they are protagonists of two different traditions. The Anzac was the protagonist of the commemorative tradition, whereas the digger was of the informal culture of soldiers in war. I will return to the construction of the Anzac soldier within the Anzac tradition in the following section. For now, let us focus on the digger.

The digger tradition was cultivated by Australian soldiers in war and was exclusively intended for the diggers themselves. It involved a raw articulation of the diggers' common experiences, anecdotes and perceptions of war. This tradition included an in-group slang developed through the experience of war, featuring terms like the pejoratives 'gyppo' and 'wog' to speak of the Egyptians and Turkish, as well as other words borrowed from other languages encountered by the soldiers. Additionally, it incorporated sarcasm and heavy swearing characteristic of working-class soldiers in war. This slang served both as a means of camaraderie and as a tool for cultivating a distinct identity that set Australians apart from other White soldiers. The digger slang and image demonstrated the presence of entrenched nationalist feelings among the Australian soldiers, notwithstanding their allegiance to the Empire and imperial patriotism. Furthermore, the digger slang often served as a tool to express an aggressive form of nationalism that positioned Australians as a group opposed not just to the enemy, but also to fellow allied soldiers, most notably the British. In fact, a central motif of the digger culture revolved around the interaction between diggers and British officers, portraying the latter as haughty and dismissive of the former, while depicting the diggers as openly resistant to the authority of British officers. For example, the diggers often complained about military discipline, hierarchy and life. They showed dispassionate humour in the face of adverse circumstances and made fun of the British for not understanding Australian slang (Seal 2004). In this respect, the digger culture was important to distinguish the Australian nation within the Empire and from the embattled people of Europe more broadly.

While a military man, the digger was not a fully-fledged militarised masculinity capable of legitimising national identity. In fact, he was too closely associated with a civilian identity and, more precisely, that of the bushman. Already the term digger suggests a connection with the civilian worker of the goldfields. Just like the bushman, the digger had a distaste for authority and a strong sense of camaraderie, in Australia referred as mateship. As Seal (2004: 3) notes, the digger saw himself as 'an ordinary bloke doing a job of work for a reasonable day's pay'. The digger was primarily a civilian man and a worker, who wore the uniform with unease and temporarily and only to do a job. His attitude was irreverent, typical of the Australian larrikin,[2] and had a nonchalant attitude to life and death. The connotation of the digger being more of a civilian donning a uniform rather than a born soldier reflected the absence of an enduring military tradition that could have imprinted both the identity of the Australian soldier and the broader Australian national identity. As I noted earlier, besides the very early period, Australian settler masculinity was primarily defined in relation to the worker, the sportsman and the bushman. To some extent, all these types of settler masculinity were accustomed to violence, so they could be dressed in military uniform, but none of them was specifically a military type. The closest to a military type was the sportsman to the extent that sport matches were in some respects akin to military warfare in the ways that teams, just like nations, fought against one another and on equal grounds.

We can glean visual references to the digger in *The Anzac Book*, a volume edited by Charles Bean in which he collected sketches and text produced by Australian soldiers in Gallipoli. *The Anzac Book* was initially conceived as a trench magazine to maintain the morale of the soldiers in Gallipoli. By the end of the Gallipoli campaign, however, Bean edited and curated the material submitted by the soldiers to produce a more polished representation of Australian soldiers in Gallipoli to send home and for posterity. In this respect, *The Anzac Book* straddles across to the commemorative Anzac tradition. However, although Bean was the editor of *The Anzac Book* he did not include his own writing in it. He wanted to maintain an authentic feel and therefore preserve the soldiers' exclusive authorship. Therefore, we can be confident that despite of editing, *The Anzac Book* offers an authentic depiction of the soldiers in their own eyes. Generally, besides the soldier on the front cover, there is little heroism in *The Anzac Book*. Most of the representations of the soldiers are comical and sarcastic and depict everyday activities rather than scenes of battle. The soldiers are often bare-chested or wearing shorts and are rarely represented wearing their full uniform, suggesting that the formalities and prestige of war were of little importance to them. The men represented in *The Anzac Book* can barely be characterised as military men and instead they look like civilians adapting to the realities of war with humour and drawing from their civilian experiences. The book shows that the soldiers had a profound awareness of their virility and Australian identity derived from the worker and the bushman.

As an example of the digger represented in *The Anzac Book*, consider the drawing by David Crothers Barker (see Figure 3.1). Before enlisting, Barker was an artist, and in Gallipoli he served in the 5th Field Ambulance. In his representation of the digger, Barker wanted

"AT THE LANDING, AND HERE EVER SINCE"
Drawn in Blue and Red Pencil by DAVID BARKER

Figure 3.1 'At the Landing, and Here Ever Since', by David Crothers Barker, 1915. Private Collection Peter Newark Military Pictures/Bridgeman Images.

to capture and convey the typical Australian 'bloke' who enlisted for the war. He drew a simple man wearing a casual unbuttoned collar shirt, smoking a bent cigarette, and smiling with few teeth. His masculinity can hardly be described as militarised, but it references the bushman in his defiance of death. There is little heroism in the portrait of this man who looks more like a worker coming back from the fields than a soldier going to war. He is irreverent and appears casual about his participation in the Gallipoli mission that made the nation. The hint of stubble on his face suggests a nonchalant attitude. There is a sense of good-naturedness in his face underscored by his crinkled eyes and broad smile. He seems to have had a hard day of work suggested by the bandage and the crooked cigarette. But he can still have a laugh with his mates at the end of the day, unbuttoning his collar and lighting his cigarette. He seems to suggest that there is nothing that a plaster, a laugh and a cigarette cannot fix.

The Anzacs

Firmly established at the end of the First World War, the figure of the Anzac soldier drew from a selection of the qualities of the digger that were ennobled to inspire national pride and stand to represent the nation. The figure of the Anzac soldier dropped the anti-authoritarian streak of the digger and the confrontational stance towards other national soldiers. He also dispensed with the worker identity of the digger, instead elevating his sense of duty and bravery in the face of adversity. As for the digger, mateship was a key feature of the Anzac soldier too. However, while for the digger mateship evoked a sense of egalitarianism, in the Anzac it assumed a stronger connotation of brotherhood and camaraderie in war. Seal (2004: 82) also notes that the digger's humour was reframed as expression of his profound insight into life and his defiance of authority as simply 'a pose', a virtue of leadership and an expression of his democratic spirit. The Anzac soldier embodied duty, courage and sacrifice, which were only undertones of the digger.

Conversely to the somewhat organic development of the digger tradition created by soldiers for soldiers, the figure of the Anzac soldier emerged within a commemorative tradition and played a central role in the establishment and institutionalisation of the official commemorative framework and the nation. As a commemorative figure, the invention of the figure of the Anzac soldier was strictly linked to the establishment of the Australian War Memorial and, above all, to the War Art Scheme discussed in Chapter 2. The Anzac soldier was the protagonist of the war art collection, Anzac Day and the Australian War Memorial. The figure of the Anzac soldier was not an accurate representation of the Australian soldier in war, unlike the digger. Instead, it was a deliberate creation of a national symbol. This is evident, for example, in the conspicuous lack of representation of the horrors of war and death in the war art collection. The Fist World War was characterised by the use of unprecedented instruments of death that blew bodies apart. This central reality of war was notably absent in the emerging representation of the Anzac soldier. The body of the Anzac soldier was represented intact as a symbol of his prowess and spiritual power to represent the nation (Nicoll 2001: ch. 2).

The Anzac soldier in battle is a key representation in the Anzac tradition which commemorates the actions that made the nation. A key visual reference to the Anzac soldier in action is the painting by George Lambert *Anzac, The Landing 1915*. This painting is iconic among the hundreds produced by the Australian official war artists to date because it represents the very moment that has come to define the birth of the nation, that is, the landing at Gallipoli. As already discussed, the landing at Gallipoli has been codified as the birth of the nation, her baptism of fire, and the event that bookmarked the maturity of the newly established Australian nation. The importance of this canvas in the official war art collection is demonstrated by the fact that it has been shown continuously since the Memorial's first temporary exhibition in Melbourne in 1922. It is enormous – measuring 200 cm by 370 cm – and is the largest in the Memorial's collection. Today, the canvas hangs on the walls of the gallery devoted to the First World War, which is the first one a visitor encounters when they enter the Memorial. The location and size of this canvas make it impossible to miss and it continues to be a frequently cited visual representation of the inception of the Australian nation.

This painting captures the Anzac Spirit, the heroism and the suffering of the Australian soldiers in their act of forging the nation in war. As the first official representation of the Anzacs in Gallipoli, the Anzac soldiers are spotlighted and depicted with a uniquely national flavour. Lambert produced this painting after the war between 1920 and 1922. *The Landing* was the first public visualisation of the military campaign that baptised the nation. In fact, prior to this painting there were only a handful of private visualisations of the Gallipoli campaign because soldiers were restricted from taking photographs (Travers 2017: 73). The completion and presentation of *The Landing* to Australians occurred seven years after the actual event. This gap and the post-war recession made the depiction of the Anzac soldiers as national heroes a necessity for post-war reconstruction. Australians needed an anchor of hope and national pride. Given the importance of the mission, Lambert's representation needed to be grandiose but also realistic. Lambert was chosen to represent the landing at Gallipoli because he was renowned for his historical accuracy and attention to detail. His representation of the landing was meant to draw credibility from the reputation of the artist as well as the artistic realism of the representation. Defying modernism (which was the prevalent post-war artistic style in Europe, including Britain), Lambert deployed realism and produced a representation rich in detail and national symbolism.

Despite the photographic realism of the painting and attention to detail, *The Landing* is neither a historical record nor an eyewitness account. Lambert was not part of the Anzac contingent that undertook the Gallipoli mission, and the painting was produced from secondary material, including the memories of Gallipoli veterans, his post-war travel to Gallipoli and, of course, the Anzac myth crafted by Bean. And although Lambert saw himself as an 'artist historian' and was given this commission because of his renowned accuracy (Travers 2017: 141), he used his artistic licence to enhance the soldiers' heroism and tweak the historical facts to emphasise the national symbolism. Let us review the most politically salient features of *The Landing* and its representation of the Anzacs.

A most notable technique used to convey national heroism is the use of what today we might call 'cinematic view' to offer a panoramic perspective of the composite events of landing. In fact, *The Landing* captures more than a single glimpse could: the boat landing on the shore, the soldiers climbing up the mountain and the soldiers encountering the enemy. These three moments unfolded over several days, but the painting collapses them into a single representation. Furthermore, Lambert chose the point of view of the outside spectator rather than that of a fellow soldier, and the viewer is offered a god's eye view of the Gallipoli mission. The dramatic mountainous line breaks the horizon and carries the viewer's gaze across the battle scene. This cinematic view conveys a sense of dramatic anticipation, combining the excitement of seeing Australian soldiers in action for the first time and apprehension for the young Australians who lost their lives in the name of the nation.

The dramatic perspective emphasises the landscape over the soldiers. In fact, the soldiers appear somewhat insignificant compared with the landscape. This was not intended to devalue the soldiers but to emphasise the landscape, which, as already noted in Chapter 2, was an artistic feature of Australian identity popularised by the nationalist artistic group, the Heidelberg School. Thus, the prominence of the landscape was to create a nationalist effect. Furthermore, the imposing landscape accentuates the heroism of the Anzacs who are represented as tiny figures, resolutely taking on the challenge of clambering uphill in inhospitable terrain. The use of the same colour palette to paint the soldiers and the soil implies that the terrain was swallowing the soldiers and creating another obstacle to an already arduous mission. In *The Landing*, the terrain is as much an enemy as the Turks are. This reflected the view that Australians were shaped by their environment and recalled a well-known Australian war tradition, that against the wilderness (Gilfedder 2021: 104). There is only one Turkish soldier in the painting, and he is dead. This is to keep the spotlight on the Anzacs but also to divert attention from the fact that, after all, the Gallipoli mission ended in the retreat of the Anzacs and the Allied forces. The representation of the hostile terrain as the main challenge for the Anzacs conveys that the landscape was more of a problem than the Turks. But despite the terrain, the soldiers nevertheless endure and courageously ascend the hill. The tenacity of the soldiers in the face of the hostile terrain recalls the bushman rendered heroic against the overwhelming forces of nature.

The Anzacs are presented as tragic heroes but, importantly, the emphasis is not on any one of them as an individual hero. The Anzacs are a national hero as a collective noun. This is conveyed by the absence of details in the faces of the soldiers. Some of the soldiers' faces are absent altogether and none of them can be recognised individually. This is a stylistic choice to emphasise equality and mateship and the importance of the collective over the individual. The painting is designed in such a way that the viewer's eye does not fall on any individual soldier but instead captures the troop as a collective that stands for the nation. While the faces of the soldiers have little to no detail, the soldiers are recognisable as the Anzacs because of the white of the calico ration bags that are attached to their belts. In both of my guided tours, the tour guides noted that this is where the Anzacs kept their Anzac biscuits, sweet, oat-based cookies that remain very popular in Australia today.

A final feature of the painting that shows the construction of the Anzac tradition is the soldiers' uniform. Lambert diverged from the historical record and used artistic licence to change the uniform and paint a nationalist version. On the day of the landing, the Anzacs were wearing the peak cap, which was a standard feature of the imperial uniform. In 1885, the peak hat was adopted by the Victorian Mounted Rifles, and after federation it became the standard gear of the Australian Commonwealth Army (Rutherford 2014). This headwear, however, was associated with Britishness (Pedersen 2014: 124; Travers 2017: 205). Instead of the peak cap, Lambert painted the Anzac soldiers wearing the slouch hat which was more readily recognisable as Australian. For example, the representation of the digger by David Barker discussed above wears a type of slouch hat. This headwear has long been associated with the Australian bushman who used it because it offered more protection from the harsh sun of the Australian outback. As Marti (2018: 10) remarks, the slouch hat connected the soldier to the Australian masculinity of the bushman and aligned the bush and the military narratives. Lambert also tweaked the sleeves of the uniform. In the painting, the Anzacs wear sleeves down, despite evidence suggesting that on the day of the landing, the Anzacs were ordered to wear their sleeves up so as to be more readily distinguishable from the Turks (Pedersen 2014: 124; Travers 2017: 205). One reason that can explain this change is that the Australian soldiers created for themselves a reputation that they lacked order and discipline. The representation of sleeves down countered that and created an image of the Anzacs as orderly and disciplined. Thus, in *The Landing*, the Anzacs were no longer unruly diggers and bushmen wearing the uniform with unease, but proper soldiers in the service of their nation embodying militarised masculinity.

The Landing does not merely represent the event and the soldiers landing in Gallipoli; instead, it constructs a representation of the birth of the nation, and in so doing, defines the qualities of the Australian nation. It depicts the Australian soldiers as natural soldiers and fully militarised men who can legitimise the nation. From the perspective of settler analysis, this iconic painting creates a visual reference to the birth of the settler nation and establishes a racialised hierarchy of heroism and suffering. It legitimates White belonging and possession through the grammar of heroism and suffering and the representation of the homogeneous Whiteness of the settler nation. The Anzac soldiers making the nation as in *The Landing* mythologises the White soldier as national hero and enshrines the White history of war as the pillar of the nation at the expense of the history of colonisation.

The Soldier as Victim

The figure of the Anzac after the First World War was the pinnacle of Australian militarised masculinity, and it stood as a representation of

Australian heroism and national maturity within the British Empire. However, the figure of the Anzac soldier began to change in the second half of the twentieth century when it acquired a victim identity. Despite the nationalist rhetoric that animated Australian society in the First World War and its aftermath, Australia was hit hard by the economic recession after the war. Furthermore, in 1939, Australia found itself at war again because of its imperial ties with Britain. The Second World War held less allure for Australians, as the Japanese attack on Australia from Singapore instilled the realisation that war had come uncomfortably close to home for the first time. Many Australian soldiers were also captured as prisoners of war and therefore could not 'live up to the warrior ideal established by their [Anzac] fathers' (Garton 2008: 49). This was particularly emasculating for Australian soldiers because imprisonment was at the hands of the Japanese, a race that they perceived as inferior (ibid.).

Ivor Hele, Australian official war artist in the Second World War and the Korean War, produced notable visual references to the soldier as victim. He was the longest serving Australian official war artist and produced a large amount of work. Animated by social realism and its critique of power, Hele was interested in depicting the real socio-political conditions of men at war. Consequentially, his depiction of Australian soldiers reveals minimal heroism. The typical representation of Hele's soldier is injured, exhausted and struggling. Hele's perspective is diametrically opposed to Lambert's and instead of a cinematic view, he offers a close-up of the faces and bodies of soldiers in pain. The soldiers are depicted as weary, with their bodies frequently blending into their surroundings, whether the jungle landscapes or military machinery. This effectively symbolises the soldiers' lack of agency and control. Hele's art from the war in Korea, the second war that he covered, accentuates the pain in the faces of soldiers who are cadaveric and depicted used a green and orange palette, perhaps in reflection of the growing unease with Australia's involvement in war after the Second World War (Fry 2003: 123).

As an example of Hele's representation of the soldier as victim, consider the painting titled *Bardia* (see Figure 3.2). The battle of Bardia, Libya, in 1941, was a significant military action for Australians. It was the first battle fought by Australians in the Second World War and the offensive was planned and commanded by the Australians. Overall, the battle was a success: the Allied forces won, 36,000 Italians who were occupying the town were captured, and the Allied forces continued to advance through Libya. According to the Australian War Memorial records, Australia lost 130 men and 326 were wounded

Figure 3.2 *Bardia*, by Ivor Hele, 1967. Copyright expired, image in the public domain.

compared with 1,703 Italians killed and 3,740 wounded. The Australian casualties were from the 6th Division which was deployed in a diversionary role, but a series of misunderstandings led to heavy losses. The Memorial's description of Hele's *Bardia* states, 'To many Australians, this battle had been a test of their equality with the men of the First World War, and they believed they had passed it.' Although Bardia was a military success characterised by Australian actions and decisions, Hele decided to focus on the casualties of the 6th Division, as indicated by the uniform patch of the soldier on the right. *Bardia* zooms in on a scene after the Italian attack that caused the casualties from the 6th Division. There is a tone of contestation in this painting that represents the victims of a victorious battle. Hele seems to reject the official narrative that Bardia was a victory to show the casualties and represent the soldiers as victims of war. He put the viewer right in the scene by adopting the perspective of one of the soldiers who also suffered in the attack. There is no blood, but the soldiers are dead and injured, with those at the front comatose and clenching, while those at the back are pulling the injured to save them. The painting features a prominent green palette that makes the soldiers look homogeneous and thus replaceable.

Hele's representation of the soldier is nonetheless a dignified victim. Hele's soldier is a victim of the harsh conditions of war, but there is an undertone of heroism in his ability to withstand them. Hele is the only artist who was commissioned to represent two wars and he won numerous awards for his art; neither the repeat commission nor the plaudits to the artist would have been possible had his representations been hostile to the soldiers and veterans who were sanctioned as national heroes and founding fathers on the nation. While struggling, fatigued and injured, the soldiers in Hele's war art are still resilient and enduring. In *Bardia*, this is evident from the soldiers at the back who are pulling the injured back to safety. With his art, Hele wanted to show the realities and struggles of war, including its physical and emotional toll, a sentiment that resonated in Australia after the two world wars. Although the soldiers are not combative like they are in the war art collection of the First World War, they retain their masculinity in their physicality and resilience. Their bodies are intact and there is no blood, allowing the viewer to contemplate the suffering of soldiers without feeling disturbed by the visceral effects of war.

By the 1980s, the identity of the soldier as victim became a mainstay in Australia and served to distance Australia from the dissolved British Empire. The consolidation of the soldier as victim was possible because of the unpopular Vietnam War and the introduction of conscription for overseas service for the first time in Australia. The public perception was that the men conscripted to fight in Vietnam were victims of politics and were sent to die in a war that had little moral purpose. Moreover, the 1970s marked the emergence of an international culture of trauma in response to the Vietnam War, which led to the acknowledgement of post-traumatic stress disorder as a medical condition (Fassin and Rechtman 2009). In this political climate, soldiers were suffering men rather than national heroes and they were to be protected and compensated. Seizing this trauma culture and the emphasis on soldiers as victim, in 1981, the Australian filmmaker Peter Weir released his blockbuster *Gallipoli* which represented the Anzac soldiers as victims of war and of British imperialism. Holbrook explains that the film did a great deal of work to distance Australia from imperialism and militarism and presented the First World War as a story of personal tragedy. Banking on the culture of victimhood, it presented the Anzac soldiers as naive young men who were sent to war to be 'sacrificed to the stupidity of the British command' (2018: 57). Holbrook's view is shared also by McKenna (2010: 133), who comments that the representation in *Gallipoli* of the Anzac soldiers as victims of the incompetence of British 'hedgehog-moustached officers who spoke in plummy accents' offered 'the perfect antidote to the problem of Anzac's imperial past'.

The representation of the soldier as victim in the 1980s not only dealt with Australia's imperial past, but also silenced the feminist critique of war and military masculinity in such a way that singularly reinforced martial settler nationalism. Twomey (2013) contends that the Australian feminist movement against war that emerged in the late 1970s and was active in the early 1980s (see Chapter 4), set in motion a nationalist response to protect the soldier as victim. The feminist critique of war was construed as an attack on soldiers and disrespect towards their families and the nation. The culture of trauma and victimhood fuelled the belief that the feminist anti-war movement was exposing soldiers to unwarranted and unjustified criticism and doubt. The body of the veteran as victim was at the forefront of the public reaction against feminists. For example, in 1985, veteran Mike Lahey interrupted a feminist protest against war by waving his prosthetic leg from the top of a truck and crying that these women made him feel inadequate (Twomey 2013: 104). The newly acquired status as victims allowed soldiers and veterans to discredit the message of the feminist anti-war movement. The feminist protests were met with public indignation, policies restricting demonstrations on Anzac Day, and misogynist comments such as this from a man to the press: 'if it weren't for these guys [the soldiers] these little bitches wouldn't even be here' (ibid., 101). In the face of public and government reactions against the feminist critique of war on Anzac Day, the feminist anti-war movement dissolved by mid-1980s. Twomey also finds that the feminist protests against war and military masculinity catalysed the reinvigoration of Anzac Day and the resurgence of the language of pride for the soldiers following the controversial Vietnam War. As Twomey (2013: 102) puts it, 'feminist actions ultimately prompted a defence of Anzac Day, even from those who admitted to having previously felt disengaged from it'.

More recently, the figure of the soldier as victim has been brought back into the spotlight by Ben Quilty's art on Afghanistan veterans suffering with post-traumatic stress disorder and combat fatigue. Quilty was commissioned to be Australia's official war artist in Afghanistan in 2011 and his body of work was exhibited at the Australian War Memorial in 2014. The work collected in the exhibition titled *After Afghanistan* presented large-scale portraits of soldiers across different ranks. Notably, only a single portrait depicted a female soldier, and all soldiers were White or White-passing. Many soldiers were painted naked, in contorted poses that evoke suffering, fatigue and death. Quilty's collection of soldiers' portraits exhibit an expressionist style achieved with a thick impasto of oil paint applied on the canvas to build layers of colour. The human forms are only sketched and present little detail. Positioned on very large canvases, the viewer's eye can perceive the human forms only from a distance, but they disappear with proximity. The soldiers are positioned against dark or dull backgrounds of blue, grey and purple. Quilty focuses on shadows and lights to convey psychological states of being such as fear, anxiety, sadness and resignation.

The soldiers of Quilty's art are vulnerable bodies. They are diametrically opposite to Lambert's representation of the Anzacs as small action figures in uniform. Quilty also offers an even closer zoom-in than Hele's art and an insight into the inner emotional world of the soldiers. Well-versed in the subject of Australian masculinity, Quilty has developed an artistic language to capture the soft side of toxic masculinity. The soldiers' vulnerability is underscored by the naked body sustaining intense emotions. Naked as they are, the soldiers have nowhere to hide their emotions and the marks of war. For Quilty, the naked body is a way to access and express the emotions associated with the experience of soldiering which are ordinarily covered by the uniform and buried under body armour. Upon returning from Afghanistan, Quilty invited some of the soldiers he had met there to pose for him and talk about their experiences as soldiers and veterans. All shared stories of intense operational stress and post-deployment distress, and some talked about their experience of battling with post-traumatic stress disorder upon return to civilian life. With the naked body, Quilty wanted to capture vulnerability but without conveying weakness. Admittedly, there is a certain bravery and boldness in soldiers stripping themselves bare before the public for whom they fight wars.

The body of the soldier in pain in Quilty's art lends itself to the narrative that soldiers are victims of war and that publics owe them compassion. Quilty's work has received an overwhelmingly positive response and the artist has become an advocate for supporting returned veterans. He has been vocal about the limited resources available to soldiers returning from war with post-traumatic stress disorder and the stigmatisation of soldiers' mental health. This rhetoric and aesthetics have fed the culture of trauma that frames the soldier as a victim in need of empathy. As Butler (2017) notes, the personalisation of war trauma in Quilty's art tends to depoliticise war and promotes sympathy for the soldier. Quilty's soldiers are completely removed from the context of war and in most paintings, there is nothing that suggests that these are the bodies of soldiers; they can be apprehended as veterans and soldiers only within the narrative that identifies them as such. Because of Quilty's advocacy, this narrative is loud and resonant, but nonetheless lacking a political perspective that problematises why soldiers are sent to war and what type of wars they fight. Butler (2017: 442) analyses that the removal of references to war is a subtle suggestion to the viewer that they do not need to know about the details of the war that injured and stressed the soldiers; all that they are asked to do is to feel empathy for them. Bulter argues that Quilty's art creates the illusion of offering an intimate insight into the experience of war without saying anything about war itself. As he puts it, the public success of Quilty's war art lies in the fact that it offers the viewer an opportunity to be part of the public spectacle of care and responsibility towards the soldier without any real encounter with war (ibid., 443).

Multiculturalism and the Ethnic Anzac Soldier

The last iteration of settler militarisation that I wish to consider in this chapter is the ethnic soldier. I will discuss the militarisation of First Nations people in detail in Chapter 5, while here I focus on culturally and linguistically diverse groups only. The ethnic soldier is predominantly a male figure that emerged from the settler politics of multiculturalism that have developed in Australia since the late 1970s. When Britain joined the European Union in the early 1970s, Australia was prompted to reflect on its colonial identity and relationship with Britain, coming to the realisation that it was largely one-sided. This sparked the need to craft a new national identity away from Britain and the legacies of empire and reinvent the civic and racial qualities of the nation. Facing the demise of the British Empire and the influx of migrants since the end of the Second World War, under the leadership of the Whitlam government, Australia recognised the necessity of breaking free from its past policies of racial exclusion and discrimination. The repeal of the White Australia Policy marked a pivotal moment in the nation's history, signalling a departure from the ethno-centric practices that had characterised Australia's immigration and social policies for decades. This transition was crucial in moving away from the imperial past and establishing the foundation for a new nationalism premised on the rhetoric of multiculturalism and unity in diversity (Curran and Ward 2010).

But Australia's embrace of multiculturalism was fraught with racism and imperial nostalgia. The language of multicultural national identity

contended with that of nationalism tied to the British race and the legacies of empire. And while Australia was trying on the rhetoric of multi-
culturism, some politicians adopted military heritage to tell Australians
who they really were without Britain. For example, Prime Minister Bob
Hawke mobilised a Gallipoli-centred narrative of the Anzac Legend to
foster a sense of independent nationalism, whereas his successor, Paul
Keating, used the Anzac Legend and the Second World War to position
Australia in the Asian neighbourhood. According to Holbrook (2016),
politicians were able to utilise military heritage to shape a sense of
nationhood facilitated by the influence of popular culture, most notably
Peter Weir's acclaimed film *Gallipoli*. This cinematic portrayal stripped
the Anzac Legend of its imperialistic and militaristic undertones,
reimagining the Gallipoli narrative as a tale of poignant tragedy and
courageous young soldiers embroiled in a war that was not their own.
To remark the influence of Weir's *Gallipoli*, Holbrook quotes the prominent Australian historian, Bill Gammage, who called the film 'easily the
most influential of all depictions of Australians at war' (ibid., 172). The
representation of the Anzacs as victims of war took hold in the climate
described in the previous section and served to distance Australia from
its imperial history.

In the 1990s, military heritage got caught in the Australian project
of multiculturalism as demonstrated by the burial of the Unknown
Soldier at the Australian War Memorial discussed in Chapter 2. In
the eulogy to the soldier, then Prime Minister Paul Keating said:

> This unknown soldier is not interred here to glorify war over peace; or
> to assert a soldier's character above a civilian's; or one race or nation
> above another or one religion above another; or men above women;
> or the war in which he fought and died above any other war; or one
> generation above any other that has been or will come later . . . He is
> all of them. And he is one of us.

Keating's eulogy for the Unknown Soldier sought to reaffirm Australia
as the united, multicultural and postcolonial nation that he promoted
in his ministerial agenda (Nicoll 2001: 29). In the early 2000s, the
rules allowing participation in the commemorative rituals of Anzac
Day were also relaxed to allow diversity of representation.

This environment created opportunities to retrieve the history
of ethnic soldiers who served in the Australian Defence Force. The
late nineteenth-century gold rush in Australia attracted a significant
influx of immigrants from both Europe and Asia. Despite the prevailing restrictions and occasional hostilities between Australia and

the migrants' countries of origin, some of these immigrants chose to actively contribute to the defence of Australia. However, history erased their identity in the name of national homogeneity and the association of Australianness with the Anglo-Saxon race. The Australian embrace of multiculturalism offered the space where historians could unravel the stories of ethnic soldiers, including Chinese, Italian, Greek, Russian, German and from other nationalities. Their primary drive was to challenge the monocultural identity that characterised the nation and the Anzac Legend and to establish concomitant histories of belonging. However, their work and perspective reinforced the perception, especially among conservatives, that multiculturalism was a force of societal fragmentation (Bongiorno 2014: 92). Instead of generating possibilities for a more inclusive nation, the retrieval of the ethnic soldier produced the belief that cultural diversity was a threat to national unity and identity. This was evident, for example, in a 2011 report commissioned by the Department of Veterans' Affairs on community expectations about multiculturalism at the 100th anniversary of the landings at Gallipoli. This report identified and framed multiculturalism as a 'risk and issue to consider' and as a 'potential area of divisiveness' (Drozdzewski 2016: 7–8).

The official response to the challenge of multiculturalism was to use the centenary of the landing at Gallipoli as an opportunity to give ethnic groups a better understanding and stake in the Anzac Legend. Thus, subcommittees of ethnic veterans were invited to register and participate in war commemorative events on Anzac Day. When I went to Canberra on Anzac Day in 2017, many ethnic groups, including Europeans, but also Indians, Pakistani, Turkish and others, registered to march in the Anzac March (see Figure 3.3). The Turkish contingent is particularly interesting because Turkey was Australia's enemy in the First World War and in the pivotal Gallipoli mission. However, as Bongiorno explains (2014: 95), Turkish people may feel a strong need to participate in Anzac commemoration because they are a 'vulnerable recent migrant group' which has 'concerns about racism and being made feel unwelcome' insofar as they are 'Muslim, Brown, and were enemies in World War I'. At the Anzac March in Canberra, I also encountered and briefly spoke to a small representation from Tonga who told me that they march on Anzac Day in Australia because they are proud of their military history. They did not seem to be interested in the complexities of race and the restrictions to migration for Pacific Islanders. It is evident that while Australia embraces the ethnic soldiers, it is not producing a concomitant engagement with the history and politics of migration that allowed and allows ethnic soldiers to

Figure 3.3 Banners identifying ethnic contingents marching on Anzac Day.
Photograph taken by the author in Canberra, 2017. © the author.

serve and be included in the Anzac Legend. The lack of engagement
of migrant communities with the politics of race and migration on
Anzac Day and in the Anzac Legend can be explained with Bongiorno's reflection that inclusion in the Anzac tradition has come at the
price of chauvinism that equates national history with military history. As he puts it:

> once a tradition is defined in more inclusive terms, those who refuse
> to participate can readily be represented as beyond the pale. To
> question, to criticize – even to analyse – can become un-Australian.
> (Bongiorno 2014: 86)

Ethnic minorities joining the Anzac March walk the line between
assimilation and fear of rejection from the nation, if not expulsion
from the country. Their participation on Anzac Day is a political statement that they embrace Australian values and tradition as a necessary
condition to be accepted in a predominantly White society. It is also
a relinquishment to raise their voice against war, military culture, and
structural and casual racism for fear of being labelled un-Australian.
Sumartojo and Wellings (2021: 173) further explain that multiculturalism in Australia has given rise to a new form of racism which

emphasises cultural difference and incompatibility over hierarchy, and which they characterise as xenophobia. Accordingly, belonging is defined less overtly in terms of skin colour, and more in respect to how a group can claim a connection with the civic traditions. This is evident, for example, in a comment by the Minister of Education in 2005, Brendan Nelson (who then became the Director of the Australian War Memorial), who said to the press: '[I]f people don't want to be Australians and they don't want to live by Australian values and understand them, well then they can basically clear off' (quoted in Bongiorno 2014: 95–6). Immigrants finding inclusion within the Anzac Legend are afforded a platform for connecting with a nation that historically upheld a White identity, irrespective of their own ethnicity. Their right to belong to the Australian nation is gauged by the degree to which they can identify with the Anzac Legend and connect with Australian military values. Thus, the settler politics of multiculturalism in war commemoration functions to reinforce the history of White achievements as the foundation of the nation and the reluctance to speak against racism. This is most evident in the ongoing debate about the Indigenous Voice to Parliament where many ethnic Australians do not support Indigenous people in this political process on the ground that it would divide the nation and give Indigenous people an "unfair" advantage over other ethnic communities that constitute the nation.

Notes

1. Escaped convicts who hid in the bush.
2. An Australian term denoting a mischievous and uncultivated young man, but with a good heart.

CHAPTER 4

The Militarisation of Women

Introduction

Following from Chapter 3 which discussed the militarisation of masculinity and the male soldier protagonist of the aesthetics of war commemoration, this chapter focuses on how women have contributed to the aesthetics of war commemoration and have been militarised in the process. War played a significant role in shaping Australian femininity and did so within a settler colonial framework. In this chapter, I flesh out women's dual identity as oppressed within a patriarchal system and oppressor within settler colonialism. I show that the feminist struggles that relied on war to achieve women's emancipation and equality with men were inevitably entangled with the settler colonial project. Within the hyper-masculinist conditions that shaped the Australian nation, Australian White women have historically banked on race to move up the social hierarchy, and have established the Australian White middle class by navigating the crossroad between nation and empire. War offered White women a prop in these manoeuvres in ways that advanced their status in society as well as the Australian settler colonial project.

I argue that the militarisation of women has been an important part of the Australian settler colonial project. I examine the logics governing women, femininity and race brought about by war, the involvement of women with war, and the engagement of women in the aesthetics of war commemoration. The chapter maps the history of Australian women at war and frames the emancipation of White women through war opportunities within the 'coloniality of gender'. This concept reminds us that in colonial contexts, gender is shaped by colonial and imperial relations predicated on the construction of racial hierarchies.

Women were largely excluded from the construction and narrative of war as myth of origin but nonetheless occupied a role in settler military politics. While excluded from military ranks, in the First World War women were the counterpart of the citizen-soldier as citizen-mothers. The enfranchisement of Australian White women in 1902 gave them a stake in the war and they engaged in supporting the war as mothers of the White race. Women embraced their patriotic duty to reproduce the nation as White and developed a maternal feminism predicated on their contribution to war and the nation as mothers of the White race. I demonstrate that this was the continuation of the central role that women played in establishing the British White settlement in Australia. Australian women were influenced by imperial feminism, a transnational women's movement across the British Empire that enabled White women to acquire social capital and political rights in the metropole and colonies by virtue of racial differentiation and hierarchies (Woollacott 2000; Midgley 2007; Oppenheimer 2010). In their position of enfranchised citizen-mothers, Australian White women largely supported war, militarism and the racial hierarchies of the empire.

The establishment of the Australian Women's Auxiliary Services and the work of women in munition factories in the Second World War created space for their entry into the Australian civic pantheon sanctioned by their representation in the aesthetics of war commemoration. The involvement of women in war was the source of social anxieties around gender. These anxieties were managed with visual representations of women as patriots who did not lose their femininity. I discuss how the commission of the first three female war artists operated in this order. The representation of women in the aesthetics of war commemoration and the militarisation of White women after the Second World War also worked to manage race relations. In fact, in the Second World War, Indigenous people were becoming more involved in the war effort. Some Indigenous women enlisted in the Women's Auxiliary Services, over 3,000 Indigenous men enlisted in the Australian regular forces, and Aboriginal and Torres Strait Islander men from northern Australia were engaged by the military to form Indigenous-only battalions for reconnaissance. The spotlighting of White women in war shifted attention away from the Indigenous contribution to war and towards Whiteness.

In the final part of this chapter, I also consider two potentially disruptive engagements of women with war commemoration, namely, the feminist anti-war activist and the female Aboriginal soldier. I say "potentially disruptive" because, as I will discuss in this chapter, they both work within the settler military politics that have consolidated the Australian settler nation-state. The feminist anti-war movement emerged in the 1960s and rose to prominence in the late 1970s. It ceased in the early 1980s because of nationalist pressure to defend the soldier as victim. As already noted in Chapter 3, the feminist anti-war movement was instrumental in the revival of Anzac Day and prompted support for soldiers as victims. In this chapter, I go into the detail of the history and representation of the feminist anti-war movement. As for Aboriginal women, although they sought military service to improve their living conditions under settler colonialism, within settler military politics their service has been signified as the ultimate token of postcolonial progress and settler legitimacy. The Indigenous female soldier represents the progress of both the Australian armed forces and the nation in terms of gender and racial equality. Within this discourse, the service of Indigenous women fails to represent an act of resistance against settler colonialism.

Women and War in Australia

Australian women gained the right to vote soon after federation in 1902, and yet the Australian public sphere was dominated by men. The gendered division of society was reinforced at the start of the First World War when men were sanctioned as warriors and creators of history, and women were relegated to the passive flesh of mothers at the mercy of history (Shute 1995: 23). As enfranchised citizens, however, women were not completely excluded from the public deliberations about war. They were engaged as citizens and, more specifically, they took on the civic duty to be citizen-mothers and the responsibility to produce children, reproduce the nation, and support their husbands and sons to step into war. Given the absence of conscription in Australia, women's duty to uphold belligerent masculinity was particularly important, and some joined the British and Imperial White Feather Campaign[1] to hand out white feathers to young men who did not enlist.

The First World War did not represent a groundbreaking moment for Australian women like it did for their European counterparts. For many women in Europe, war represented an unprecedented employment opportunity. By the end of the war, the employment of women in France and Britain had increased by more than 20 per cent, and in 1917 women comprised 30 per cent of the workers at Krupp, a German armament manufacturer (Grayzel 2002). In Australia, the figures show an increase in the order of 2,000–3,000, which is inconspicuous compared with almost a million in Britain (Beaumont 2000: 274). Conversely to Europe, Australia did not have a large munitions industry where women could have gained employment. But as Beaumont (2000: 275) notes, this was hardly the only reason for Australia's inability to expand the employment of women, and conservative views on femininity largely contributed to keep women in traditional roles. Women in male positions and jobs were considered a threat to morals and society, and women who attempted to enter men's spaces were met with resistance and violence (Damousi 1995; Haskins 2017). Australia did not introduce paramilitary women's auxiliary groups of the British kind, and the only way that women could join the war was as nurses in the Australian Army Nursing Service (AANS). The nurse was the only authorised female figure in war because she conformed to the role of women as carers and citizen-mothers. Female doctors were refused service (Holmes 1995).

Despite the limitations imposed by the authorities and society, Australian women wanted to be more involved in the war effort. They performed their patriotic duty mostly as volunteers and unpaid workers (Beaumont 2000). Notably, in 1916, a group of women formed the Australian Women's Service Corps to train women to work in jobs new to them and make the government aware of women's intent to participate in the war. They regularly petitioned the Department of Defence to create an official women auxiliary corps like Britain, but Defence was adamant that they did not need (or want) women. The government did not support women's active service, but encouraged their voluntary mobilisation to contribute to the war on the domestic front. This was, after all, their duty as citizen-mothers. It is estimated that 10,000 patriotic clubs, societies and sewing circles made up of volunteers were established across Australia to support the war, and they involved large numbers of women (Scates 2001). Affluent women were particularly active in the Red Cross which supported imperial feminism[2] through wartime philanthropy across the British Empire (Oppenheimer 2016).

During the First World War, the nature of Australian feminism was remarkably imperialist and militaristic. Australian feminists were well connected to feminists elsewhere in the Empire. As Australian women were enfranchised, the Australian feminist movement was at the vanguard of feminism in the whole of the Empire and supported the

British, Canadian and South African suffragettes. When the war started, feminists across the Empire suspended their suffrage activism and used the suffrage channels to send charity and support the war. Imperial feminists were concerned that if Britain lost the war, the imperial order that supported their privileged position as White imperial women would have collapsed (Woollacott 2000: 212). For Anglo-Australian women, Whiteness was a means of elevating their social standing within the colony in comparison with Indigenous women. Similarly, in the British metropole, it served as a way to distinguish themselves from other women of colour within the Empire (Lake 1993; Woollacott 2000). Imperial feminism's concern with the racial and imperial order influenced Australian women to embrace their patriotic duty as mothers of the White race. They 'spoke the language of imperial loyalty and militarism, and supported with a growing passion the official efforts to persuade more men to enlist' (Beaumont 2013: 100). After the war, Australian feminists used the militarised discourse of the wartime service of the citizen-mothers to campaign for maternity allowance separated from wifehood, a discourse which became implicated in the racist nationalist policies that excluded Aboriginal and Asian mothers from citizenship and maternity allowances (Lake 1992).

The Second World War represented a more significant shift for Australian women. The domestic experience in voluntary positions during the First World War and the expansion of women's rights in the Empire set the conditions for Australian women to become more actively involved in the Second World War. This war is often presented as a pivotal moment for Australian women (Adam-Smith 1984; Lake 1995; Bassett 1998; Bomford 2001). Following the example of other nations like Britain and Canada that established women's service and under the pressure from the Japanese threat at home, Australia mobilised the female workforce to meet its war needs. Thus, in the Second World War, Australia witnessed a shift from the voluntary work of mostly affluent women who supported the First World War to paid employment and the involvement of working-class women in the Second World War. Women were largely employed in feminised industries such as clothing and textiles. As men went to war, women also took on men's employment positions in banking and heavy industry, although without receiving equal pay. Women in men's jobs received up to 90 per cent of men's wages while those in jobs classified as women's work only received up to 65 per cent of the men's wage (McWatters 2005: 43). Although women rarely remained in men's jobs after the war, their war employment paved the way for the post-war societal acceptance of women in the work-force and for the struggles for equal pay and fair work conditions.

In the Second World War, women were also given military ranks for the first time. The creation of the Women's Auxiliary Services in 1940 and the establishment of the Australian Women's Army Service (AWAS), Women's Auxiliary Australian Air Force (WAAAF), Women's Royal Australian Naval Service (WRANS) in 1941, and of the Australian Women's Land Army (AWLA) in 1942, expanded the direct involvement of women beyond nursing. These services were created to relieve men from non-essential and non-specialised duties while they were fighting. Initially, women were given tasks associated with femininity such as cooking and typing and were only deployed domestically. As the war progressed, however, women took on more specialised tasks such as operating military technology and some 6,000 volunteers were deployed abroad. Some women like Colonel Sybil Irving, founder and controller of AWAS, had the militarised privilege to experience positions of power in the military that were unprecedented to Australian women (Howard 1990).

The Second World War changed Australian femininity. More women experienced earning a wage, unprecedented freedom from domestic life, and a sense of power and camaraderie in work. This 'new woman' had skills and a sense of entrepreneurship, and she saw herself repre-sented glamorously in posters and public campaigns. They also experi-enced sexual freedom. Some Australian women had extramarital sexual relationships, often with American soldiers (Lake 1995). Women-only auxiliary services also created opportunities for women to find and experience lesbian love (Ford 1995). As Australian women gained a wage, they became targeted as consumers by advertisers selling makeup and fashion clothing, which further contributed to women's desire to earn a wage independent from men (Finch 1995).

The transformation of Australian femininity brought about by the war caused social anxieties about women and gender which ultimately led to the disbandment of the women's auxiliary services and the return of men to their pre-war employment. The anxieties revolved around women taking men's jobs and wages, the sexualisa-tion of women, and women abandoning their maternal and domestic duties. After the war, women were assigned the task of repopulating the nation, and the Australian government mobilised local politics, the church and the media to encourage them to return to their pre-war life and role of mothers of the nation (White 1988: 410–1). While many Australian women returned to their traditional gen-der roles under the government incentives to repopulate Australia, migrant women from Europe increased the number of women in the post-war Australian workforce. This created new opportunities for Anglo White women to enter the middle class and differentiate themselves from the White migrant working class. Female wages went down because migrant women were prepared to take lower wages than those received by Australian women during the war in order to secure a permanent place in Australian society (Sheridan 2002). At the bottom of this hierarchy were Indigenous women who were channelled by institutions of the Aboriginal Protections System to work as servants in middle-class families.

The emergence of the Cold War created new opportunities for Australian women. While some women returned to their pre-war life and duties, others pushed for the establishment of a permanent women's auxiliary service in defence. In the early 1950s, the War Cabinet approved the employment of women in women-only defence services. These were made permanent at the end of the 1950s. The rationale was that women were already trained and could supplement the shortage of manpower. WRAAAF, WRANS and AWAS now renamed the Women Royal Australian Army Corps (WRAAC) were reformed and gathered in a gender-segregated service that was not part of the regular forces but still conferred military rank. Because of the social anxieties around women in uniform, women of the auxiliary services were employed in positions deemed suitable for women such as signallers, telephonists, administrative and office workers, cooks, and occasionally in mechanical and driving positions. They could not be deployed overseas and received honourable discharge when they married. Women of the auxiliary services did not go to Vietnam; only nurses did.

While some women were looking for social and economic opportunities in the national armed forces, others were mobilising to mount strong opposition against Australia's military involvement in Vietnam. Australian women have been involved in anti-war movements since the First World War (Damousi 1995). During the Vietnam War, women were particularly triggered by the institution for the first time of overseas conscription in 1964. The prominent anti-war and anti-conscription women's movement, Save Our Sons (SOS) emerged in 1965 and involved mothers campaigning against the conscription of their sons for war. This movement was voluntary and relied on the unpaid labour of women who were primarily middle class, married and with sons approaching or at the age of conscription (McHugh 1993; Curthoys 1995). In the 1970s, some women were involved in the anti-war movement as unionists, and they often clashed with union members who subordinated women's liberation to class struggle (Curthoys 1995). In the late 1970s and early 1980s, anti-war women's groups were particularly inspired by the rise of radical feminism in the West and in Australia. Notably, in the early 1980s, a group of radical women founded Women Against Rape in War, often abbreviated as WAR. The group marched on Anzac Day demanding recognition for the victims of rape in war and in all countries. This movement brought to the fore a critique of patriarchal militarism in Australia and generated an examination of the Australian soldier as potential rapist (Elder 2005). This movement was met with a strong national resistance by veterans and women alike. Twomey (2013) contends that the feminist critique of WAR can help to explain the revival of Anzac Day since the 1980s on the ground that it led to the emergence of a counter-movement in support of the soldiers and the Vietnam veterans who were just starting to receive national recognition for their service. WAR ended up softening its tone and excluding Australian soldiers from their critique, and eventually it crumbled under the inability to articulate its message in the face of nationalist sentiment (Elder 2005: 80).

Starting from the mid-1970s, women became integrated in the Australian military. WRAAF, WRAAC and WRANS were abolished in 1977, 1979 and 1985, respectively, and female soldiers were integrated into regular services. In 1979, servicewomen were guaranteed equal pay, but the Australian Defence Force was granted an exemption from the Sex Discrimination Act 1984 to exclude women from combat roles. The ban on women in combat positions started to lift in 1990, and was fully lifted in 2011. Full integration was achieved in 2016. As of 2022, women make up 20 per cent of the Australian Defence Force. The Australian Department for Veterans' Affairs has provisions to support female veterans after service (DVA 2022), which suggests that military service can be an opportunity for social mobility for women – though data on this is missing. In the last decade, Australian women have also achieved positions of power at the highest levels of defence and foreign policy. In 2013, Julie Bishop was named as Australia's first female foreign minister, followed by Marise Payne and Penny Wong, while in 2015, Marise Payne became the first female defence minister, followed by Linda Reynolds.

The Coloniality of Gender

In line with the feminist theory that war and gender are mutually constitutive (Goldstein 2001; Sjoberg and Via 2010; Åhäll 2015), as Australian women became involved in war, war shaped Australian femininity. War created unprecedented opportunities for female emancipation, and since the Second World War, Australian women have seized these opportunities to their advantage. But 'women' is an abstract category that does not capture the female experience at the intersection of race, class and sexuality. Feminist scholars like Crenshaw (1991) have long established that the experience of women varies along intersectional lines, and Henry (2017) reminds us of the importance of understanding the position of Black and minority women when analysing gender, the military and war. An intersectional analysis of Australian women and war reveals that war did not empower all women equally. As discussed in the previous section, the First World War offered opportunities for White mothers and upper-class women to contribute to the nationalist project as citizen-mothers and to establish their influence through imperial feminism. Middle- and working-class White women had more opportunities in the Second World War when the national workforce embraced female labour for a wage. Lesbians and single women also found spaces to exist during this war, and the return of Anglo women to their role of mothers of the White nation after the war created new employment opportunities for European immigrant women.

For Aboriginal women, the war was primarily an experience of exclusion or assimilation in the settler society. In the First World War, Aboriginal women were excluded from serving as nurses. In the Second World War, sixty-nine Aboriginal and Torres Strait Islander women served in the women's auxiliary forces, mostly in the AWAS and WAAAF. Many of them were from the Stolen Generations[3] and joined-up to escape mistreatment in institutions run by the Aboriginal Protection System. Some joined to bypass the racist policies of segregation and exclusion, while others joined for financial reasons and to avoid becoming servants in the homes of wealthy White women (Riseman 2015; Cadzow 2019). Their racial background was not always recorded, and some women decided to pass as White or were not aware of their Indigenous heritage because they were part of the Stolen Generations. The service of Aboriginal and Torres Strait Islander women was often characterised by episodes of racism such as being treated as a curiosity and being refused entry in public spaces with other servicewomen (Cadzow 2019). Those who served used their skills and status to better their position in White society, but for the authorities, military service was a way to assimilate Aboriginal and Torres Strait Islander men and women in White society. The wartime opportunities for Aboriginal and Torres Strait Islander women were severely impacted by racist policies. For example, Hughes (2017) highlights the politics of resistance that emerged when Aboriginal women met African American soldiers stationed in Australia. Their intimate relationships cross-pollinated ideas and activism and contravened and challenged the racist ideologies of these two countries. Nevertheless, racist policies, including the White Australia Policy that prohibited the immigration of African Americans and blood quantum logics that governed marriage of Indigenous people, limited and negatively impacted the lives of Indigenous women who could not build a life with African Americans.

In colonial societies, race and coloniality are key intersections of gender. Lugones (2008) explains that colonisation introduces gender as a system of oppression of colonised people. She calls the intersection of gender and race to reproduce systems of colonial oppression the 'coloniality of gender'. Colonisation institutes racial hierarchies that construct Indigenous people as an inferior race and introduces gender relations that position colonised racialised women at the bottom of the hierarchy of power. The coloniality of gender identifies the racialisation of women as a key feature of colonisation and colonial power structures.

Most often when we hear the word 'race' we think of Blackness or Asian identities. Whiteness is rarely identified as race and instead is characterised as the default identity. Australian critical scholars recognise Whiteness as a defining feature of colonisation in Australia (Moreton-Robinson 2004). Non-White people have been managed and governed in relation to White people and society to create and maintain White supremacy (Elder, Ellis and Pratt 2004; Carey and McLisky 2009; Moreton-Robinson 2015). The construction of Whiteness is particularly important in the context of Australia, a land located in the southern hemisphere and that, prior to British colonisation, was populated only by Black people. Leading scholar in critical race studies in Australia, Goenpul woman Aileen Moreton-Robinson (2020) demonstrates that White women were crucial for the consolidation of Whiteness and the colonisation of Australia. This is important to note because the coloniality of gender and the construction of Whiteness are key to explain why the emancipation of Australian women did not spread evenly across all Australian women.

Because of the coloniality of gender, the emancipation and privileges of some Australian women are strictly tied to colonisation and Indigenous dispossession. Moreton-Robinson (2020) notes in particular the role of the middle-class woman and the tension between liberal feminists and Indigenous women. The achievements of the White middle-class woman are implicated in colonial rule and governance and the figure of the emancipated (White) woman masks the dispossession of Indigenous people. Moreton-Robinson's (2020: 24) point is summed up as:

> White women participated in gendered racial oppression by deploying the subject position middle-class woman both consciously and unconsciously, informed by an ideology of true white womanhood, which positioned Indigenous women as less feminine, less human, less spiritual than themselves.

To go into greater depth into the coloniality of gender in Australia, let us consider the history of gender relations and feminism in Australia. Colonial Australia was born as a British penal colony with a strong demographic sexual imbalance. Records indicate that the ratio of men to women in 1822 was five to one, and only started to even out in the early twentieth century (Woollacott 2010: 315). The first women in colonial Australia were convicts and were characterised as 'whores', degraded and morally corrupted (Farrell 2001: 123). Women had the important role of reproducing society, but, first, the moral character of women had to be redeemed. Marriage and imperial and Christian ideologies promoted by elite imperialist women through transnational organisations such as the Red Cross, the Mothers' Union and the Woman's Christian Temperance Union were primary vectors for redeeming convict women. Furthermore, in order to incentivise emancipated female convicts to get married, colonial governments restricted employment opportunities and wages for single women (Farrell 2001: 124–5). Inspired by the opportunities to improve colonial society and women's role within it, and by the imperialist and Christian women's movements, upper-class women in Australia took on the task of promoting moral purity by policing men's drinking and unchecked sexual behaviour (Smart 2000). Lake (1998a) examines 'frontier feminism', the politicisation of women in colonial Australia to protect mothers and wives from the shame and misery brought about by the immorality of White men raping Aboriginal women and having them as concubines, making mixed-race babies, drinking and gambling. Frontier masculinity represented a danger to the new White society and frontier feminists positioned themselves as the protectors of White women as well as the guardians of White civilisation in the colonies. Women's patriotic duty at the junction between the empire and the new emerging nation was to domesticate frontier masculinity and safeguard the purity of the White race.

With the coming of federation, Australian feminists and suffragists mobilised the colonial discourse of women as guardians of civilisation to gain the right to vote. In a campaign, they juxtaposed the disenfranchised educated White woman with enfranchised men, including drunken men and wife-beaters but also Aborigines and Chinese men as inferior people (Smart 2000: 54). In the late 1890s, women founded the National Council of Women, the largest women's organisation in Australia, through which they advocated for women's rights on the ground that they performed the patriotic duty to populate the nation with healthy White babies. Carey (2009; 2011) discusses the National Council of Women's enthusiastic promotion of eugenics and racist ideology that not only advocated for White motherhood but also for the segregation and sterilisation of Aboriginal women. As Australian White women gained political rights on these grounds, the new Commonwealth government embraced their maternal contribution to the nation as mothers of the race and instituted policies to encourage women to stay at home and care for the children, such as the family wage paid to the man (Swain, Grimshaw and Warne 2009: 218). Although the family wage freed some women from the burden to work for low wages, it did not give women economic and sexual independence from men. Thus, feminists further endorsed the notion of the mother of the nation to campaign for women's rights as citizen-mothers. They achieved maternity allowance, a one-off payment to be paid for the birth of each child. The maternity allowance was not a pension or gratuity but a remuneration for the service of women to the state. Notably, the allowance covered even unmarried White women, but excluded Aboriginal, Pacific and Asian mothers, whose children were not considered to be a benefit to the settler state (Lake 1992; Lake 1999b).

The relationship between Australian feminists and Indigenous women was fought with settler structures and racist ideology, but most White feminists were not oblivious to the discrimination and violence faced by Indigenous women. While deriving their superiority from racial differentiation, White women recognised that they shared a condition of sexual exploitation with Aboriginal women (Lake 1998a: 131). Some White feminists campaigned against Aboriginal child removal practices and for the economic and political empowerment of Aboriginal women (Lake 1999b), but their most successful efforts were achieved with campaigns that increased the institutional "protection" of Aboriginal women, which often resulted in more settler control and governance over the latter's lives (Eveline 2001: 172). While acknowledging the good intentions, Moreton-Robinson (2020: 102) reads these efforts as civilising manoeuvres that were intended to 'deconstruct and reconstruct Indigenous women in the image of true white (middle-class) woman'. These efforts were imprinted by the racist ideology to rescue the "primitive" people by inserting them into Western civilisation and White society. Moreton-Robinson (2020: ch. 1) remarks that Australian White women have long been implicated in the settler colonial mission to civilise Aboriginal women, as is most evident in their work as missionaries in the Aboriginal Protection System designed to confine and micromanage Aboriginal people, and in their role as social workers involved in the removal of Aboriginal children from their families. On moralist grounds, White middle-class feminists insisted on being part of the mission to civilise Indigenous women through education, training and paid work under their service, and envisioned the advancement of Indigenous women in assimilationist terms. Most often, this meant a reformation of Indigenous girls and women under the employment of White middle-class women that reinforced race division through the hierarchy of class.

In the aftermath of the Second World War, White women moved away from being the police of White civilisation and sexual purity and feminists campaigned for sexual liberation outside marriage (Lake 1998a: 126). While the government and men wanted women to return to their maternal and domestic positions, White feminists were articulating women's rights more on the model of male independence. The icon of the female worker began replacing that of the citizen-mother and women were demanding rights to earn wages equal to men (Lake 1999a: 173). To affirm the status of women as workers, White feminists recorded and elevated the work of their colonialist forbearers who were implicated in the dispossession of Indigenous land through their work in the Aboriginal Protection System. Despite its racist undertones, this feminist movement attracted the participation of Indigenous women not only because it was more inclusive, but also because Indigenous women were interested in claiming their status as workers and stopping the colonial practice of exploiting their unpaid labour (Lake 1998b: 103). The involvement of Indigenous women in the feminist movement contributed to their increasing participation in the workforce, which nevertheless involved assimilationist conditions and subordination to White bosses (Moreton-Robinson 2015: ch. 7).

From the 1960s, Australian feminists became involved in the international civil movement and the anti-war movement. The Australian feminist movement endorsed the open condemnation of racism and invited Indigenous women to participate as equals in the feminist struggles for the emancipation of women. However, there was little understanding of the differences between Indigenous women's and White women's feminist demands. For example, while White feminists were fighting for equal pay with men, Aboriginal women were twice as likely as White women to be unemployed (Eveline 2001: 168). White feminists were campaigning for sexual liberation, contraception and abortion rights, while Indigenous women wanted the ability to say no to sexual exploitation, the end of forced sterilisation and the ability to have as many children as they wanted. White feminists were campaigning for childcare to enable them to work, whereas Indigenous women wanted the end of interventionist welfare policies that removed their children from families (Huggins 1994: 71). White feminism's endorsement of individualism and its attempt to pass it on to Indigenous women operated as a practice of settler colonialism because it overshadowed issues of kinship, community and land rights which are primary concerns of Indigenous women (Moreton-Robinson 2020: 163). White feminists prioritised gender over race and universalised the experience of White woman with little acknowledgement of the historical involvement of White women and Australian feminists in the settler project.

In colonial Australia, the coloniality of gender works to differentiate between White and Indigenous women on both racial and class lines. This intersection of gender and race means that when women gain emancipation, including through military inclusion, the coloniality of gender differentiates between colonising women as the default female position that can progress, and colonised racialised women who remain at the bottom of the structures of power. The progress of colonised racialised women is envisioned only in assimilationist terms whereby the Aboriginal woman can advance her status by aspiring to become like the emancipated White middle-class woman.

Women and the Aesthetics of War Commemoration

Now that we have established the historical context of Australian women in war and the settler and racial relations that shaped it, I want to focus on the representation of women and their involvement in the aesthetics of war. This will further reveal the involvement of women and femininity at the intersection of race and class in settler military governance. It also allows us to flesh out in more detail the ways in which the colonial and masculinist logics of war subjected women and femininity to control and governance, as well as how they opened up opportunities for transformation and change. In this second part of the chapter, I map four key representations of women in war: the citizen-mother, the worker, the anti-war activist and the Aboriginal soldier. First, however, I want to discuss the context in which women accessed and contributed to the Australian aesthetics of war commemoration.

Women were largely excluded from the official war efforts as they were from the establishment of the aesthetics of war commemoration. Only one woman was officially commissioned within the War Art Scheme as a war artist in the First World War, Florence Rodway. She was commissioned in 1920, after the war and after all the other war artists were commissioned. Her commission was to produce a portrait of General William Bridges, a high-ranking military man memorialised as 'the first great soldier Australia possessed' (Speck 2004: 76). This suggests that there was no interest in the female perspective of war. In 1921, the War Art Scheme acquired the first painting by a woman, *Departure of the Last Australian Hospital Ship from Southampton, England, 1919*, by Dora Meeson, wife of George Coates who was a commissioned war artist. Meeson's painting depicts a ship used as a hospital departing from England back to Australia after the war. There is no evidence to suggest that this painting was acquired because it offered a female perspective on war. Nonetheless, it introduced an element of femininity in a largely masculinist war art collection. In fact, this painting represents a scene about caring for the war wounded and includes a female nurse who can be recognised from her unique uniform and can be spotted on the ship in the far background of the painting.

The conspicuous underrepresentation of women in the early days of the Australian War Art Scheme was neither for a lack of female artists nor international models. Australia had a good contingent of women trained in art, some of whom also joined the war in nursing positions. Notable Australian female artists include Iso Rae, Hilda Rix, Dora Meeson, Vida Lahey, and Dora Ohlfsen. Some Australian nurses were also artists, including Bessie Davidson, Jessie Traill, Nora Gurdon and Louise Riggall (Hutchison 2018: 74). The newly established British and

Canadian Wart Art Schemes officially commissioned female artists to represent the contribution of women to war, including from the home front (Nicoll 2001: 70; Speck 2004: 20–1). But conversely to the British and Canadian War Memorials, the Australian War Memorial showed no desire to make space for a female perspective on the war.

The lack of representation of women in the Australian War Art Scheme can be explained by the masculinist trajectory of the Memorial to elevate the male soldier to maker of the nation. Charles Bean envisioned the Memorial as a project to collect and produce commemorative material for 'the great sacrifices, and the sacred memory of the *great men* to whose bravery these pictures should be a monument' (Bean quoted in Speck 2004: 24; emphasis added). Discounting the nurses, Bean believed that painting war was a job for men, because they had direct experience of it. And even when women had witnessed the war, for example, as nurses, their perspective was deemed to lack objectivity which, as noted in Chapter 2, was a feature of art dear to Bean. The female perspective was considered biased and personal, and therefore not up to for the task of crafting the image of the nation as sacred, indivisible and whole (Nicoll 2001: 73).

A case in point is that of Iso Rae, an artist and nurse who produced about 200 pastel drawings while stationed in France at the army base of Étaples between 1915 and 1919. She was not commissioned by the Australian War Memorial. Her work captured the war behind the front lines, including the preparations for battle, soldiers' entertainment activities and soldiers' recovery. Étaples also housed German prisoners and was the place where soldiers rioted due to poor living conditions. Rae captured and documented these events in artistic form, but her work did not feature in the War Art collection of the First World War because it did not represent great battles or events that testify to the mythical birth of the nation (Speck 2004: 42). Rae fulfilled the essential requirement for becoming an official war artist, which was to possess a 'close and intimate acquaintance with the life and activities of our men', as established by the Australian High Commission when introducing the War Art Scheme. However, despite meeting this criterion, she was not even considered for the position of official war artist. Her work was too far from the heroic iconography that was envisioned to commemorate Australia's involvement in the First World War (Speck 2004: 44).

The Memorial's lack of interest in the female perspective on war and the commitment to craft a highly curated representation of the war experience is further demonstrated by the rejection, in 1922, of Hilda Rix's triptych *Pro Humanitate, 1917*. During the war, Rix lost her sister, mother and husband, Major George Matson Nicholas, and used her art to express her grief and make sense of her loss. She intentionally produced commemorative art and wished it to feature in the Memorial once established. She was particularly interested in representations of grief which she believed fitted the theme of the Memorial. *Pro Humanitate* represented the path to her grief in a sequence of three images. The painting was lost in a fire, but we still have some of the sketches that help us to reconstruct the representation. The first panel represented two lovers; the second, the death of the husband-soldier; and the third, a grieving widow. The Memorial Art Committee found it 'of too intimate a character for inclusion in a public collection' (quoted in Speck 2009: 279), but commented that they would have taken the middle panel if it was sufficiently accurate. Rix refused to break the triptych up and rejected the claim that the painting was a representation of her marriage, instead claiming that it was a representation of the national spirit.

Representations of women in early official war art are inconspicuous and the rare depictions are at the hand of male artists. The focus was largely on action and on men, despite female nurses being present with the troops. The subordination of the female nurse to male figures is evident not only in the abundant representations of male soldiers, but also in the preference for the representation of the male nurse. Notably, the male nurse Simpson and his donkey immediately secured a position in Anzac mythology as they were memorialised with a human-size statue that is still in the garden of the Memorial. The memorialisation of Simpson and his donkey is in contrast to the representation of female nurses who were rarely given names and faces and were represented as angelic figures rather than as earthly women (Inglis 1987; Nicoll 2001: 82). George Lambert's painting *Balcony of Troopers' Ward, 14th Australian General Hospital, Abbassia*, is emblematic of the representation of female nurses. The woman in this painting is a generic nurse. Her face is sideways and has minimal features. She looks down and holds her hands together to her chest as if praying. Her figure is light, almost floating above the ground. She is angelic, dressed in white and positioned in the light of a sunbeam. This representation is important to note because the proximity of nurses to male bodies and emotions was a source of social anxiety (Holmes 1995). The representation of nurses as angels was a sign of gratitude as much as a mechanism to manage social anxieties about gender and sexual relations sparked by female nurses' proximity to men who were not their husbands. In fact, the nurse as angel is not fully human and therefore her sex does not pose a threat to the morality of the soldier and sexual relations.

The more active role of women during the Second World War led to the appointment of three official women war artists, Stella Bowen, Sybil Craig and Nora Heysen. They all operated during the war and offered a representation of women in war and a female perspective on war. Their art had more than commemorative functions; it also configured and presented to the public a new Australian woman, one that was no longer a mother of the nation only, but a worker for the nation. In this respect, these three artists sanctioned the role of women as workers that developed in the Second World War and the official entry of women as workers in the Australian civic pantheon.

The Citizen-Mother

The under-representation of female artists and perspectives in the War Art Scheme instituted at the end of the First World War did not preclude femininity from being invested by militarisation. The project for the Australian War Memorial was developing in line with a masculinist trajectory that elevated male soldiers to the status of makers of the nation. In feminist theory, masculinity and femininity are complementary and need one another to create a gender system. The position of male soldiers as makers of the nation needed a female counterpart, which, as noted above, was the citizen-mother. War art from the First World War attests to the militarisation of women as citizen-mothers. Although women did not wear a uniform in the war, their lives were nevertheless militarised when they were called upon to fulfil their patriotic duty as mothers of the nation, to encourage men to go to war, and to care for the wounded and sick. Women were militarised to the extent that femininity was governed by military logics, including that male soldiers must protect women and women must care for male soldiers.

The architects of the Memorial endorsed the role of women as citizen-mothers by excluding them from the public role of official war artists. This exclusion reinforced the idea that women's appropriate place was the private and domestic sphere. The role of women as citizen-mothers was officially endorsed in 1920 when the Australian War Art programme purchased Hilda Rix's painting, *A Mother of France, 1914*. The painting represents, in Rix's words, 'an old French woman, resigned to her existence but not broken by it, [who] had twice seen the invader desecrate her native soil. In 1914, war laid claim to her sons just as in 1870, it called her husband' (quoted in Speck 2009: 280). The old French lady was Rix's neighbour in France. The War Art Committee commented that the painting would be 'of the most value to us and . . . that would fill the gap in our collections' (Speck 2009: 281). This gap was the representation of the citizen-mother. Albeit of a different nation, the French woman embodied the qualities of the citizen-mother: domesticated, dignified in her pain caused by the loss of her men due to war, and White. The old French woman is represented sitting in her home. The domesticity of the environment is further conveyed by a line of decorative plates, a glass and a jar set in the background. The woman holds her hands on her thighs. The artistic rendering of her hands is impressive. One hand grips the other almost in a comforting gesture, or perhaps to maintain a grip on reality. The woman wears a black dress indicating that she is in mourning. Her modesty is conveyed by her headdress which covers her hair and neck with a big white ribbon.

The endorsement of figure of the citizen-mother served to domesticate Australian femininity after the war. Prior to the war, the role of women in Australian society was confined to the mother, and feminists linked women's rights to this maternal identity. Their public presence was limited to being private influencers of public men. The war gave upper- and middle-class White women a taste of public life. Although they did not join the workforce as in other countries, they were present in the public sphere through their volunteer work. The anti-war activists were a particular source of social anxiety because they spoused socialism and the masculine rhetoric to reject the war (Damousi 1995). After the war there was widespread concern that women would have shaken their social positions and demanded to be more involved in public life. For example, in an editorial of the *Age* in 1919, the editors wrote that 'the greatest and perhaps most threatening social change that has been worked by the conditions of nearly five years of war has been the enormous influx of women into industry and commerce' (Lake and Damousi 1995: 7). Despite the lack of evidence of this influx in Australia, this editorial demonstrates the social anxiety around the possibility that women chose freedom and independence over their family duties. After the war, Australian society held strong onto traditional gender roles and pushed to reposition women in the domestic space and as mothers. This gender role was endorsed and amplified through the acquisition and display of Rix's *A Mother of France* by the emerging War Memorial which was defining the contours of the new nation.

The endorsement of women as citizen-mothers also had a settler colonial function. Women departing from their social role as citizen-mothers represented a security threat to the settler society because they compromised the gender order of colonial governance – and the coloniality of gender. The settler society was invested in maintaining White women in the position of mothers and wives because the war had claimed the lives of 60,000 Australian men, and women had the duty to repopulate the nation with White babies. Women as wives also had the duty to police White civilisation and prevent White men having babies with Aboriginal and Asiatic women, which, according to the racist ideology of that time, would have led to the degradation of the White race. The return of affluent women to their role of mothers was also important to maintain the racialised class system that governed settler Australia.

The Worker

The development of an Australian war industry by the outbreak of the Second World War and Japan's proximity to Australia created the conditions for Australian women to enter the workforce in large numbers. Just as in the First World War, however, the entry of women in men's jobs was a source of social anxiety because it challenged the gendered division of labour and the sexual contract upon which the Australian society was founded. This time though, social anxiety needed to be managed by accounting for the new role of women as workers because they were needed in industries to meet the war needs. The first measure taken to manage social anxieties was to allow women to work in men's jobs, but only for the duration of the war and at a lower wage than men (Lake 1995: 62). This, however, did not address the concern that women doing men's jobs would lead to a loss of their femininity and damage their prospects for marriage. Ford (1995) notes that women in men's jobs were often caricatured in magazines as manly, muscular and commanding subordinate men. The masculine woman also created fears around women turning lesbians or becoming sexually promiscuous. This was countered with a public campaign to reassure Australians that women in uniform and in the workforce would not lose their femininity. In this campaign, women were represented as highly feminine, heterosexual and attractive, with make-up, fashionable clothes and hairstyles, and doing hard work but without sweating (of course!). As a condition of women entering the workforce, workplaces had to ensure that women maintained a ladylike appearance, behaviours and sex appeal through cosmetics, feminine uniforms and upholding social norms around marriage.

The ladylike appearance of women at work in the war industry was captured by the female war artists commissioned in the Second World War, and especially by Sybil Craig and Nora Heysen. In their commissions to represent the female experience of war, these war artists engaged with the public debate – and the social anxieties – around women in uniform and at work. In doing so, they created the representation of woman at work as the icon of femininity in war. While the Memorial's commission did not come with an obligation to produce paintings for propaganda or recruitment, the artists were confronted with a sense of patriotism and national duty that came with their appointment, including the duty to show to the nation how women maintained their femininity in war.

A notable example is Nora Heysen's *Transport Driver (Aircraftwoman Florence Miles), 1945* (see Figure 4.1), which captures the idealised aesthetics of women in Australia during the Second World War. The painting is an iconic representation of Australian women at war that is often reproduced in books and blogs because it represents the contribution of women to the nation in need through their work in the war industry. As discussed above, this was a pivotal moment for Australian White women from the middle and working classes that allowed them to taste an unprecedented freedom and independence and want more of it. Therefore, in the present day, Heysen's painting is often used to represent women's emancipation. However, this painting captures the temporary nature of women's work during the war and reflects the prevailing belief of that time that women would return to domesticity at war's end. This is evident in Heysen's painting and, in particular, in the eyes of her subject, Florence Miles. She stares ahead as she drives, her eyes angled slightly downward. If she is looking at the road, she does not seem to be paying much attention to it. Maybe she knows the road very well. Regardless, her eyes suggest that her mind is somewhere else. She looks pensive and distracted from her task. Is she thinking about the war? Her children? Or maybe her faraway husband? Or simply about the monotony and repetitiveness of her job? As viewers, we could imagine ourselves sitting on the passenger seat of Miles' vehicle, listening to her innermost thoughts and secrets. Whatever she is thinking, she is not there, and she is not invested in a future being there.

Figure 4.1 *Transport Driver (Aircraftwoman Florence Miles)*, by Nora Heysen, 1945.
Copyright expired, image in the public domain.

This painting also represents how the aesthetics of war commemoration worked to govern gender. Notably, Florence Miles does not
compromise on her femininity regardless of the circumstances in
which she finds herself. She is working in the war industry and wears
a rugged blue overall, thick rubber or leather gloves and a peaked cap.
She drives a heavy vehicle that requires strength and skill to manoeuvre. But this does not come at the expense of her femininity. Her
hair is up, in a fashionable and orderly hairstyle typical of the 1940s.
She wears make-up: red lipstick, black mascara and pink blusher.
Her body looks soft and curvy, not deprived by the war. She looks
comfortable, with one arm resting on the window. She looks com-
petent, although not particularly interested in what she is doing. Her
femininity is non-negotiable. This commemorative representation of
women at war and their uncompromised femininity served to sooth
the social anxieties around women who entered spaces considered to
be inappropriate for their gender. Indeed, this representation is very
different from the satirical ones circulating in some magazines that
represented women involved in war as commanding, muscular and
masculine. This latter representation was not how the nation wanted

to commemorate the contribution of women because of the threat that it posed to the social order.

Sybil Craig's art offers a more progressive view of women at work. Craig's commission was to paint the employment of women in munitions and other industries and thus her art directly engaged with the figure of the woman at work in factories. When Craig assumed the position, the significance of munition work as a patriotic and esteemed female contribution to the war had already been firmly established. Extensive propaganda efforts had previously been dedicated to disseminating the message that women could engage in munitions work without compromising their femininity (Speck 2004: 164). Craig herself defied conventional femininity, leaning more towards a masculine demeanour. She adopted the masculine moniker 'Bill' (a diminutive of her first name), wore men's trousers and a brown beret, and drove a distinctive green Morris car (Speck 2019: 302). When the Memorial nominated her for the position, she experienced profound self-doubt about her ability to represent women effectively. She reluctantly agreed to the appointment, compelled by her mother's insistence and her sense of patriotism. She also felt apprehensive about 'portraying subjects who appeared so proficient and brave working with dangerous materials', but started easing into her position when she realised that the women were, after all, very similar to her (Speck 2004: 165). They were women but were not caged by the stereotypes of femininity of their time. They were brave and bold, and put themselves on the line.

Well-versed in modernist art, Craig deployed a modernist style in her representations of women at work. She was appointed as war artist under the pressure that the Memorial should include more modernist art in its mostly classical and conservative collection (Speck 2019: 303). Craig depicted working women in the distance which allowed her to represent the work environment as well as the women. The artist's utilisation of a distant perspective precludes the viewer's ability to juxtapose the scene with the domestic environment. The women in her paintings are clearly feminine, but they are too far away to give any emphasis to the details of femininity such as make-up and hairstyle. Unlike Heysen's *Transport Diver*, the women represented by Craig look intent and immersed in their work. They are doing dangerous work; they work with explosive materials and heavy machinery. While their femininity is unmistakable, it is not their defining feature. Speck (2019: 305) concludes that Craig 'is therefore not complicit in the patriarchal policies of seeing women as a mobile workforce who can be moved into paid work, then returned to private sphere as it suited government policy'.

The commemorative representation of working women in the Australian War Art Scheme sanctioned the emergence of a new archetype of the Australian woman that departed from the citizen-mother. Women were no longer simply mothers of the nation relegated to the private sphere, but fully militarised citizens publicly involved in the war effort. Their militarisation was carefully crafted through the management of their femininity such that it did not upset the masculinist representation of the nation constructed thus far. The introduction of working women into the Australian civic pantheon also had a settler colonial function of reaffirming the nation as White. In fact, while the majority of the Australian population during the Second World War traced their ancestry back to Britain, during the war, the Australian government conducted trials with exclusively Indigenous soldier battalions which could have been a challenge to the Whiteness of the Anzac soldier (see Chapter 5 below). Furthermore, after the war, the country experienced an influx of immigrants from southern Europe. Notably, these individuals were not regarded as fully fitting the definition of White, and therefore represented a challenge to the racial composition of the nation. The representation of White working women in commemorative art showcased Australia's forward-looking position, yet concurrently perpetuated an image of the nation as predominantly White.

The Anti-War Activist

In the 1960s and 1970s, women inserted themselves in the aesthetics of war commemoration to disrupt militarisation. As already noted in Chapter 3, the Vietnam War was unpopular in Australia, and it made Anzac Day and war commemoration lose momentum. During the Vietnam War, the Memorial engaged only a small number of artists, all of whom were men. This void enabled women to carve out their own place beyond the confines of official war commemoration and create the archetype the female anti-war activist.

The anti-war activist was a new form of femininity, largely facilitated by the transformation of Australian women brought about by the Second World War. Their increased presence in public life allowed them to create avenues for themselves to influence and mould society. Immediately after the war, the Women's Auxiliary Services were disbanded, and women were invited to return to their pre-war roles.

Some women were happy to return to domestic life, while others pushed to stay in employment and re-establish the Women's Auxiliary Services. When the Cold War started, the War Office approved the re-establishment on the condition that the Women's Auxiliary Services remained gender segregated, and women in the defence forces did not neglect their femininity. The reinstatement of the Women's Auxiliary Services created economic opportunities and social mobility for working-class women. While women were free to choose the military as an employer of choice and opportunity, the National Service Act 1964 introduced the draft for young men, which agitated White middle-class women with children of conscription age. These women gave rise to an aesthetic of women and war centred on anti-conscription and anti-war activism.

In the late 1960s, the aesthetics of women and war was dominated by the maternal activism of Save Our Sons (SOS), a nationwide movement predominantly composed of women and mothers who demonstrated against conscription in Australia (Collins 2021). SOS demonstrations against conscription consisted of silent vigils, the circulation of petitions and the distribution of leaflets. Some of the members were demonstrating for the first time in their life and came from suburbs that traditionally voted for the Liberal Party (the Australian right). The movement mobilised a maternal rhetoric, but it also involved women without children and a few men who rejected the war. While SOS operated in major Australian cities, the movement lacked cohesive national unity due to challenges arising from costly intercity coordination, the technological limitations of the era, and governmental oversight and surveillance.

SOS created an aesthetic of middle-class respectability that banked on the figure of the mother to send its message against conscription. SOS members made themselves visible in public spaces carrying anti-conscription banners, carrying handbags and wearing sensible shoes, hats, gloves, silk dresses and pearls (see Figure 4.2). This strategic essentialism served two functions. First, the aesthetics of middle-class respectability and motherhood aided SOS to differentiate their movement from the international anti-war movements primarily led by young, communist university students. In an interview with the media, one member of SOS, Mary McNish, said that their middle-class aesthetic was intentional and strategic to appeal to other middle-class people who were 'terrified of war protesters because they equated them with the unwashed and the long-haired and the uni students and the Communists who would blow

Figure 4.2 Save Our Sons protest in Sydney against conscription, 1 October 1965.
© FAIRFAX MEDIA/*Sydney Morning Herald* and The Age Photos.

up things and rape your daughters and the whole thing' (quoted in Curthoys 1995: 325). Secondly, SOS embraced the image and discourse of motherhood to speak to an Australian audience because of the country's history of the citizen-mother. As already discussed, in Australia motherhood was considered the appropriate role for women. Furthermore, SOS learned from the social backlash suffered by the anti-conscription feminists in the First World War who used a socialist rhetoric. The backlash was against the anti-conscription message as much as it was against women adopting a masculine rhetoric and social position (Damousi 1995). SOS's middle-class aesthetics and emphasis on maternalism played to its advantage. This was evident in a notable incident in 1971 when five women associated with the movement were arrested for trespassing after distributing anti-conscription leaflets at a barracks. The subsequent media coverage of the case spurred vigils and rallies outside the prison where the women were held, thus drawing attention to SOS among individuals who had previously been unaware of its existence. The media emphasised the maternal role of the imprisoned women and remarked that 'between them they had 25 children, all of whom would have to spend Easter that year without their mothers' (DVA 2019).

Nonetheless, due to the prevailing class divisions, SOS's presentation of middle-class respectability and maternal values also posed challenges to the movement. In the post-war era, the working class had become increasingly outspoken and politically engaged, often opposing the middle class when its privileges seemed to encroach upon the opportunities of the working class. This dynamic was evident in the anti-conscription and anti-Vietnam War movements, which the working class perceived as a threat against the employment and social mobility prospects generated by the war and military service (Curthoys 1995). Moreover, the general public frequently cast doubt on the maternalism of SOS women, despite the movement's own rhetoric. Members of SOS recall instances of passers-by making comments such as 'Why don't you go home and get your husband's dinner, love?' or 'Why aren't you home looking after your husband and kids?' or 'Why aren't you home doing the washing?' (quoted in Curthoys 1995: 325). These remarks undermined the femininity and maternalism of the women who became politically active and took to the streets to participate in demonstrations against war. Some other comments made overt reference to class and the aesthetics of middle-class respectability of SOS activists. For example, a member recalls a comment along the lines of: 'Shut up, you bourgeois bitch. What would you know?' (quoted in Curthoys 1995: 352). This statement and rhetorical question insinuated that the women of SOS were incapable of understanding the challenges faced by working-class individuals.

By the late 1970s, the aesthetics of women against war moved away from maternalism and blended with the more radical international anti-war movement. In 1977, another women's group appeared in Australia: Women Against Rape in War (WAR). This movement was animated by a radical feminist political agenda and in particular by Susan Brownmiller's book, *Against Our Will*, which argues that rape is 'a conscious process of intimidation by which all men keep all women in a state of fear' (Elder 2005: 76; Radford 2019). WAR was vehemently against war rather than just against conscription and wanted to make the female experience of rape in war known. It was a peace-movement-meets-women's-liberation-movement that demanded the end of war and militarism on the ground that they enabled the rape of women. The women of WAR developed their anti-war rhetoric drawing attention to the Vietnamese women who suffered from sexual violence during the war and thus were grounded in transnational feminist solidarity. Within this rhetoric, they framed all male soldiers, including those from Australia, as potential perpetrators of rape.

WAR came to national attention when members started using Anzac Day as a platform for their anti-war demonstrations. They chose Anzac Day not only because it represented Australia's martial nationalism, but also because it conspicuously commemorated the male experience of war only and excluded women's perspectives. However, WAR was not interested in commemorating the female experience in defence despite the fact that Australian women were just being integrated into the regular forces. Instead, they wanted to commemorate the female victims of rape in war. In 1978, about twenty women joined Anzac Day and marched on Anzac Parade at the War Memorial in Canberra carrying a banner reading 'Women Against Rape'. The crowd frowned in disapproval. The following year, women from WAR marched again, but this time without a banner. They were aware that they were entering dangerous territory by challenging the Anzac mythology on Anzac Day. In 1980, sixteen women marched again, and attempted to lay a wreath in memory of women raped in war. Fourteen of those women were arrested. In the court case, the police claimed to have arrested the women for fear that the public would have turned violent on them. The court found no evidence of this (Radford 2019). The court case attracted more women to join the following year. However, they were met by a police force empowered by the newly minted Traffic Ordinances issued specifically to counter anti-war activists on Anzac Day. The Traffic Ordinances allowed police to arrest individuals who were 'offensive or insulting, or likely to give offence or cause insult' to the people participating in the services (Davies 1996: 368). That year, police arrested more than sixty women.

What particularly appealed to the women who joined in 1981 was WAR's endeavour to render women and girls affected by war as visible within the predominantly masculine framework of war commemoration on Anzac Day (Howe 1995; Davies 1996; Elder 2005). Participants believed that their actions were not a form of protest to disrupt Anzac Day, but an extension of commemoration to encompass the issue of violence against women during wartime. This was conveyed by WAR's strategy of intervention that mirrored the Anzac Day syntax of war commemoration, including the marching contingent carrying a banner and laying wreaths in memory of those who suffered in war. The following year, in 1982, WAR's aesthetics of commemoration was further consolidated in line with that of Anzac Day. A group of 750 women dressed in black gathered before the official Anzac Day March and staged their own ritual of commemoration that mirrored that of the Dawn Service. Women read from the letters written by women raped in war, just like soldiers read from soldiers' diaries; just like the mourning veterans, WAR members sang *Lest We Forget* and laid wreaths and flowers on the Stone of Remembrance. Then, they gathered on one side and watched the official Anzac Day March standing behind a big banner 'In Memory of All Women of All Countries Raped in Wars'.

Public opinion was vehemently against the women of WAR as it was believed that their demonstrations were offensive to the Australian veterans who sacrificed their lives for the freedom of the nation, including women's freedom. The women of WAR were accused of being lesbian Marxists, un-Australian and against the Anzacs who they included in their discourse of male soldiers as potential perpetrators of rape. They were urged to go back to their family or to find a husband and make a family and were told that they should have opened their doors to the victims of rape rather than demonstrate against the Anzac soldiers (Elder 2005). The adoption of the aesthetics and rhetoric of war commemoration in line with the official Anzac Day services was a strategic move to minimise the backlash against their message to remember women victims of rape in war and the repercussions against its members.

Ultimately, the movement lost relevance and the ability to articulate its message and was eventually dissolved. In 1983, WAR demonstrated again using Anzac Day's syntax of commemoration. This time, however, its message focused on the women raped in South America, a context where the Australian military were absent. As WAR gained proximity to Anzac Day by mirroring its syntax of war commemoration, the argument that all soldiers, including Australian soldiers, were potential rapists clashed with the desire to represent the female experience of rape in war in national war commemoration. Anzac Day revolved around the Anzac soldier as national hero, and increasingly he was recognised as a victim of war himself following the welcome home marches for the Vietnam veterans (Twomey 2013; see also Chapter 3). Anzac Day could have not accommodated the representation of the female experience of rape in war if it accused the Anzacs of being rapists, especially not in a national climate in which the soldier was being actively reframed as victim to be protected. WAR's focus on the victims of rape in South America in 1983 allowed them to commemorate the female experience of rape in war while maintaining a suitable distance from the Anzac soldier who did not serve in that part of the world. In 1984, WAR did not march at all.

By utilising Anzac Day as a platform to convey its message, WAR inadvertently revealed internal contradictions within the movement that led to its dissolution. The movement found itself simultaneously appealing to a universal experience of female victimisation in war at hands of men while engaging with the martial nationalism that celebrated the male soldier in Australian war commemoration. In order to use martial nationalism, WAR had to drop the Anzac soldier from its critique of male soldiers as potential perpetrators of rape. Radford (2019) notes that this gave a pass to the emerging stories of Japanese women raped by Australian soldiers in the Second World War and cleared the Australian man from the colonial history of rape of Aboriginal women in the Frontier Wars. As Elder (2005: 78–9) notes, this move revealed the subject position of the women of WAR as White and themselves implicated in the settler colonial project of Australia and the global racial colour lines.

The Aboriginal Female Soldier

Today, the commemorative aesthetics of women and war in Australia pivot around the figure of the female soldier. Since 2016, Australian women have been recruited into the frontlines of combat and have been present in Australia's military interventions. On the website of the Australian War Memorial, women are represented donning the uniform, carrying weapons and with heavy military equipment. Women have become so seamlessly integrated in the aesthetics and rhetoric of war commemoration both at the Australian War Memorial and on Anzac Day to the extent that their gender often goes unmentioned. They are depicted simply as Australian soldiers. As the figure of the female soldier takes shape within the Australian aesthetics of war commemoration, there is a clear attempt to diversify her race to identify and render visible the Aboriginal female soldier. The female ethnic soldier is virtually absent, and so is the data that disaggregate gender and race in the Australian Defence Forces.

In war commemoration, the Aboriginal female soldier is often represented with the picture of Kath Walker wearing the Army uniform and a big bright smile (see Figure 4.3). She stands to represent the historical participation of Aboriginal women in the Women's Auxiliary Services and the more recent integration of Aboriginal women in the Australian Defence Forces. Born in Stradbroke Island in 1920 as Kathleen Ruska, Kath Walker was an Aboriginal woman who enlisted in AWAS in 1942. She worked as a switchboard/radio operator and achieved the rank of corporal. She served for two years only and was discharged due to ongoing medical conditions. In AWAS, she completed a course as a stenographer and other vocational education which allowed her to get clerical middle-class jobs as a civilian after military discharge. In the 1960s, Walker became a vocal activist for Aboriginal rights and a prominent Aboriginal poet. In 1988, she adopted the name Oodgeroo Noonuccal to re-establish a connection with her cultural heritage and to reflect her Aboriginal origins.

Figure 4.3 Kath Walker in Army uniform, today known as Oodgeroo Noonuccal.
© expired, image in the public domain.

The portrait of young Oodgeroo Noonuccal in Army uniform in the aesthetics of war commemoration stands for the idea that the Australian Defence Forces are progressive and inclusive, and implies that the nation has reconciled with its Aboriginal population. This representation is often accompanied by Noonuccal's quotes about the army as a place where she did not experience racism and where she could gain an education as an Aboriginal woman (see, for example, Riseman 2015: 762; Cadzow 2019: 245; Cadzow and Jebb 2019: 165). I encountered Noonuccal's portrait at the Memorial's temporary exhibition *For Country, For Nation* in 2017, and it was accompanied by the quote:

> And all of a sudden the colour line disappeared, it just completely disappeared. And it happened in so many different ways too. Like . . . there was a tremendous colour bar here [in Australian society] . . . it was the women who broke down the silly barrier of racial discrimination because it was the white women who went to the black women here on the island and said, 'Look, you make socks better than us, you are better at all these things' and they came together in the Australian Comfort Fund.

Another quote by Noonuccal in the exhibition speaks about the army as her sole opportunity to gain an education:

> So [one of the reasons] I joined the army was that it was the only way I would be allowed to learn. And I thought, after the war, if I am still alive, I'll be able to take extra studies through the 'dimwits' course and it was the only way that the Aboriginals could learn extra education.

The portrait of Noonuccal in army uniform purports to represent the opportunities and respectability that she gained through her military service. Together with her portrait as a servicewoman, it is frequently noted that she emerged as a prominent Australian and Aboriginal poet. This conveys a sense, also openly expressed by White people close to her, that 'We [White society] have made Kath Walker what she is' (quote from a White member of the Queensland Council for the Advancement of Aborigines and Torres Strait Islanders found in Riseman 2018a: 272; see also Cochrane 1994: 80–4). Noonuccal was a well-known Australian poet, often credited as the first Aboriginal woman to have published a book of poetry. She was also a leading member of the movement that led to the 1967 referendum to include Indigenous people in the national census. She was elected secretary of the Queensland Council for the Advancement of Aborigines and Torres Strait Islanders. Reading about Noonuccal, I have often come across her being described as a 'campaigner' for Aboriginal rights, rather than as an activist, in a way that minimises her radical politics and political interventions. Her achievements are often linked to her (brief) military service (Riseman 2015; Cadzow 2019). For example, a quote by Noonuccal which emphasises the role of the military as stepping-stone to her post-military achievements is:

> I joined the Australian Women's Army which really opened my eyes to the injustices suffered by Aboriginals. I'd always known, of course, but the war made people more equal in a way, and I got a taste of not just being a maid in a white's man's house. (Noonuccal quoted in Cadzow 2019: 145)

This critique is not to say that the military did not have a role in the advancement of Noonuccal's life and career in settler colonial society. Rather, it is to emphasise that she made a life and career despite living under adverse and racist conditions.

What Noonuccal's portrait in uniform and attendant quotes and remarks often omit is how much bigger her life as an activist was compared with her military service. During her time in Brisbane with the army, she met several African American soldiers with whom she cross-pollinated her political activism for Indigenous rights. After her time in the army, she joined the Communist Party, the only Australian political party that did not restrict Indigenous participation (Riseman 2018a: 265). Subsequently, she joined the Queensland Council for the Advancement of Aborigines and Torres Strait Islanders, of which she became the secretary in late in 1960s.

Her son, Danis, was a founding member of the Brisbane chapter of the Black Panther Party in Australia, and Noonuccal was involved in some of the protests associated with the Black Power movement, including the demonstration against the re-enactment of Captain Cook's arrival at Botany Bay for the bicentennial of Australia.

Moreover, Noonuccal's portrait and quotes about equality in the military obscure the racist conditions that led Aboriginal women to enlist. While Noonuccal was disconnected from her country and culture and her mother was from the Stolen Generations, in some respects, she was a privileged Aboriginal child who was not taken from her family. Her parents encouraged her to succeed in White society and wanted her to gain an education. Many Indigenous women who joined the military when Noonuccal did were from the Stolen Generations and were raised in orphanages by White matrons or by White families and under assimilationist conditions. The prescribed path for these women was to become servants in middle-class families. The military represented an opportunity to escape the racist limitations of civilian life (Riseman 2015). As I will discuss in detail in Chapter 5, the military was an institution of assimilation. At that time, Indigenous policy was governed by the logic that fair-skinned Indigenous individuals and so-called "half-caste" had to be assimilated in White society and made in the likeness of White people. Therefore, the Indigenous women who embarked on military paths to escape racism in civilian society were not set for freedom but for assimilation.

Taken outside the bigger picture of structural racism and Noonuccal's life of national and international activism, her portrait in uniform can be mobilised within settler colonial institutions and discourses to signify the advancement of Aboriginal people and the end of racism and colonialism in Australia. In Australia's martial nationalism that elevates the military as pillar of the nation, the commemoration of Noonuccal's military service presents the military as the institution that enabled Indigenous people to achieve civil rights, but discounts the logic of assimilation that enveloped the military service of Indigenous people, something that I consider in more detail in the next chapter.

Notes

1. Founded in Britain, this movement involved women pressurising men in their family and friends to join the war. Women gave white feathers to young, fit men who did not enlist to shame them, while giving badges to men discharged due to injury and age.

2. Imperial feminism was a transnational feminist movement that united women across the empire in their struggles to advance the rights of women. The advancement of women was often predicated on racial hierarchies and the privileging of White women as superior to women of colour and Indigenous women (see Midgley 1998; Woollacott 2006; Oppenheimer 2016).
3. The Stolen Generations refers to a dark chapter in Australian history during which Indigenous Australian children were forcibly removed from their families, communities and cultural heritage by government authorities and institutions. These removals occurred over a span of several decades, primarily from the late nineteenth century to the mid-twentieth century, up until the 1970s.

CHAPTER 5

Indigenous Militarised Recognition

Introduction

In this chapter, I consider the history of Indigenous military service and its representation in the aesthetics of war commemoration. Indigenous people were barred from enlisting in the Australian Defence Forces officially until 1951. There were some exceptions during the two world wars when Indigenous individuals served regardless of the ban and were allowed to enlist to meet Australia's war needs and address shortages. I begin the chapter outlining the assimilationist logics that accompanied this history and explain how they extended into the second half of the twentieth century, after the official lift of the ban on Indigenous enlistment. Emphasising the assimilationist logics that governed Indigenous military service is crucial. This is because the contemporary aesthetics of war commemoration increasingly showcase the involvement of Indigenous soldiers to portray Australia's commitment to reconciliation and multiculturalism. Nevertheless, the official aesthetics of war commemoration neglect how the assimilationist logics intertwined with the history of Indigenous military service. This omission overlooks how the settler nation leveraged Indigenous military participation to advance the settler colonial project.

The argument that I put forth in this chapter is that the present of inclusion must be historicised and understood in its settler colonial context. Indigenous military inclusion is not a breakthrough in history, but rather the continuation of the settler colonial project through other means. I articulate it as a form of militarised recognition intended to govern Indigenous identities and steer settler nation-building. Under settler conditions, recognition serves to adapt settler colonialism and further settler authority and legitimacy.

I build upon the scholarship of Indigenous Canadian author Glen Coulthard, who propounds that the recognition of Indigenous people under settler colonialism is a practice of colonial governance 'that co-opts Indigenous people into becoming instruments of their own dispossession' (Coulthard 2014: 156). In a nation such as Australia, where military service and its history hold significant reverence, the celebration of Indigenous soldiers and their contributions to national defence serve as a symbol of settler legitimacy. They attest to the incorporation of Indigenous individuals in vital settler institutions and, most notably, their readiness to make the ultimate sacrifice for the defence of the settler state. Thus, the state recognises Indigenous military service such that Indigenous people can recognise the state as a legitimate source of authority and governance. Although recognition is disguised as mutual, it is in fact fraught with unequal power relations. Through recognition, Indigenous people may achieve integration in settler society but at the expense of their sovereign autonomy. Militarised recognition is a strategy to consolidate settler colonial power, serving as evidence of Indigenous integration into settler society and equal participation in settler sovereignty and its defence. This, however, leaves unaccounted the legacies of colonisation, the enduring power imbalance, and the disciplinary implications of military inclusion as discussed in this chapter.

I end this chapter with some considerations about the aesthetics of Indigenous counter-memory. Indigenous people have been articulating their memories of war to include the history of racism, marginalisation and, above all, colonial warfare. Militarised recognition emerged from the efforts of the settler state to administer the politics of memory and erase or downplay these Indigenous memories and experiences considered to be threatening to settler legitimacy. The Indigenous aesthetics of war commemoration contest the hegemonic settler narrative of war memory and produce interventions that affect the politics of war commemoration. They bring to the fore pressing questions about colonisation and its legacies that settler authorities and society cannot ignore. Ultimately, the responsibility lies with Australia to confront Indigenous counter-memory and authentically depict its history of war and the military. This entails re-examining the nation's myth of militarised origin and dismantling the hierarchical differentiation between military warfare and colonial conflict. Such actions have the potential to bring about a transformative change in colonial power dynamics.

Militarised Assimilation

First World War

First Nations people have only recently been included and recognised in the Australian Defence Forces and official practices and institutions of war commemoration. Following the 1909 amendment to the 1903 Defence Act which established the Australian Defence Forces, Aboriginal and Torres Strait Islander people were excluded from enlisting in the military because they were 'not substantially of European origins and descent'. Just like Chinese, Pacific Islanders, and other ethnic minorities, Aboriginal and Torres Strait Islander people also faced discrimination in the context of military enlistment and were frequently rejected for not meeting the physical 'fitness' requirements of race (Scarlett 2015). Despite this restriction, which was only officially permanently lifted in 1951, more than a 1,000 Indigenous people served in the First World War and over 4,000 in the Second World War. However, these numbers remain uncertain because there is no official record documenting the racial identity of the soldiers.

Indigenous people were far from being a homogeneous group, differentiated not only by their traditional belonging to over 500 nations each with their own language, tradition and geography, but also by their skin colour and the colonial caste system that distinguished between the "half-caste" and the "full blood".[1] This was further complicated by the fact that every state had different laws defining Aboriginality, and that Torres Strait Islander peoples were subsumed under the nomenclature and legislations governing Aboriginal people. Thus, not only there were different Indigenous people but there was also a heterogeneous definition of Aboriginality.[2] This, coupled with the vagueness of the racial exclusion of the 1909 amendment to the Defence Act, meant that some Indigenous individuals managed to enlist despite not being 'substantially of European origin'. Some enlisted by disguising their identity or travelling to different jurisdictions where they were not known to be Aboriginal. Many enlisted when the government eased race restrictions on military service to meet war needs. The stories of service are varied, and every person had their own individual reason for enlisting (see Cadzow and Jebb 2019), including seeking opportunities and campaigning for equal rights (Furphy 2018; Maynard 2018).

There is a conundrum about Indigenous individuals seeking military enlistment at a time when they were excluded from serving by legislation, and above all, when the Frontier Wars of colonisation were still ongoing (the end of these wars tends to be dated in 1928, despite contestation and some maintaining that they are still ongoing). While there are no easy answers and generalisable positions, Indigenous military service must be contextualised within the dynamics of Australia's settler colonialism. First, it is important to acknowledge the effects of the Protection System as a pull factor for Indigenous military service (Scarlett 2015; McDonnell and Dodson 2018). The Protection System was a series of restrictive legislative Acts that confined Indigenous people to missions and stations, appropriated their wages, and limited their life options in the name of a racist and paternalistic ideology. For some Indigenous people, military service represented a way to escape the Protection System and be freer than they were in civilian society.

In addition, assimilationist logics played a central role in Indigenous military service in the First World War. Defined as the attempts to eliminate a racial minority by erasing their difference with the dominant group, assimilation is a key practice of settler colonialism. In Australia, Wolfe (1998: 30–2) finds evidence of legislative assimilation as early as 1886 when the colony of Victoria passed an Act that expelled so-called "half-caste" individuals – a racist term that was used to refer to Indigenous people with one White parent under the caste system – from the Indigenous reserves. This Act was justified on the ground that they did not belong with the so-called "full blood" individuals, those with both Aboriginal parents.[3] The caste system was an essential component of assimilation in the early twentieth century. It was a strategy of dispossession ultimately intended to assimilate the "half-caste" in settler society and reduce the number of Aboriginal people. To this end, the "half-castes" were legally determined to be non-Aboriginal despite being subjected to racial discrimination nonetheless (Birch 1995). The caste system held a crucial role in establishing the social hierarchy among Aboriginal people, also delineating those eligible to enlist in the military and those who were systematically excluded from such opportunities.

Military service was a way to promote the assimilation of the "half-castes". For most of the First World War, military assimilation was not a systematic approach and was instead administered and managed locally and at the discretion of medical officers. The 1909 Defence Act gave medical officers the infamous task of determining who was 'substantially of European origin' and to approve or reject the enlistment of Aboriginal people in accordance with their perception of race and the legal definition of Aboriginality in their state. The medical forms for enlistment included the check box 'unsuitable physique aboriginal' or 'unsuitable physical colour' which medical officers could check at their discretion (McDonnell and Dodson 2018: 34). In 1917, the Australian government became more explicit about the permission to enlist "half-castes" to combat a shortage of soldiers. However, the recruitment of the "half-castes" had to be accompanied by a signed declaration stating that they had 'associated with White people all my life' (Scarlett 2015: 168). Thus, being "half-caste" was not enough and military inclusion necessitated a deliberate stance on loyalty and integration into White society. This approach emerged from the realisation that being "half-caste" fell short of achieving successful assimilation. In fact, some of the "half-castes" recruited prior to 1917 proved to be not yet as assimilated as imagined and continued to have connections with their Indigenous communities and culture (Scarlett 2011).

The principle of assimilation can also explain the enlistment of the few "full bloods" who served in the First World War. While uncommon, their enlistment was not entirely absent. A case in point is that of Douglas Grant who enlisted in the army in 1916 despite being identified as a "full blood" under the caste system. Grant was born of Aboriginal parents who were both killed in a punitive expedition by the Native Police when he was only a child. He was adopted by a Scottish immigrant family, the Grants, and brought up and educated in settler society. When the war started, he volunteered and was admitted to military training. However, he was discharged just before leaving Australia for overseas active service because he was recognised as Aboriginal and therefore could not leave the country without government approval (Maynard 2018). He managed to re-enlist and eventually left for France with special permission obtained with the aid of his adoptive father (Riseman 2014: 158). Grant's permission was given because, despite being considered "full blood", he was assimilated into settler society. He was a "rescued" young Aboriginal child who was already trained in the manners of White society (Riseman 2014: 159). Grant became a media phenomenon and was hailed as a prodigious Aboriginal man for assimilating so well into White society. For example, an article from 1916 in *The West Australian* commented:

> Douglas has many accomplishments. He writes a splendid hand, draws well, recites Shakespeare with histrionic ability, plays the Scottish bagpipes, and can earn a very good living any time by following

his profession – that of a draughtsman. This brief history demonstrates what may be done with an aboriginal when taken early and trained. (quoted in Riseman 2014: 159)

Despite this praise, when Grant came back from war, he faced racism and discrimination, just like all the other Aboriginal men who were recruited. They were also denied access to soldier settlement schemes that entitled veterans to land and compensation for their service (Riseman and Trembath 2016: 8). Regardless of assimilation, granting land to Aboriginal veterans undermined the settler project of dispossessing Indigenous people of their land to consolidate a White society of settlers. Furthermore, after a very short period, the racist bar to Indigenous military service was fully reinstated after the war's end.

Second World War

At the start of the Second World War, restrictions to Indigenous military service were reinstated. However, new opportunities for militarised assimilation emerged when the government authorised so-called "half-castes" to serve and when it established Indigenous-only military units to meet war needs. In the very early months of the war, some Indigenous men managed to enlist thanks to confusion about the racist ban and local memories of Indigenous military service in the First World War. These were predominantly men with one White parent, including fifty from Darwin and some twenty from Queensland. Some of these even left Australia for the Middle East and London (Beaumont and Moss 2018).

However, in 1940, Prime Minister Robert Menzies wrote to the departments of the Army and Navy to clarify that 'the admission of aliens or of British subjects of non-European origin or descent to the Australian Defence Forces is undesirable in principle' (quoted in Riseman and Trembath 2016: 10). This command also explicitly excluded "half-caste" people, possibly because of the threat to White Australia that was posed by Indigenous First World War veterans who linked their service to civil rights (Beaumont and Moss 2018: 95; see also Maynard 2018). Menzies nonetheless made room for exceptions 'to provide for the special needs of any of the Services during the war' (quoted in Riseman and Trembath 2016: 10). This included entry to the Royal Australian Air Force which was more relaxed. Beaumont and Moss (2018: 95) explain this 'in view of the heavy commitments already made in late 1939 to provide air crew for the Empire Air Training Scheme'. The decision to exclude all Aboriginal men from enlisting in the army and navy was opposed by both Aboriginal veterans and communities who claimed their right to serve on account of their loyalty to Australia and the Empire, and by White settlers who were adamant that military service was a path to assimilated integration.

The ban was contested, especially on the ground that "half-caste" should be given full citizenship status, including the right to serve. There were also controversial cases where Indigenous men underwent military training but were subsequently prevented from departing for the warfront, resulting in wasted training resources and a reduction in the count of active soldiers. These sparked campaigns and petitions with the intention of pressuring authorities to grant suitable (read, "half-caste") Indigenous individuals the opportunity to serve. They were often infused with an assimilationist language which emphasised that the men who were refused enlistment were fair skin and therefore would have not upset White soldiers, they spoke good English, and their educational standards were higher than average. While it was confirmed that "full bloods" could have not served, by the end of 1940, the enlistment of "half-caste" individuals was again left to the discretion of medical officers (Beaumont and Moss 2018: 96–7).

The Japanese threat and attack on Australia in 1941 changed the Australian strategic landscape by bringing the war home for the first time. This created a special war need to reconsider Indigenous military service. However, instead of considering integration, the strategy involved creating Indigenous-only military units. This approach aimed not only to leverage Indigenous local knowledge of the territory and survival skills to monitor remote areas of the country vulnerable to Japanese attacks, but also to exert control and governance over Indigenous populations from northern isolated communities. Gray (2018: 107) notes that the Japanese threat to Australia heightened colonial anxieties about the loyalty of Indigenous people. Some generals and officials were concerned that the Japanese could have persuaded Indigenous individuals to support the enemy, rather than the British settlers who had stolen their land. This concern was particularly pronounced regarding remote Indigenous people of far north Australia, an area not yet fully colonised at that time. To mitigate this concern, the government sanctioned the creation of special units and auxiliary positions for Indigenous individuals from remote communities of the north. Consequently, this strategy further contributed to the consolidation of colonisation in northern Australia (Caso 2023).

The first battalion that was created was the Papuan Infantry Battalion comprising Indigenous Papuans. Papua had been an Australian protectorate and colony since 1906, and was therefore a space where authorities could test the idea of Indigenous-only battalions with limited domestic repercussions. Following this experiment, Australia created a unit of Torres Strait Islanders operating in non-combat roles in the northern islands of Australia. Torres Strait Islanders were presented as a martial race suitable for service (Beaumont and Moss 2018). There were more reservations about recruiting Aboriginal people from the mainland and fears about arming them. Eventually, the Northern Territory Special Reconnaissance Unit was instituted recruiting Aboriginal people from the Arnhem who were not armed (Beaumont and Moss 2018; more on this below).

As Riseman (2007: 81) remarks, the institution of these battalions and reconnaissance units in the north and islands did not represent a sudden appreciation of Indigenous skills in warfare. Indigenous people's inclusion in segregated units commanded by White officers was an opportunity to secure their loyalty through wages and goods offered as compensation for their military service. Indigenous people were exploited for their knowledge of territory, and they were also cheap labour. In fact, the Aboriginal and Torres Strait Islanders who were recruited in the Northern Territory Special Reconnaissance Unit and the Torres Strait Light Infantry Battalion were "full blood" and were governed by the Protection System which limited their wage. Low wages and unequal working conditions were sources of resentment among Indigenous soldiers and their voices against injustice and protests heightened colonial insecurities which led to the disbandment of these services.

Women in the Auxiliary Services

In 1940, the Australian government also approved the establishment of the Women's Auxiliary Services, which, as discussed in Chapter 4, also included Aboriginal and Torres Strait Islander women. As of 2023, the Australian War Memorial has identified sixty-nine of them. Many of these were removed from their families when they were children and were part of the Stolen Generations. Some were not aware of their Indigenous origins, while others enlisted to escape the restrictions of the Protection System like their male counterparts.

Aboriginal and Torres Strait Islander women's service in the Women's Auxiliary Services enabled them to gain skills valued in White society (Riseman 2015), but also simultaneously put them on the path to assimilation. Having previously explored the assimilationist discourse surrounding Oodgeroo Noonuccal's service in Chapter 4, let us now turn our attention to another exemplary case: Sue Gordon.

Unlike Noonuccal, Gordon was from the Stolen Generations. Military service was the continuation of the assimilationist project of removing children from their families. Separated from her family at the age of four, Gordon spent her formative years in a religious mission in Perth. Enlisting was a decision driven by her desire to evade the fate of becoming a domestic servant, a common path for many Aboriginal women raised in missions. In the military, she also saw an opportunity to escape a future of poverty and marginalisation that typically awaited women departing the mission. She did not join for patriotic reasons but for the security of having accommodation and an income outside the mission (Cadzow and Jebb 2019: 181). For Aboriginal women like Gordon who were raised in missions, enlisting in the Women's Auxiliary Services was a relatively smooth transition. As Gordon commented, 'I swapped one institution for another, but it was the only way I could get away [from Sister Kate's and working as a domestic]' (quoted in Riseman 2015: 764). Coming from the Stolen Generations, Gordon found in the military a 'family' that she never had (Cadzow and Jebb 2019: 180–2). The military gave her a sense of belonging and individual recognition that she could not experience in the family from whom she was taken.

For Gordon, Noonuccal and other Aboriginal women, military service opened a path of education and good employment within settler institutions, and gave them skills and respectability valued in settler society. While this made them rise above the ranks, it also implicated them in the assimilationist project to eradicate difference and the settler logics of elimination. Gordon worked in the National Aeronautics and Space Administration (NASA) in Western Australia and then pursued a career in State Indigenous Affairs, for example, as part of the Aboriginal Employment Committee, the Aboriginal Development Commission and as the Commissioner of Aboriginal Affairs. She also became the first Aboriginal magistrate in Western Australia's Children's Court. Like many other Indigenous veterans, Gordon used her status and privileges in settler society to help and give back to Indigenous communities. Thus, she attempted to reverse militarised assimilation. However, her service to communities from within settler institutions also put her in a difficult position, such as when she was appointed as chair of the controversial Northern Territory Emergency Response Taskforce between 2007 and 2008. In that role, Gordon supported the removal of Aboriginal children from their families on account of alleged sexual abuse. This move was extremely unpopular among Indigenous women who believe that the government never listened to them when they tried to ring alarm bells and propose preventive work (Moreton-Robinson 2015: 165–6). In this respect, Gordon was accused of being an Indigenous bureaucrat in the service of the settler state. Working from within settler institutions meant that Gordon has had greater influence and power, but also that she was caught in the settler colonial logics and frameworks that pathologised and violated Indigenous communities.

Post-Second World War

The assimilationist agenda of Indigenous military service continued after the Second World War, and is very visible when considering the media representations of Indigenous veterans. Although the military reinstated the ban on Indigenous service soon after the war, the media nevertheless presented Indigenous military service as an example of assimilation in White society (Riseman and Trembath 2016: ch. 1). Riseman (2014: 160) discusses Douglas Grant's re-emergence in the media after the Second World War as an example of what the "civilised life" can do for Aboriginal people. The media omitted Grant's experience of and fight against racism and discrimination that led him to become an alcoholic and be admitted to a psychiatric ward. Because of his life experience, Douglas was in favour of assimilation, but questioned whether White Australia was willing to go all the way in (ibid., 162).

In 1951, Australia adopted assimilation as its official Indigenous policy, and Indigenous military service became a primary vehicle to promote it. In the policy, assimilation was defined as the expectation that 'all persons of aboriginal blood or mixed blood [sic.] in Australia will live like white Australians do' (quoted in Riseman 2018b: 196). In the same year, section 138 of the Defence Act which banned those 'not substantially of European origin or descent' from enlisting, was repealed. Riseman (2014) documents that in the 1950s and 1960s, media representation of selected Indigenous people was an instrument by which to pursue assimilation. This strategy had a twofold objective. The media portrayal of assimilated Indigenous individuals aimed to persuade White Australians that Indigenous people could adopt a lifestyle akin to their own. Simultaneously, it sought to encourage Aboriginal and Torres Strait Islander individuals to embrace assimilation as a means to attain advantages and accomplishments. The profiles of Indigenous soldiers were particularly useful to demonstrate Indigenous people's commitment to the settler state and their willingness to fight and die for the settler nation. It also showed Indigenous people that they could achieve the right to vote[4] and the privilege to access housing.

In the 1960s, Captain Reginald Saunders became the face of militarised assimilation. Saunders joined the army in 1940 and was the first Aboriginal man known to have been invited to attend Officer Training School and become a commissioned officer. In 1950, Saunders re-enlisted in the military to fight in the war in Korea. The media presented Saunders as the epitome of the assimilated Aboriginal man (Riseman 2014: 165). His assimilation was considered complete by the fact that he volunteered and served settler society in two wars. His commitment to settler society also led him to distinguish himself and become a captain. Saunders' assimilation was further confirmed by the fact that after divorcing from his first wife – who was also Aboriginal and a servicewoman, Dorothy Mary Saunders – he married a White Irish woman and nurse, Patricia Montgomery. Like Douglas and others, Saunders faced discrimination and racism in civilian society that significantly impacted his ability to find a civilian job, rent a house and live with dignity. His experience of racism was unsurprisingly omitted in the media heralding of assimilation.

Indigenous soldiers like Saunders and Douglas, among others, endorsed Indigenous assimilation and saw the military as a promising pathway. Sue Gordon, for example, noted that Indigenous veterans from the war in Korea encouraged Indigenous children from the mission where she grew up, Sister Kate's, to enlist and earn medals (Cadzow and Jebb 2019: 182). They believed in assimilation as a path to equality and opportunities that were foreclosed to them by a history of exclusion and racism. Saunders' enthusiasm for assimilation is captured in his autobiography when he speaks about his son, Chris:

> He [Chris] could be totally assimilated. He's a good-looking boy, not too dark, very popular, better than average at sport. And he's very bright at school. You never know . . . Chris might one day get to university. And he'll certainly marry a white girl. (quoted in Riseman 2014: 166)

This endorsement of assimilation is an expression of hope for his Aboriginal child who had the disadvantage of being born in a racist society. It also goes to show how powerful the rhetoric of assimilation was. Whiteness was a potent signifier of status, belonging and virtue. The negative impact of racism and discrimination was so powerful that Indigenous people like Saunders considered loosening or even giving up their identity and connection to culture for the promise of equal opportunities and a better life for their children. But by the mid-1970s, Indigenous people had begun to realise that 'the right to fight for King and Empire' (Beaumont and Moss 2018: 96) did not translate to respect and equal rights. Despite the claims that in the military Indigenous people experienced little racism, in civilian society they continued to face racial barriers, prejudice and police harassment (Riseman and Trembath 2016: ch. 5). Assimilation also perpetuated the removal of Aboriginal children from their families and relocation into White families, which was effectively destroying Aboriginal communities and culture.

Finally, it is also important to note that assimilation was sold to Indigenous people as a promise of (a future) equality. Thus, for Indigenous people who supported assimilation like Saunders, assimilation did not mean the suppression of their Aboriginality or the breeding out of their Aboriginal blood. Instead, it was 'an opportunity to bring Aboriginal culture into the mainstream of Australian life' (Riseman and Trembath 2016: 32). This is also demonstrated by the fact that many Aboriginal veterans pursued careers in rights activism and community service.

Reconciliation and the Emerging Aesthetics of Indigenous War Commemoration

Despite the service of Indigenous individuals in both world wars, Indigenous people were excluded from war commemoration services and representations. They developed their own local and family commemorative practices but were largely omitted from official and national war commemoration (Riseman 2017). As already noted in Chapter 2, they were absent in the War Art Scheme and the newly established Australian War Memorial. Furthermore, their ability to march on Anzac Day was contested. While there is historical evidence of Indigenous participation on Anzac Day events, they were often denied membership to local Returned Service League Clubs (RSLs) and could not participate in the attendant social activities because they were banned from accessing pubs. The landscape begun to shift in the 1980s, driven by a changing national identity that embraced multiculturalism and the rising influence of Indigenous activism.

During the 1970s, the discourse of assimilation gradually yielded ground to that of recognition and diversity. This era marked a period of profound change, as Australia began to loosen its symbolic connections with the British Empire and grip on Whiteness, ushering in its identity as a postcolonial nation. In 1973, the government repealed the White Australia Policy and, in 1978, it started implementing policies to promote multiculturalism. Post-war Indigenous activism, including from Indigenous veterans, was an important factor that contributed to this change (Furphy 2018; Maynard 2018). The decade-long campaign to bring about constitutional changes to address the exclusion of Indigenous people eventually led to the national referendum of 1967 which changed the constitution by removing two clauses that discriminated against Indigenous people. Won with an overwhelming majority (90.77 per cent), the referendum enabled the inclusion of Indigenous Australians in the national census and gave legislative power over Indigenous Affairs to the Commonwealth.[5] This represented a historical moment when Indigenous people came to be officially and constitutionally included in the nation. However, the referendum happened at a time when assimilation was still the guiding policy for Indigenous affairs and activists were wary that the constitutional inclusion of Indigenous people was, in fact, part of the assimilation agenda (Maddison 2019a: 5). To counter a possible assimilationist project, activists became more vocal about Indigenous self-determination and the recognition of Indigenous sovereignty. The 1970s was a time of raising Aboriginal Black Power as demonstrated by the fervent activism around the country and the establishment of the Aboriginal Tent Embassy which was the emblem of Indigenous resistance and resurgence (Foley, Schaap and Howell 2014). Activism for Indigenous self-determination and sovereignty led to the campaign for treaties between the settler state and First Nations (initiated in 1979), the legal proceeding of the *Mabo* case (initiated in 1982), the recognition of native title rights (1992), the official recognition of the Aboriginal and Torres Strait Islander flag (1995), the establishment of the National Inquiry into the Separation of Aboriginal and Torres Strait Islander Children from their Families (1995) and the landmark *Bring Them Home* report which documents the history of removing children from Aboriginal and Torres Strait Islander families (1997).

Against this background of political ferment, Indigenous veterans and soldiers wanted more than military assimilation. As immigrant communities gained authorisation to utilise war memorials nationwide for their own commemorative ceremonies under the banner of multiculturalism (Riseman 2017: 85), Indigenous veterans capitalised on the evolving multicultural political atmosphere and harnessed the vigour of the Indigenous self-determination and sovereignty movement. This empowered them to advocate for acknowledgement of their military service and wartime encounters as Aboriginal and Torres Strait Islander individuals rather than as just soldiers. Effectively, they were demanding the recognition of their identity and difference to counter the years of silence and neglect. In 1985, about fifteen Aboriginal veterans formed the National Aboriginal and Islanders Ex-Services Association and attempted to march under their own banner at the Melbourne Anzac Day March, but were refused permission by the Returned Service League's president, Bruce Ruxton. They were refused on the ground that 'marching as their own group would make the gap wider and wider between Black and White' (Ruxton, quoted in Riseman 2017: 85). This refusal did not stop the veterans from parading in the northern suburbs of Melbourne rather than at the Shrine of Remembrance[6] with the other soldiers and veterans (Beaumont 2018: 203). This separate march occurred for three more years and then picked up again in 2007 in the predominantly Aboriginal suburb of Redfern in Sydney.

Indigenous veterans also led several attempts to erect monuments in memory of Aboriginal and Torres Strait Islander service people and those who died in war. As documented by Riseman (2017) and Beaumont (2018), in 1987, the National Aborigines and Islander Ex-Services Association applied for a grant managed by the authority organising the celebration of the Australian bicentennial to erect a memorial to Aboriginal and Torres Strait Islander people killed in Australia's wars. This project was rejected, but undeterred, two of the veterans who lodged the grant application erected their own simple memorial without the support of the state. The following year, a White woman and private citizen, Honor Thwaites, erected a small memorial to Aboriginal and Torres Strait Islander military service on Mount Ainslie behind the Australian War Memorial. This became the site where Indigenous people commemorated their own military service on Anzac Day, as discussed below.

The launch of the Reconciliation campaign by the government in 1991 prompted a significant shift towards the inclusion and commemoration of Indigenous military service. After a decade of refusal and neglect of Indigenous veterans' efforts to promote recognition, Reconciliation finally propelled the recognition of Indigenous military service. However, Reconciliation was a fraught process. It emerged in response to Indigenous activism demanding treaties and self-determination which the government perceived to be divisive and a threat to national unity. Reconciliation was proposed as an alternative to pacify activists and foster racial and postcolonial unification under the banner of 'moving forward as a united Australia' (Short 2008: 154; see also Robbins 2007: 319). In 1991, the government formally established the Council for Aboriginal Reconciliation (CAR), which was tasked with promoting education about Indigenous disadvantage and history and making policy recommendations to the government. At that time, Reconciliation was conceived as a decade-long initiative aimed at accomplishing harmonisation between Indigenous communities and the settler state by the time of the Australian Federation's centenary in 2001. However, in 2001, CAR produced a report declaring that ten years of reconciliation was insufficient to address 200 years of colonisation. Reconciliation came under fire, especially from Indigenous communities. Even its own chair, Patrick Dodson, resigned in 1997 objecting to the constraints on Reconciliation imposed by the newly elected prime minister, John Howard (Dodson 2007). Howard maintained that the historical injustices were not central to the reconciliation effort and steered Reconciliation in the direction of what he termed a 'practical approach'. This approach aimed to tackle Indigenous socio-economic disparities through an assimilationist strategy (see also Short 2008: ch. 8; Maddison 2019a: ch. 8).

Although Reconciliation faced criticism from Indigenous communities and treaty activists, in wider Australia it bolstered a rhetoric of postcolonial government and multiculturalism. In relation to Indigenous military service, the Reconciliation movement spurred the exploration of the history of Indigenous individuals contributing to the defence of Australia. It also emphasised the significance of narratives highlighting the cooperation between Indigenous and non-Indigenous soldiers. It supported the production of cultural events about Indigenous military service such as the plays *The Sunshine Club* (staged in 1999), *Seems Like Yesterday* (staged in 2001) and *Black Diggers* (staged in 2014). Reconciliation also prompted national institutions such as the Australian War Memorial and the Department of Veterans' Affairs to become actively involved in the promotion of Indigenous military service. In 1993, the Australian War Memorial curated the exhibition *Too Dark for the Light Horse*, followed by the unveiling of the *For Country, For Nation* exhibition in 2016. Additionally, in 2004, the War Memorial endorsed the plaque commemorating Indigenous service personnel, installed by Honor Thwaites, on Mount Ainslie. Furthermore, in 2009, Gary Oakley was appointed as the first Indigenous Liaison Officer by the War Memorial. Then, in 2012, the War Memorial appointed the first official Indigenous war artist, Tony Albert, followed by Torres Strait Islander artist Alick Tipoti in 2016, and the first female Aboriginal war artist Megan Cope in 2017. The Department of Veterans' Affairs has been sponsoring commemorative services on Reconciliation Week in honour of Indigenous soldiers, and it has been collaborating with schools around the country to disseminate educational resources, with art organisations to produce and tour art exhibitions, and with community organisations to support commemorative events (Riseman 2017; Beaumont 2018).

Reconciliation also prompted the Department of Defence to actively pursue Indigenous recruitment. In 2007, the Australian Defence Forces (ADF) launched the first Defence Reconciliation Action Plan[7] (D-RAP), which involved the design and implementation of programmes to recruit and retain Aboriginal and Torres Strait Islander personnel. In 2008, the Department of Defence created the Directorate for Indigenous Affairs to manage and promote the recruitment of Indigenous people in the ADF, and, in 2009, inaugurated the Defence Indigenous Development Programme to help channel Indigenous people in defence careers. Since 2007, the Department of Defence has issued four D-RAPs and the number of Aboriginal and Torres Strait Islander service people has grown from 1.3 per cent of defence personnel in 1999 to 3.7 per cent in 2020, to a total of 3,160 service men and women (Department of Defence 2020). Of the three services, the army has the largest representation with 1,720 personnel employed as either permanent (60 per cent) or reservist (40 per cent). Indigenous soldiers tend to be concentrated in the Regional Force Surveillance Units (RFSUs), domestic army units tasked with the patrol and reconnaissance of the remote northern national borders; in the North-West Mobile Force (NORFORCE), for example, one of the RFSUs, Indigenous soldiers represent 60 per cent of the force.

Militarised Recognition

The recent inclusion of Indigenous people in the national aesthetics of war commemoration and in the Australian Defence Forces is intricately tied to the ongoing dynamics of settler colonialism and settler military politics. Reconciliation prompted what that I call 'militarised recognition'. In political terms, recognition is generally understood to be a practice of acknowledgement and inclusion of diversity that addresses experiences of exclusion and injustice (Taylor 1994; Honneth 1995). In the debate between two of the main theorists of recognition – Axel Honneth and Nancy Fraser – recognition emerges as the premise for self-identification and access to political rights and the precondition for economic opportunities (Fraser and Honneth 2003). In essence, recognition plays a vital role in fostering self-esteem and shaping one's identity within a broader community. However, its significance is truly realised when combined with the equitable distribution of resources and opportunities among the recognised group. This combination is crucial for effectively addressing social inequalities that exist within society.

Indigenous Canadian scholar Glen Coulthard (2014) criticises recognition as a practice of liberal politics that fails to address the underlying power imbalances faced by Indigenous people in settler colonial societies. He also argues that recognition reproduces colonial power relations that keep Indigenous people from transforming colonial societies. I maintain that Indigenous militarisation is part of settler recognition as described by Coulthard.

Coulthard sees recognition as a form of colonial governmentality that implicates Indigenous people in their own dispossession. It operates by producing subjectivities that are integral for the existence of the colonial state. In order to maintain its legitimacy in a liberal order, the settler state requires Indigenous subjectivities that recognise the state. Through state-led recognition, Indigenous people get piecemeal freedom and rights, and in exchange, they come to recognise the settler state as the provider of their freedom and guarantor of their existence. Under settler colonial conditions, Indigenous recognition originates from the very settler state that is responsible for the historical oppression of Indigenous people and their ongoing marginalisation. Therefore, their freedom and existence are already constrained by settler logics. The settler state sets the term of recognition to craft a domesticated version of Indigeneity that can coexist with the settler state. Thus, settler recognition precludes Indigeneity in its own terms and selectively chooses which aspects of Indigeneity can be recognised and which cannot be accommodated.

Although Coulthard theorises from the Canadian experience of settler colonialism, his insights resonate in Australia and other settler societies. Aboriginal and Torres Strait Islanders have been wary about the language and practices of recognition in Australia which have mostly revolved around the inclusion of Indigenous people in the constitution. They have been concerned that constitutional recognition would remove the possibility of signing treaties with the state and nominally erase the Indigenous difference while leaving untouched the legacies of colonisation (Davies and Langton 2016; M. Davis 2016; Maddison 2017). This same concern animated the Indigenous debate about the Voice to Parliament in 2023 (see Tong 2023). Ultimately, Aboriginal and Torres Strait Islanders are wary that recognition will assimilate Indigenous people as citizens of the settler state, deny their sovereignty and nationhood, and preclude self-determination (Moreton-Robinson 2007).

In the context of Australia, too, recognition has been identified as a strategy to manage colonial relations and produce obedient Indigenous subjects (Povinelli 2002; Strakosch 2015). Moreton-Robinson (2015) exemplifies this with reference to the constitutional changes brought about by the 1967 referendum mentioned above. Despite being acknowledged in the census and incorporated into Commonwealth legislation, Indigenous communities have faced persisting systemic disadvantages. Paradoxically, due to the perception of equality implied by constitutional reforms, the ongoing Indigenous disadvantage has often been portrayed as an inherent shortcoming of Indigenous individuals. Moreton-Robison discusses how those individuals and communities which fail to adhere to settler norms and lifestyles are pathologised, thus creating a framework that empowers the settler state to intrude upon Indigenous sovereignty. This is evident in instances such as the Northern Intervention, which involved the removal of children from Indigenous families based on alleged sexual abuse. These communities were pathologised as inherently and culturally abusive rather than understood within a framework of protracted and ignored socio-economic disadvantage. Additionally, Moreton-Robison points out that Indigenous recognition prompted by the 1967 referendum subjected Indigenous people to settler control mechanisms imposed as prerequisites for accessing the economic means necessary for survival.

Recognition of Indigenous military service works in the order of settler recognition as outlined by Indigenous scholars such as Coulthard and Moreton-Robinson. As already noted in Chapter 3, it took hold in the context of colonial reckoning when the historiography of colonial violence was also becoming popular in Australia for the first time (Reynolds 2013: 30; Riseman 2017: 85). This history represented a threat to the legitimacy of the settler state because it revealed that Australia was built on the bloodshed of Indigenous people perpetrated in order to steal and appropriate their land. It called into question the authenticity of a state that took every measure possible to hide the history of violence and implement Indigenous dispossession behind a facade of paternalistic benevolence. This colonial reckoning sparked a sense of national shame which the government addressed by promoting military heritage as a point of national pride (McKenna 2010). The resurgence of modern military history to dissipate national shame over colonial history opened the door for the inclusion of Indigenous military service in the national military canon (Due 2008: 26; Reynolds 2013: 4; Riseman 2017: 88). In this context, Indigenous military service has been presented as a story of collaboration between Indigenous and non-Indigenous soldiers, and the military as an institution that galvanised Indigenous rights. Thus, recognition of Indigenous military service has been utilised to manage the emergence of a difficult history and to promote national unity under the banner of reconciliation.

The recognition of Indigenous military service is strategically employed to counter Indigenous resistance and to resolve conflict in favour of the settler state. In fact, while it allows Aboriginal communities to participate in the war narrative of nation-building, it leaves the narrative 'relatively untouched and uncomplicated by colonised people's experience of conflict' (Sumartojo and Wellings 2021: 171). The focus on the history of Indigenous military service, presented as a narrative of harmonious collaboration transcending race in defence of the settler state, serves as a mechanism to shape a specific narrative of nation-building and reconciliation. While collaboration must be celebrated, it is also important to recount the history of violence, racism and discrimination faced by Indigenous people that led them to seek military service at a time when they were barred from enlisting and were involved in the Frontier Wars. As I have discussed elsewhere (Caso 2020), Australian institutions such as the Australian War Memorial embracing the commemoration of Indigenous military service tend to shy away from telling the history of the Defence Act that excluded people 'not substantially of European origin' from enlisting. They also omit the stories of racism faced by Indigenous people who served (Scarlett 2015; Cadzow and Jebb 2019: 104–5). Instead, military service tends to be presented as freely available and relatively uncomplicated for Indigenous people, thus erasing the settler conditions that structured Indigenous military service.

Indigenous military service narrated as a story of reconciliation also relegates colonial warfare to a bygone era, implying its irrelevance to contemporary politics. This is most evident in the fact that while Indigenous soldiers have found a place in the Australian War Memorial to promote reconciliation, colonial conflict remains excluded because it is a history considered to be divisive. The recognition of Indigenous military service and the continued exclusion of the Frontier Wars operated by the Australian War Memorial rests on the caesura between modern history and pre-modern colonisation which estranges the modern soldier who fights in the Australian Defence Forces and the anti-colonial warrior who fought against European colonisers. Thus, the militarised recognition of Indigenous people further cements the structures of settler colonialism by erasing colonial conflict from the history of Australia. Without a proper acknowledgement of the history of colonial warfare on a par with modern western wars, Indigenous history is misrecognised.

According to Coulthard, settler recognition of Indigenous people is always already a form of misrecognition. This misrecognition operates to produce an image of Indigeneity that fits the settler state. In the case of militarised recognition, the aspect of Indigeneity that is edited out is the colonial warrior fighting against the colonial settler. This omission, together with the recognition of the modern Indigenous soldier who fights for the defence of the settler state, enhance the legitimacy of the settler state, and ultimately reproduces the settler colonial relations that keep Indigenous people at bay. Strakosch and Macoun (2012) and Maddison (2019a) explain that manipulation of history to edit the present such as this are a strategy of settler colonialism. Settler colonialism relies on crafting linear narratives of progress that can mark colonial tensions as resolved. The history of settler colonial societies is narrated as a progressive move from colonisation to post-colonialism (Strakosch and Macoun 2012: 42). Post-colonialism is perceived as a phase when the distinctions between Indigenous peoples and settlers have been reconciled, resulting in the equitable sharing of the nation's wealth among both groups. This assumed accomplishment is used to validate the relegation of calls for Indigenous sovereignty, land rights and the integration of colonial history in the national identity (Maddison 2019a). The recognition of Indigenous military service is narrated as a story of reconciliation such that it sustains the narrative that Australia has overcome structural racism, has moved on from colonial history, and has become a postcolonial society.

NORFORCE

The case of NORFORCE is on point to illustrate the militarisation of Indigenous people and the misrecognition of their history. NORFORCE is a domestic army reconnaissance unit that operates in the Northern Territory and the Kimberley region. As already mentioned, Indigenous people make up 60 per cent of NORFORCE, a figure that has become a media sensation to illustrate how far post-colonial Australia has gone in including and creating opportunities for Indigenous people. NORFORCE came to public attention in 2012 when Tony Albert was appointed as the first Aboriginal official war artist to depict the unit. Some of the art produced by Albert has the flavour of recruitment propaganda, such as the piece titled *Be Deadly – NORFORCE*. This represents three Indigenous children surrounded by images taken from superhero comics and the writing 'be DEADLY NORFORCE'. 'Deadly' is an Aboriginal English expression meaning 'simply the best'. *Be Deadly – NORFORCE* seems to be a poster that encourages Indigenous children to join NORFORCE and become heroes.

Despite being hailed as a symbol of post-colonialism and Indigenous military integration, NORFORCE is not outside the settler colonial framework. It was established in the early 1980s as part of the Regional Forces Surveillance Units and the strategy to make Australia's defence autonomous. The media and defence department eagerly trace the history of NORFORCE in the Northern Territory Special Reconnaissance Unit (NTSRU), formed in 1942 and which recruited from the Yolngu people on the Arnhem Land. This was the reconnaissance unit in the Second World War composed of Aboriginal people from mainland Australia introduced above. In September 2022, the Australian army celebrated the 80th anniversary of the NTSRU, making clear that this unit is the predecessor of NORFORCE (*Defence News* 2022). This connection is a practice of militarised recognition which allows the recovery of the history of the NTRSU and the celebration of Indigenous military inclusion while erasing the stories of racism and the exploitation of Indigenous labour.

When narrated as the predecessor of NORFORCE, the enlistment of the Yolngu people in the NTSRU is presented as an unproblematic story of cooperation between Indigenous people and White generals, despite the fact that the former were subordinate to the latter and were not paid a wage comparable to regular soldiers. Riseman (2007) shows that White generals and politicians were highly suspicious of and sceptical about enlisting the Yolngu people – and

Indigenous people more broadly – because they were considered to be savages, malicious in nature and with no loyalty. The Yolngu people were also mistrustful of the White settlers and especially of the police, which were known for their punitive expeditions. The government and military officials saw the Yolngu people merely as 'a "coloured" human buffer between the "yellow peril" and white Australia' (Riseman 2007: 85). They managed to strike a deal with the Yolngu people by offering trade goods such as tobacco, pipes, fish and spears. The generals dismissed the Yolngu people as soon as the Japanese threat became serious and replaced them with the North Australian Observer Unit (NAOU) made up of White soldiers who were paid a wage. This shows the levels of mistrust and suggests that Australia could only ever be defended by troops of White soldiers (Riseman 2012: 52). The deliberate exclusion of this history of mistrust and exploitation creates a narrative that allows White Australians to perceive Indigenous military service as unproblematic, free from racism and uninterrupted. Simultaneously, Indigenous individuals may come to connect with a familial military history that seems unaffected by racism.

Coming back to the present, the recruitment of Indigenous individuals in NORFORCE serves to promote the settler disciplining of remote Indigenous communities and their proximity to settler power. Banking on a martial race rhetoric, commentators discuss Indigenous people in NORFORCE as a defence and strategic asset because of their survival skills and knowledge of territory, which are presented as natural and innate abilities (see, for example, Pastor-Elsegood 2021). The framing of Indigenous people as having innate skills that are valuable for defence promotes Indigenous proximity to the military, which for the government, has more than defence purposes. In fact, Indigenous military inclusion in NORFORCE is often praised for its contribution to Closing the Gap, a national strategy announced in 2008 to measure and improve the health and wellbeing of Indigenous Australians. In *Closing the Gap, Prime Minister's Report 2013*, NORFORCE was mentioned as an indicator of success. The report stated that 'The unit's mission of protecting country aligns with the traditional values of the Indigenous culture' (Australian Government 2013: 109). Along similar lines, more recently, a political commentator working for a prominent Australian think tank wrote that:

> The greatest gains realised so far from the involvement of Indigenous Australians in the defence of the north have been the social benefits

derived from NORFORCE programmes. Those gains have been an important contribution to the whole-of-government strategy for closing the gap on Indigenous disadvantage. (Clark 2019)

Military integration, and particularly in NORFORCE is a political strategy to bring Indigenous people from remote communities closer to the social heart of Australia and promote integration into settler disciplinary institutions such as the military. This is not dissimilar to the recruitment of the Yolngu in the Second World War, which was ultimately intended to discipline remote Indigenous populations and consolidate the settlement of the north of Australia (Caso 2023).

The settler disciplinary effects of Indigenous military integration are evident in the many testimonies of Indigenous people from remote Australia praising the military for having a job and for not being in prison. A society in which minorities resort to military service to escape the risk of incarceration highlights significant power imbalances and underlying issues. In this context, it is insightful to consider Coulthard's assertion that recognition functions as a disciplinary mechanism prompting Indigenous individuals to develop psycho-affective attachments towards the settler state. This connection then becomes a means of survival for Indigenous communities. Building on the work of Fanon, he contends that recognition encourages Indigenous individuals to identify with the values and freedom proposed by the settler state and at the expense of Indigenous conceptions (Coulthard 2014: 39). In this respect, recognition effectively leads Indigenous individuals to internalise the impact of colonisation, thereby subduing the Indigenous subject and eroding Indigenous sovereignty and self-determination. In the case of Indigenous military integration, militarised recognition promotes the view among Indigenous people, especially in remote communities, that military service is the path to economic empowerment and to be outside the carceral system.

The most infamous example of how militarised recognition disciplined Indigenous people and promoted their identification with the settler colonial project is the involvement of Indigenous soldiers from NORFORCE in the Northern Intervention. Launched in 2007 by the Howard government against seventy-four Indigenous communities in the Northern Territory, the Northern Intervention was intended to remove children from their families following allegations of sexual abuse. The Australian military was deployed domestically against "its own" people through Operation Outreach, and NORFORCE supplied 400 of the 600-plus soldiers involved (Riseman and Trembath

2016: 156). The task of Indigenous soldiers was to mediate (or ingra-
tiate) community elders and facilitate the operation of social workers
to remove children. Indigenous soldiers in the Northern Intervention
effectively became the hand of the settler colonial state to remove
children from their families, a longstanding settler colonial practice
in Australia. The Northern Intervention also epitomised the success
of the "good Indigenous citizen" (Moreton-Robinson 2015: ch. 11) –
aka the Indigenous soldier – who became modern through Indigenous policy and settler institutions, set against the "problematic"
and "dysfunctional" primitivism and disadvantage of those Indigenous people who did not enter the settler system (Caso 2021; 2023).

Through militarised recognition, Indigenous people are interpellated as colonial subjects who belong to the settler state. It is
according to this logic that the Indigenous soldiers deployed in the
Northern Intervention internalised settler colonial rule and became
primary actors of settler colonial policies. Here it is important to
note the psychological dimension of recognition which makes colonised subjects internalise their oppressor's image of themselves as a
practice of survival and adaptation. Coulthard explains this recalling
Fanon's experience of being interpellated by the child as a 'frighten-
ing Negro' and finding himself identify with that subject position
both viscerally and intellectually. As the child's words resonated in
Fanon's body, he found himself examining the characteristics of his
Blackness only to be battered down by 'cannibalism, intellectual
deficiency, fetishism, racial defects' (Fanon, quoted in Coulthard
2014: 32). In this episode, Fanon internalised the racist, colonial
misrecognition of Blackness and lost his subjectivity to become an
object of White culture and denigration. Regardless of recognition,
in settler societies like Australia, Indigenous people still deal with
the characterisation of Indigeneity as being dysfunctional, primitive, lawless and incapable of governing its subjects (Macoun 2011:
523; Strakosch and Macoun 2012: 60; Watego 2021). Alongside
economic disparities, the internalisation of this discourse holds significant importance in comprehending why Indigenous individuals
engage with settler institutions like the military and participate in
initiatives like the Northern Intervention.

Counter-Memory

The militarised recognition of Indigenous people and their inclusion in the official national aesthetics of war commemoration are

recent phenomenon compared with the longstanding efforts of Aboriginal and Torres Strait Islander communities to commemorate their military service and experiences of war (Riseman 2017; Beaumont 2018: 360–8). In this final section, I delve into the concept of self-recognition as a means of counter-memory and sovereignty. Self-representation is an essential component for recognition that is not dictated by others, and therefore, is a crucial aspect of sovereignty (Tuhiwai Smith 2012: 178). First Nation Australian scholar Irene Watson (2007: 27) notes that colonisation involves imposing on Indigenous people a representation of themselves that comes from the colonisers. Therefore, by contrast, Indigenous sovereignty involves acts of self-representation, including how colonisation has shaped Indigenous subjectivity, life and history. I examine how Indigenous-driven war commemoration endeavours to present a more comprehensive narrative of war in contrast to the selective official nationalist perspective. In particular, Indigenous commemoration invariably links Indigenous military service in modern warfare with the Frontier Wars, thus offering a fuller picture of the Indigenous experience of war. This is a form of resistance against the half-story of settler nationalist commemoration which distinguishes between the modern Indigenous soldier who fought for the settler state and the traditional Indigenous warrior who fought against the birth of the modern settler state.

Counter-memory refers to the establishment of collective memories and commemorative practices that are attuned to the temporalities and subjectivity of marginalised groups. Tello (2019: 2) defines counter-memory as 'a conceptual tool, and indeed method, to mobilise the memories and struggles of the vanquished in the face of abject violence and dispossession'. Tello notes that counter-memory is often configured in oppositional terms against the 'the nationalist-normativity of remembrance', thus creating the formula of *either* this history *or* that other history. Using the concept of montage, she proposes a conceptualisation of counter-memory through the structure of *and-and* that can accommodate multiple histories at the same time. Tello's conceptualisation of counter-memory is relevant to Indigenous war commemoration because Indigenous veterans and activists involved in commemorating Indigenous experiences of war elude the framework of either modern warfare or colonial warfare. Instead, Indigenous war commemoration is predicated on the convergence of modern *and* traditional practices of commemoration and the link between the modern soldier *and* the traditional warrior.

There are three relevant examples that I will consider in turn: the exhibition *For Country, For Nation*; the Aboriginal and Torres Strait Islander Commemoration Service on Anzac Day; and the march commemorating the Frontier Wars on Anzac Day at the Australian War Memorial in Canberra.

For Country, For Nation

The first example of counter-memory is the temporary exhibition *For Country, For Nation* inaugurated at the Australian War Memorial in 2016. *For Country, For Nation* was produced by the Australian War Memorial in consultation with Aboriginal curator Amanda Jane Reynolds to address the absence of Indigenous military service in official war commemoration. It gathered the work of thirty-two Indigenous artists from Australia and the Pacific Islands, six of whom were specifically commissioned for the exhibition. The final product was an eclectic combination of art, photography and documents that celebrated and commemorated Indigenous military service. This exhibition provided an extraordinary platform for Indigenous individuals to narrate their stories, share their experiences, and showcase the enduring legacy of their military service using their own unique voices within the Memorial. This marks a significant departure from the institution's historical exclusion of their perspectives.

As I have argued elsewhere (Caso 2020), *For Country, For Nation* largely worked within the institutional framework of militarised recognition and the settler narrative of postcolonial nation-building through reconciliation. The exhibition lacked a temporal narrative which made it impossible to reconstruct the history of military exclusion and assimilation. Instead, it was organised thematically to exalt collaboration between Indigenous and White soldiers and present the military as a platform for Indigenous inclusion and rights. Excerpts from Indigenous soldiers and veterans were carefully curated to illustrate that their military encounters were free from racism, and that their service was motivated by a deep sense of allegiance to the nation. Additionally, pre-colonial history was invoked to portray Aboriginal people as innately possessing martial qualities. For example, the quote by Army Reservist Garth O'Connell read:

> We come from a long-standing tradition of military service in this nation. The Anzac Legend Spirit comes out of this greater service to our Country that's been here for 40000 years. Anzac is a modern incarnation of that spirit in defending Country.

Nevertheless, *For Country, For Nation* also offered an unexpected take on Indigenous military service that linked the modern soldier who fought in international wars for White Australia with the traditional warrior who fought against European settlers. This approach brought the Frontier Wars into the Memorial for the very first time. Indeed, the curatorial text completely omitted a discussion of this link. For example, the exhibition included a display of Indigenous traditional weapons including spears, boomerangs and shields. The curatorial text next to it read:

> Australian military forces have always drawn inspiration from Indigenous cultural tradition. Characterised sometimes as pride in our history and sometimes as appropriation, this trend has also underpinned the creation of Australian identity.

Avoiding a direct reference to the Frontier Wars, this curatorial text creates a connection between the Indigenous martial tradition and the Australian Defence Forces that is timeless and uncomplicated by racial and colonial politics. Nevertheless, this display of traditional weapons manifested the Frontier Wars by showing the equipment of Indigenous warriors which they used to defend their country from the British invasion. There was also a digital display showing Indigenous people in uniform that included the Aboriginal warrior. Defiant of the institutional exclusion of colonial warfare in the Memoria, *For Country, For Nation* was an act of visual sovereignty (Rickard 2011; Fullenwieder 2017) that camouflaged and manifested the Frontier Wars in the undertones of its representations. This was an act of self-representation and sovereignty insofar as it exceeded the terms of recognition of Indigenous military service imposed by settler recognition.

Another notable representation of colonial warfare in *For Country, For Nation* was Rover Thomas Joolama's *Ruby Plains Massacre 1*. Positioned just before the entry into the gallery space hosting *For Country, For Nation*, this large painting depicts and commemorates an episode of the colonial massacres in the East Kimberley region in Western Australia. The curatorial text provided a title for this painting but did not include a story or an explanation. When I visited the exhibition, this large and colourful painting captured my attention, but there was no way for me to know what it represents if I had not researched it myself. The beautiful aesthetics of this painting does not immediately convey the bloodshed of the Frontier Wars and the colonial massacres of Aboriginal people. However, it uses an Aboriginal aesthetic syntax of dots, lines and colours that is descriptive and can be decoded by the trained, expert eye. This painting could be accommodated in the Memorial because of its ambiguity. Nevertheless, it was an act of Indigenous sovereignty whereby the artist and the curator wanted to reach Indigenous viewers primarily and represent to them their history and experience of colonial conflict and suffering.

The Aboriginal and Torres Strait Islander Commemoration Service

The second case of counter-memory is the Aboriginal and Torres Strait Islander Commemoration Service on Anzac Day held in Canberra at the Aboriginal Memorial Plaque on Mount Ainslie, just behind the Australian War Memorial. The service starts at 6.30 am, just after the Dawn Service (see Chapter 3) and takes place in front of the Aboriginal Memorial Plaque, a small commemorative plate installed by a White woman to commemorate Indigenous military service in 1988. Indigenous veterans have been using this space to commemorate their service since the early 2000s, and the service is organised by the Aboriginal and Torres Strait Islander Veterans and Services Association. It is thus independent from the Australian War Memorial, which nevertheless has been a sponsor since 2004. According to Brennan (2011: 42), the Memorial's endorsement of the service relieved it from 'the responsibility of incorporating Indigenous experience into its own commemorative role'.

I attended this service in 2017, and I described my experience in the Introduction of this book. After the Dawn Service, there was no announcement about the Aboriginal and Torres Strait Islander Commemorative Service and the Memorial's volunteers were oblivious to it. I found it just in time before it started. It was more informal than the Dawn Service, and there were just over 100 people attending, significantly less than the 38,000 people who attended the official Dawn Service just before. This intimacy created a space for resistance that I did not immediately recognise. At first, I felt outraged that there were so few participants, but then it became evident that this was a commemoration by Indigenous people primarily for Indigenous people. The service opened with a Welcome to Country, followed by the introduction of the representatives that were going to lead the service and speak. There was a special guest, Colonel Glenn King, a Maori officer of the New Zealand Army, a reminder of the shared experience and struggles between the Indigenous people of the two countries. After the commemoration of various service people, Lieutenant Colonel Chaplain Ivan Grant recited a prayer for Aboriginal and Torres Strait Islander servicemen and women, followed by the

Ode to Remembrance, which was accompanied by the sound of the didgeridoo, an iconic Indigenous musical instrument. At the end, all were invited to say 'we will remember them' – rather than 'lest we forget' as in the official Dawn Service.

One could argue that the Aboriginal and Torres Strait Islander Commemoration Service uncannily resembles the Dawn Service, with military authorities donning the uniform and addressing the crowd in a solemn tone to remember the soldiers who gave their lives for the country. One could even speak of the Anzacisation of Indigenous history to describe the tendency to see Indigenous history and practices as relevant only in relation to Anzac nationalism (Furniss 2001). But the exclusivity of the Aboriginal and Torres Strait Islander Commemoration Service, and its location and timing separate from the Dawn Service and other official nationalist sites of war commemoration underscore Indigenous distinctiveness and difference, countering the notion of assimilation. This is important because the erasure of difference between colonised and colonisers is a strategy of settler colonialism and assimilation (Strackosch and Maccoun 2012). The Aboriginal and Torres Strait Islander Commemoration Service evades that by maintaining a level of distinction as well as Indigenous ownership. Thus, instead of the Anzacisation of Indigenous history, one could speak instead of the attempt to 'indigenise Anzac Day', a term proposed by Beaumont (2018: 207) to identify the practice of 'combin[ing] traditional Western rituals [of war commemoration] with Indigenous cultural forms to produce a new fusion'.

The Aboriginal and Torres Strait Islander Commemoration Service has provided Indigenous veterans and their families with a platform to remember and honour the distinctive contributions of Indigenous individuals in times of war and service, without the expectation to conform to the conventional Anzac Legend. Central to this commemoration is the recognition of Indigenous people as survivors on a land that was forcibly taken from them. This event serves as an important avenue for acknowledging their experiences of survival and the natural location of the service on Mount Ainslie is particularly symbolic. The service took place away from the Australian War Memorial, a grandiose building that, as discussed in Chapter 2, was implicated in constructing the settler nation and excluding Indigenous people. There was no stage or altar that divided the attendees from the military authorities conducting the service, and there was only a small commemorative plaque mounted on a rock that I could not even see from where I was standing. Everything was down to

Figure 5.1 The Aboriginal and Torres Strait Islander Commemoration Service, Canberra, 2017. © the author.

earth. We assembled in an informal circle, with the commemorative plaque forming an integral part of the circular arrangement. We took position in an improvised and creative manner, finding spots to either sit or stand where suitable – whether it was a smooth rock, a comfortable spot or an area cleared of foliage and branches (see Figure 5.1). The land was the only authority, dictating where people could stand and sit. This resonated with one of the basic precepts of the Aboriginal worldview that 'the Land is the Law', meaning that political ordering emerges from land as it holds traces of ancestor beings (Graham 1999: 106; Brigg, Graham and Murphy 2019: 427). The natural location and the insignificant size of the plaque provided an invitation to consider that, for Indigenous people, the site of memory is the land that was stolen at the time of colonisation, as opposed to some man-made building or a monument, and that their survival was the subject of reverence and commemoration.

The March for the Frontier Wars

The third example of counter-memory is the march commemorating the Frontier Wars at the Australian War Memorial in Canberra led by the Indigenous activists of the Aboriginal Tent Embassy.[8] This march started in 2011 when a group of activists led by Aboriginal man Mick Thorpe joined the tail of the Anzac March in Canberra carrying banners in memory of the Frontier Wars. Thorpe wore the medals of his grandfather who fought and died in the Somme in 1918 and carried traditional Indigenous weapons to embody the two figures at the heart of Indigenous war commemoration, the modern soldier and the traditional warrior (Nicoll 2014: 279). The demonstration was met with resistance from marching veterans and was stopped by the police. The following year the activists of the Tent Embassy were asked to abstain from further demonstrations. However, they defied the request and continued to march year after year, advocating for their cause.

In 2017, I joined the activists commemorating the Frontier Wars. We were at the end of Anzac Parade, perfectly mirroring the structure of the Anzac March itself. Our leading banner read, 'Lest We Forget the Frontier Wars', accompanied by the emblematic Aboriginal and Torres Strait Islander flags and smaller banners that recounted the specific locations where Indigenous lives were tragically taken by the British colonisers (see Figure 5.2). With utmost discipline, we proceeded in a solemn manner, maintaining silence as we progressed.

Figure 5.2 Activists commemorating the Frontier Wars on Anzac Day, Canberra, 2017. © the author.

Our march continued until we reached a line of police officers barring our entry into the courtyard where different contingents were being introduced to the spectators. In the face of this obstacle, we remained composed, standing in silence while gripping our banners. Despite being unable to lay wreaths in alternative locations due to police intervention, we placed them before us as an act of commemoration. Throughout the demonstration, our conduct remained peaceful, even in the face of the authoritative police presence.

Despite the challenges and opposition, the presence of these activists and their unyielding commitment to their cause has earned a place of recognition within this commemorative event. While this march still encounters a line of police officers preventing activists from laying wreaths at the War Memorial (see Figure 5.3), it has gradually become an integral part of the Anzac Day March in Canberra, thus bringing the unrecognised colonial wars into the space of national war commemoration. Nicoll (2014: 279) suggests that this accomplishment has been made possible by the mimetic nature of this march. The activists mirror the aesthetics, ritual and rhythms of the Anzac March to commemorate the Frontier Wars and insert them in national war commemoration. Furthermore, when the activists were asked to not march anymore, their response emphasised that their action was not merely a protest but an act of war commemoration. They asserted that their participation aligned with the spirit of Anzac Day and thus should be embraced as a meaningful contribution to the event (Riseman 2017: 94). Thus, they have ingeniously woven colonial warfare into Anzac Day through a subtle form of camouflage.

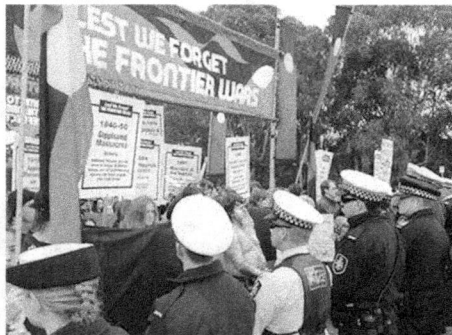

Figure 5.3 The Frontier War march meets a line of police, Australian War Memorial, 2016. Reproduced with permission from the author, Rebecca Horridge.

Notes

1. The caste or blood-quantum system differentiated Aboriginal people based on whether they had one White parent (half-caste) or two Aboriginal parents (full-blood). The system involved 'formal and extensive policies of "protection" aimed at isolating and segregating full-blood Aborigines on reserves and at restricting contact (and interbreeding) between them and outsiders, while attempting to assimilate half-castes, and especially their children' (Australian Law Reform Council 1986).
2. Since the time of British settlement, the National Library of Australia reports that governments have used no less than sixty-seven classifications, descriptions or definitions to determine who is an Aboriginal person.
3. Indeed, there are also prior examples of assimilation, such as the enlistment of selected Aboriginal individuals in the Native Police to promote their civilisation and entry into White society as discussed in Chapter 1 (see also Nettelbeck and Ryan 2018; Caso 2021).
4. At Federation, Indigenous Australians were not granted the right to vote. In 1949, the Electoral Act was amended to extend the federal vote to Aboriginal and Torres Strait Islander peoples who had served in the armed forces. In 1962, the Electoral Act was amended again to give all Aboriginal and Torres Strait Islander adults the right to vote in federal elections, although enrolling was not made compulsory like it was for settler Australians.
5. Prior to this, the constitution stipulated that laws regulating Aboriginal and Torres Strait Islander people fell under state legislation rather than the federal government.
6. Melbourne's war memorial.
7. Since 2006, Australia has launched a Reconciliation programme that invites organisations to develop reconciliation action plans, in-house strategies to advance reconciliation.
8. This is an institution that emerged in 1972 from the Aboriginal rights movement of the 1960s and 1970s to mediate land and civil rights for First Nations Peoples in Australia (Foley, Schaap and Howell 2014).

Conclusion: Settler Military Politics

Summary of Chapters

This book began with the question: does Indigenous inclusion in the military and national war commemoration signify the end of settler colonialism and a departure from Australia's colonial history? I have argued that Indigenous military inclusion is part of what I call *settler military politics*, that is, manoeuvres that mobilise military organisation, war history and war commemoration to advance settler colonialism and adapt it to the changing political environment. I have theorised militarisation as a governing practice and an intrinsic component of settler military politics. Consequently, my answer to the research question of this book is that Indigenous military inclusion is a practice of militarisation that ultimately advances settler military politics.

In Chapter 1, I mapped the origin of Australia's settler military politics to the early days of colonisation. The enduring narrative that the colonisation of Australia proceeded peacefully has contributed to the perception that the military was only a marginal actor in the process of colonisation. This must be understood as a key manifestation of settler military politics which today allows the military to be celebrated as an institution of reconciliation and inclusion of Indigenous people. Conversely to the belief that the military was a marginal actor of colonisation, I demonstrated that the British military was a key actor involved in the colonisation of Australia and the development of the settler colonial society. The military man was a prominent figure in early colonial society and had governing and administrative roles that imprinted colonial society. Military men were also engaged in colonial warfare against Indigenous populations, primarily through their roles in the Native Police. Despite the name, the Native Police was a paramilitary organisation comprising former soldiers and operated using military tactics. Colonial conflict is often dismissed as warfare because it did not mirror the European experience of two military parties meeting each other in battle. Nevertheless, a decolonised definition of war allows us to identify actors and actions of warfare even when they do not resemble those of the Western-centric experience. These include the Native Police and their tactics of selective inclusion of and reprisal against Aboriginal people. Consequently, a decolonial definition of war allows us to appreciate that the colonial conflict was a peculiar type of warfare that relied on tactics of repression and bursts of direct violence and confrontation between settlers and Indigenous people.

The definition of warfare that excludes the Frontier Wars of colonisation from the history of war in Australia is a function of settler military politics. As I discussed in Chapter 2, military warfare stands as a founding pillar of settler Australia, bolstered by the framework of war commemoration that marks the First World War as the birth of the nation. The development of national war commemoration after the First World War was a tactic to assert national independence from the imperial metropole without repudiating it. Through war commemoration, Australia cultivated a distinctive national identity, thus obviating the necessity for a transformative event akin to the American Revolution. This commemorative framework allowed the nation to forge its identity from an imperial war deed, while simultaneously asserting its independence from British colonial origins. The separation of the settler colony from the imperial metropole is a key step of settler colonial politics. This manoeuvre serves to establish the settler nation's autonomy, thereby facilitating the ongoing dispossession of Indigenous populations and the subsequent appropriation of their lands. In this respect, the development of Australian war commemoration was integral to advancing settler colonialism not only by bestowing the nation with a distinctive identity, but also by furnishing Australia with a fresh origin that diverged from the narrative of colonial history and its associated violence.

The commemoration of the First World War as Australia's birth of the nation created a breakthrough between colonial and modern Australia, effectively demoting the former to a distant era that holds no relevance to the latter. This strategic narrative shift established a clear division between the two epochs. In addition, it contributed to the consolidation of the perception that prior to the First World War Australia did not know war, thus erasing colonial warfare from the country's historiography. This act of erasure lies at the core of the settler state's legitimacy, and it was facilitated by the construction of war commemoration which strategically framed military warfare as the nation's genesis. I examined this as a deliberate process of militarisation aimed at governing Australia's historical narrative and shaping its collective identity.

The emerging official aesthetics of war commemoration was a key tactic of militarisation, integral to the consolidation of the settler nation. This aesthetics provided visual references and sites of memory where the nation could congregate and ceremonially engage in the ritualistic act of perpetuating settler national identity. I discussed how the Australian War Art Collection led the development of the Australian War Memorial and influenced Australia's perception of itself as a nation. In Chapter 3, I analysed the militarisation of Australian masculinity and its function in the settler project. Since before federation, Australia had been looking for a national image that could represent its identity as a mature nation. Aided by the emergence of war commemoration, the figure of the White male soldier took this role and became the icon of Australian nationhood. The figure of the Anzac soldier gave Australia militarised standing in the international community. On the domestic front, the figure of the Anzac soldier consolidated sentiments of White affinity with the land. War commemoration centred on the White Anzac soldier and celebrated the overseas exploits of White Australian men as symbols that validated their possession of the land, grounded in the notion that these individuals made the ultimate sacrifice and endured hardship to protect their homeland. What this narrative omitted and continues to omit, however, is that the Anzacs were imperial soldiers, primarily involved in war because Britain was.

In Chapter 3, I also considered the adaptability of the figure of the Anzac soldier, which was transformed after the collapse of the British Empire. As Britain proved unable to consider Australia's defence needs in the Second World War and its empire came to end, Australia re-articulated the image of the Anzac soldier as a victim of British incompetence and a suffering man in need of compassion and support. This representation suited a nation weary of conflict, especially as it became embroiled in the contentious Vietnam War and initiated conscription for the first time. It was also well-suited to portray the psychological damage of Vietnam veterans and the need to support their reintegration. The fall of the British Empire was also an occasion to reconsider the dominance of Whiteness, and

Australia embraced policies of multiculturalism that created space for the multicultural and the Indigenous soldiers as figures of national representation. As Australia embraced greater racial diversity, it paradoxically exhibited heightened intolerance towards anti-war discourse and activism. Anzac Day was embraced as Australia's unofficial national day to celebrate diversity and inclusion, qualities that Australia Day failed to endorse. During the 1980s, Indigenous activists protested Australia Day as a celebration of the invasion of their country. Conversely, Anzac Day enjoys protection through anti-demonstration ordinances and has evolved to encompass the contributions of ethnic and Indigenous communities within the Australian Defence Forces, thus offering fewer grounds for objection and protest. Within this framework, anti-war activism has been silenced, and communities striving for recognition have been compelled to engage with Anzac Day and Australia's military history.

This scenario mirrors the experience of Indigenous activists seeking recognition of the Frontier Wars and colonial violence. Starting from the early 2010s, these activists began leveraging the Anzac Day commemoration to spotlight the Frontier Wars. Their efforts initially encountered opposition from both veterans and law enforcement, yet they persisted and adeptly evolved their approach to engage more closely with the nation's war commemoration. Particularly noteworthy is their adoption of the official commemorative aesthetics, rituals and rhythms, all the while asserting that their actions are not protests, but rather solemn acts of remembrance that fit and should be included in official national commemoration. They toned down their contestation to pursue inclusion, thus raising concerns that this strategy may make colonial conflict relevant only insofar as it fits Anzac narratives and rituals.

Chapter 4 analysed the role of women in settler military politics by looking at their inclusion in the Australian Defence Forces and in national war commemoration. Women were notably excluded from active service in the First World War and consequently from the emerging nationalist commemoration of war. However, the Second World War represented a historical shift when women entered the Australian civic pantheon through their war service. In the Second World War, the icon of the woman at war was the female factory worker. This representation also had another function, namely, to govern femininity at a time when the entry of women into the workforce and war posed a challenge to the established gender order. In fact, the entry of women into the war industry and military echelons engendered social anxieties centred around concerns about women forsaking traditional femininity, engaging in promiscuity and encroaching on male domains. The representation of women in war commemoration served to manage these social anxieties as well as to give Australian women a model of femininity at war. Additionally, the representation of the female worker in national war commemoration served to reiterate the Whiteness of the nation at a time when Australia experimented with Indigenous-only battalions and around 4,000 Indigenous people served in the Australian Defence Forces. The inclusion of White women in national war commemoration presented Australia as progressive, while simultaneously maintaining its image as a White nation.

Chapter 5 dealt with the history of exclusion and assimilation of Indigenous people in the military and war commemoration. Indigenous people were officially barred from military service until 1951, when the racist ban was lifted. Regardless of the ban, some 1,000 men served in the First World War and around 4,000 men and women served in the Second World War. They managed to serve either by disguising their identity or because they were needed to meet the war's needs. They used their service to advance their status in settler society and to campaign for equal rights, but upon their return from war they still encountered the enduring scourge of racism. Those who served prior to 1951 were predominantly so-called "half-castes", a racist term to identify Aboriginal people with one White parent. In Australia, the caste system was designed to eradicate Indigenous people by means of miscegenation and assimilation of so-called "half-caste" individuals who were not considered Aboriginal and therefore deemed to be eligible to assimilate into society. Today, Australia no longer has a caste system and Indigenous service is integrated in the Australian Defence Forces and included in national war commemoration. Indigenous military service is narrated with pride and as part of the narrative of postcolonial reconciliation. What is omitted, however, is that settler intuitions used Indigenous service to promote assimilation as I described in Chapter 5.

Furthermore, there remains a tension between how Indigenous service is included in national war commemoration and how Indigenous veterans and communities see their military service to the nation. The latter see military service in modern Australia as the continuation of their colonial history, as well as an opportunity to speak about colonial violence and the legacies of colonisation that still negatively affect communities. Conversely, settler institutions have operated a clear distinction between the modern indigenous soldier who fights for modern Australia and the anti-colonial warrior who fought against the colonisers. This separation is in operation because while the modern Indigenous soldier is a point of pride and national reconciliation, the colonial warrior is seen as divisive and a challenge to the narrative of reconciliation. Nevertheless, there cannot be reconciliation without full acknowledgement of history.

Overall, I demonstrated how Australia's management of its settler identity and history has been deeply intertwined with its military heritage and war stories, and how the country has adopted a deliberate and curated version of Indigenous military history. Notably, the government embraced the Indigenous soldier as a way of dealing with the challenge to settler legitimacy posed by the emerging research on colonial warfare as well as from activism around Indigenous sovereignty rights. As I discussed in Chapter 5, Indigenous military service has been used to demonstrate the history of unity and commonalities between settlers and Indigenous people. This version serves as a strategic tool of settler colonial governance, aiming to navigate the rising societal calls for decolonisation and heightened public consciousness regarding colonial atrocities.

The Settler Martial State

The settler state has proven to be extremely resilient and adaptable. Because war is at the very heart of the settler state, military politics play a significant role in facilitating transformation. Colonial warfare is the unsung pillar of modern Australia, covered by the veneer of modern warfare. Without the blood spilled in colonial conflict, there would be no modern Australia. And yet, colonial warfare has remained in the shadows, strategically forgotten, unspoken and denied, to maintain the legitimacy of the settler state. The British settlers did not declare war against Indigenous people due to their perception of the latter as inferior and to expedite their acquisition of the land. The fact that there was no war declaration, however, does not mean that the war did not happen. Historical records testify to the conflict, the existence of war tactics and, above all, the mutual perception of warfare by both parties involved (see Chapter 1). The centrality of an undeclared war as a pillar of Australia meant that the settlers had to invest significant amounts of energy to cover it up and uphold the legitimacy of colonial possession. Inevitably, this beginning coupled with the history of colonial subordination to Britain led to an anxious type of nationalism and a quest for a solid national identity.

The opportunity came with the First World War, which gave Australia a respectable myth of origin infused with military hero-ism. The war was remarkable for Australians because, although they were imperial soldiers, they fought as nationals for the first time. Consequently, it was portrayed as the birth of modern Australia, an idea that persists to this day. The First World War held significance not solely in reinforcing a national identity, but also in address-ing the colonial legacy. In essence, it was positioned as a deliber-ate deviation from the colonial history. The bookmarking of the First World War as the birth of the nation elevated the White nation and the deeds of White men. In fact, people of colour were offi-cially excluded from enlisting and fighting for Australia. This racial exclusion is important to note because it sanctioned citizenship as a White privilege. Although most of the colonisers were of British descent, imperialism, militarism and the gold mines brought men of different racial backgrounds to the Australian colonies. Together with Indigenous people, these migrant workers were hierarchically ordered according to racist ideology, but they were nonetheless part of the colonial society. When the colonies federated, Australia wanted to assert its Whiteness to uphold its civilisational status, and the exclusion of men of colour from the military ranks was integral part of this strategy.

Fast-forward to today, and Australia has been retrieving the his-tory of the men and women of colour who served despite the ban. While I touched upon the ethnic soldier in Chapter 3, I focused primarily on the Indigenous soldier. Today ethnic, but above all, Indigenous soldiers are celebrated as a symbol of post-colonialism and multiculturalism. They stand as a demonstration that people of colour also make valuable contributions to the nation through their military service. In a country where war is considered to be the birth of the nation and the soldier is seen as the epitome of Australian identity, the prospect of becoming a soldier equates to the chance of becoming part of the national fabric. Nevertheless, the key question remains, 'what nation do they belong to?' They come to belong to the settler nation and their service goes to legitimate the settler state and authority.

Amid the present global rise of Indigenous voices, Australian set-tler power structures are acutely aware of the "Indigenous issue" and the challenge that Aboriginal resistance poses to the legitimacy of the

state. To address this insecurity, efforts have been made to incorporate Indigenous perspectives and people and advance multiculturalism within Australian institutions. It is within this context that the
celebration of the Aboriginal soldier acquires salience, as this figure
demonstrates the legitimacy of the settler state. For the settler state,
the Indigenous soldier is a token of legitimacy that demonstrates
Indigenous people's inclusion, acceptance and loyalty to the settler
state. The Indigenous soldier also serves to dispel the idea that, in
Australia, there are multiple nations competing for legitimacy.

The history and commemoration of ethnic and Indigenous soldiers under the banner of multiculturalism and reconciliation is
part of the settler military politics. Their inclusion can be seen as
symbolic, aiming to showcase Australia's status as postcolonial and
post-racial. Additionally, this approach underscores the significance
of contemporary military history as a fundamental component of
the path towards multiculturalism and reconciliation. Nevertheless,
their inclusion also contributes to emphasising modern military history as the defining of modern Australia, while overshadowing colonial conflict. This is particularly evident in the fact that while ethnic
and Indigenous soldiers find a place in national war commemoration, colonial warfare remains excluded. In late September 2022,
the chair of the Australian War Memorial Council, Brendan Nelson,
declared that the Memorial would incorporate the Frontier Wars as
part of the A$550 million redevelopment project that will end in
2028. However, Nelson has since left his position to take a job with
Boeing, a US defence, space and security contractor, and the Memorial has failed to clarify its position on the issue. It remains unclear if
a gallery will be added to represent the Frontier Wars, or if there will
merely be material on the topic in the archival spaces.

Indigenous Soldiers and the Carceral System

There is an aspect of settler military politics that this book touched
upon only lightly, namely, the militarisation of Indigenous people in
relation to the carceral system. The connection between the carceral
system and Indigenous military service became evident to me when
I met an Aboriginal man, former military veteran, who told me that
for him, the military was a wise choice because it helped him to stay
out of prison at a time when he was often in trouble, also because
of racism and racial injustice. He used to be bullied in school and so
he often skipped it and joined his friends. He liked learning but did

not like being in school. Without much direction, he engaged in petty crime and often crossed paths with the police under less than amicable circumstances. Enlisting was a way of finding direction, learning and steering clear of trouble. He also expressed the view that the military provided him with a passport to explore the world, secure a steady income and cultivate a professional path. His words reverberated in my mind, and I could not help but ponder the constraints on his opportunities. Becoming a soldier was a decision rooted in seeking safety and opportunities in a country that systematically denies them to Aboriginal people. Furthermore, in a country where Aboriginal people die at the hands of the police, his was a choice for survival.

This Aboriginal man's story came back to me when I was researching Indigenous military recruitment and retention programmes. Under the Defence Reconciliation Action Plan, the Defence Department can wave criminal records of Indigenous individuals to facilitate their recruitment (Riseman and Trembath 2016: 149). Interestingly, Defence Force units that have large numbers of Indigenous people such as NORFORCE, recruit from the Northern Territory, a region with rates of Indigenous incarceration that Horton (2022) defines 'hyperincarceration'. More research is warranted on the link between Indigenous recruitment and the carceral system, but here there is an indication that Indigenous military service is used as an alternative to the prison system to manage recalcitrant Indigenous individuals. Both the military and the prison system are disciplinary institutions. The prison system has been a key settler institution to deal with Aboriginal resistance, working not as a place of reformation but of disappearance (Watego 2021). Conversely, the military is a place of reformation where Indigenous people can gain a wage and status within the system, as long as they conform to it. In a country where the police represent the spectre of the carceral system that induces in Indigenous people a permanent state of fear of disappearing in their own country, the allure of the military and its accompanying conformity become increasingly appealing.

Against this background, Indigenous military service is presented as an alternative to the carceral system where Indigenous people can thrive within settler colonial institutions. This is further supported by the fact that, as discussed in Chapter 5 (see also Caso 2023), for the government Indigenous military employment is an instrument to address Indigenous disadvantage more than a military strategy. In line with the critique of *Closing the Gap* (for example, M. Davis 2015; Maddison 2019a), Indigenous military employment is another tool to discipline Indigenous people in settler obedience and promote identification with the prospects of wealth and wellbeing as measured by the settler state.

If Not Decolonisation, Then What?

The conclusion of this book that Indigenous military service and inclusion in war commemoration are entwined with settler colonial logics should not be misconstrued as suggesting that contestation and resistance are not happening or working. Maddison (2019b: 183) comments that:

> Efforts by the settler state to create policy that appears benevolent in fact offer no path towards decolonisation as they remain caught in the settler's eliminatory logic.

This applies to Indigenous military inclusion. However, Indigenous people have seized inclusion to produce Indigenous resistance and disturb the settler colonial imaginaries of reconciliation. Strakosch and Macoun (2012) contend that settler colonial states appeal to reconciliation to assert that colonial injustices have been relegated to the past. This act of absolution becomes imperative to uphold the legitimacy of settler authority and to resolve the colonial conflict in favour of the settler state. Thus, instead of looking back to address the past, the settler state erases the past to focus on an imaginary future.

As I discussed in Chapter 5, Indigenous people have resisted settler reconciliation that looks forward without looking back, and have asserted their different experience of war and history of conflict that includes colonial warfare. I discussed how Indigenous artists have camouflaged the Frontier Wars in the space of the Australian War Memorial, Indigenous veterans commemorate their unique experience of war and survival, and activists stage their commemoration of the Frontier Wars on Anzac Day. These acts do not lead to decolonisation understood as a process that reverses colonisation and colonial power relations. But they are not inconsequential. Although they will not return the land to Indigenous people, they have created an unprecedented space for truth-telling, remembering, and contestation of settler narratives and strategies of dispossession. Notably, these three acts align with the Uluru Statement from the Heart which articulates the demands of First Nations Australians to the settler state to improve Indigenous–settler relations. The Uluru Statement demands acknowledgement of the colonial history of violence and its legacy, and to some degree, settler institutions and society have accepted the Indigenous counter-memory of war. This gets Australia one step closer to truth and acknowledgement of the brutal colonial history and the ongoing violence of the settler state.

Following Maddison (2019b), I find that Indigenous counter-memory creates an agonistic democratic space. This is a symbolic space where citizens can engage in dialogue and contestation without destroying the bonds of the political community. Maddison contends that agonism is necessary to 'move away from the settler desire for the "completion" of the colonial project' and create a space for national introspection and self-reflection (p. 190). While settler colonialism cannot be undone, reconciliation can be instituted as an open-ended process of democratic dialogue that counteracts the settler colonial desire for completion. Counter-memory leaves the process of reconciliation open for dialogue and for contested versions of histories to exist and represent different experiences.

Despite the dangers of assimilation, dismissal and militarised recognition, Indigenous activists, veterans and their families have engaged with Australia's official aesthetics of war commemoration, fully cognizant of its influential role in shaping the national identity. Their interventions have created unprecedented space to change the power relations and affirm Indigenous sovereignty. To the extent that Indigenous people have linked the modern soldier to the traditional warrior, the commemoration of Indigenous service does more than recognise Indigenous people as Australian citizens premised on their contribution to the country's security and defence. It acknowledges the historical presence, contribution and tradition of First Nations people and empowers them to tell the full story of how they came to be an embattled people in their own country.

There are also projects of truth-telling that are developing outside and independently of Anzac nationalist commemoration and its institutions. A notable example is the podcast series by Kooma, Murawarii and Gamilaraay man and activist Boe Spearim titled *Frontier War Stories*. In this podcast, Spearim interviews researchers and activists to retrieve the details of the Frontier Wars. Here, colonial warfare is dealt with in its own terms rather than in relation with Anzac Day, thus avoiding the Anzacification of Indigenous history. Another example of Frontier Wars commemoration independent from Anzac is Dundalli Remembrance Day. Since 2019, the activists of the Brisbane Aboriginal Tent Embassy and the

Warriors of the Aboriginal Resistance have been organising a com-memorative event in honour of Dundalli, a Dalla man from the Blackall Ranges who led the resistance against the British settlers. The commemoration happens at Brisbane's Post Office Square, the site where Dundalli was hanged in 1855 in a public execution. In January 2023, the Queensland government announced in a media statement the official recognition of Dundalli Remembrance Day as an act of truth-telling.

There is certainly a power imbalance between the Anzac nationalist commemoration and the Aboriginal and Torres Strait Islander commemoration of the Frontier Wars – a power imbalance that lies at the heart of the Australian settler colonial state and society more broadly. It would be hard to make the argument, for example, that the Queensland government's act of recognition of Dundalli Remembrance Day or the prospect of the Memorial acknowledging the Frontier Wars in its gallery represent a mutual and equal recognition of Indigenous experiences of war on a par with Anzac Day. However, these small victories are significant for Indigenous communities as they actively reshape the settler colonial state and society. By unearthing and sharing histories from diverse viewpoints, they empower Indigenous individuals to narrate and record their own stories, leading to resurgence.

BIBLIOGRAPHY

Adair, Daryl, John Nauright and Murray Phillips. 1998. 'Playing Fields Throughout to Battle Fields: The Development of Australian Sporting Manhood in Its Imperial Context, c.1850–1918', in *Australian Masculinities: Men and Their Histories*, eds Clive Moore and Kay Saunders, 51–67. Brisbane: Queensland University Press.

Adam-Smith, Patsy. 1984. *Australian Women at War*. Melbourne: Thomas Nelson.

Addis, Elizabetta. 1994. 'Women and the Economic Consequences of Being a Soldier', in *Women Soldiers: Images and Realities*, eds Elizabetta Addis, Valeria Russo and Lorenza Sebesta. London: Macmillan.

Åhäll, Linda. 2015. *Sexing War/Policing Gender: Motherhood, Myth and Women's Political Violence*. Abingdon: Routledge.

Åhäll, Linda. 2016. 'The Dance of Militarisation: A Feminist Security Studies Take on the Political', *Critical Studies on Security* 4(2): 154–68.

Anderson, Benedict. 1983. *Imagined Communities: Reflections on the Origin and Spread of Nationalism*, rev. edn. Verso: New York.

Anderson, David M. and David Killingray. 2017. 'Consent, Coercion and Colonial Control: Policing the Empire, 1830–1940', in *Policing the Empire: Government, Authority and Control, 1830–1940*, eds David M. Anderson and David Killingray, 2nd edn, 1–15. Manchester: Manchester University Press.

Ashplant, T. G., Graham Dawson and Michael Roper. 2000. 'The Politics of War Memory and Commemoration Contexts, Structures and Dynamics', in *The Politics of War Memory and Commemoration*, eds T.G. Ashplant, Graham Dawson and Michael Roper, 3–85. London: Routledge.

Australian Government. (2013). *Closing the Gap, Prime Minister's Report 2013*, available at: http://www.dpmc.gov.au/publications/docs/closing_the_gap_2014.pdf.

Australian Law Reform Council. 1986. 'Recognition of Aboriginal Customary Laws (ALRC Report 31)', *Australian Law Reform Council Report 31.* Canberra, available at: https://www.alrc.gov.au/wp-content/uploads/2019/08/ALRC31.pdf.

AWM. 2014. 'Will the Australian War Memorial Tell the Story of Colonial Conflicts?' Australian War Memorial, available at: https://www.awm.gov.au/media/press-releases/will-australian-war-memorial-tell-story-colonial-conflicts.

Bailey, Matthew and Sean Brawley. 2018. 'Why Weren't We Taught? Exploring Frontier Conflict through the Lens of Anzac', *Journal of Australian Studies* 42(1): 19–33.

Baker, Catherine. 2020. 'Making War on Bodies: Militarisation, Aesthetics and Embodiement in International Politics', in *Making War on Bodies: Militarization, Aesthetics and Embodiment in International Politics,* ed. Catherine Baker, 1–30. Edinburgh: Edinburgh University Press.

Barkawi, Tarak. 2016. 'Decolonising War', *European Journal of International Security* 1(2): 199–214.

Barkawi, Tarak. 2017. *Soldiers of Empire: Indian and British Armies in World War II.* Cambridge: Cambridge University Press.

Barkawi, Tarak and Shane Brighton. 2011. 'Powers of War: Fighting, Knowledge, and Critique', *International Political Sociology* 5(2): 126–43.

Basham, Victoria M. 2016. 'Raising an Army: The Geopolitics of Militarizing the Lives of Working-Class Boys in an Age of Austerity', International Political Sociology 10(3): 258–74.

Basham, Victoria M., Aaron Belkin and Jess Gifkins. 2015. 'What Is Critical Military Studies?' *Critical Military Studies* 1(1): 1–2.

Basham, Victoria M. and Sarah Bulmer. 2017. 'Critical Military Studies as Method: An Approach to Studying Gender and the Military', in *The Palgrave International Handbook of Gender and the Military,* eds Rachel Woodward and Claire Duncanson, 59–71. London: Palgrave Macmillan.

Bassett, Jan. 1998. *As We Wave You Goodbye: Australian Women and War.* Oxford: Oxford University Press.

Bean, Charles E. W. 1948. *Anzac to Amiens: A Shorter History of the Australian Fighting Services in the First World War.* Canberra: Australian War Memorial

Beaumont, Joan. 1990. 'The Anzac Legend', in *The Myths We Live By,* eds Alistair Thomson and Raphael Samuel, 73–82. London, New York: Routledge.

Beaumont, Joan. 1995. 'Australia's War', in *Australia's War 1914–18,* ed. Joan Beaumont, 1–34. London: Routledge.

Beaumont, Joan. 2000. 'Whatever Happened to Patriotic Women, 1914–1918?' *Australian Historical Studies* 31(115): 273–86.

Beaumont, Joan. 2013. *Broken Nation: Australians in the Great War.* Sydney: Allen & Unwin.

Beaumont, Joan. 2014. 'Remembering the Heroes of Australia's Wars: From Heroic to Post-Heroic Memory', in *Heroism and the Changing Character of War Toward Post-Heroic Warfare?*, ed. Sybille Scheipers, 334–48. London: Palgrave Macmillan.

Beaumont, Joan. 2018. 'Commemoration', in *Serving Our Country: Indigenous Australians, War, Defence and Citizenship*, eds Joan Beaumont and Allison Cadzow, 324–45. Sydney: NewSouth Publishing.

Beaumont, Joan and Allison Cadzow (eds). 2018. *Serving Our Country: Indigenous Australians, War, Defence, and Citizenship.* Sydney: NewSouth Publishing.

Beaumont, Joan and Tristan Moss. 2018. 'Australian Military Forces in the Second World War', in *Serving Our Country: Indigenous Australians, War, Defence and Citizenship*, eds Joan Beaumont and Allison Cadzow, 94–105. Sydney: NewSouth Publishing.

Bell, Duncan (ed.). 2006. *Trauma, Memory, and World Politics: Reflections on the Relationship between Past and Present.* New York: Palgrave Macmillan.

Bell, Duncan. 2020. *Dreamworlds of Race: Empire and the Utopian Destiny of Anglo-America.* Princeton: Princeton University Press.

Berlant, Lauren. 2004. 'Introduction: Compassion (and Withholding)', in *Compassion: The Culture and Politics of an Emotion*, ed. Lauren Berlant. New York: Routledge.

Bernazzoli, Richelle M. and Colin Flint. 2009. 'From Militarization to Securitization: Finding a Concept that Works', *Political Geography* 28(8): 449–50.

Best, Geoffrey. 1989. 'The Militarization of European Society: 1870–1914', in *The Militarization of the Western World*, ed. John Gillis, 13–29. New Brunswick, NJ: Rutgers University Press.

Birch, Tony. 1995. 'A Mabo Blood Test?' *Australian Journal of Anthropology* 6(1): 32–42.

Birch, Tony. 1997. '"Black Armbands and White Veils": John Howard's Moral Amnesia', *Melbourne Historical Journal* 25(1): 8–16.

Birch, Tony. 2021. *Dark as Last Night.* Brisbane: University of Queensland Press.

Blackwell, James and Julie Ballangarry. 2022. 'Indigenous Foreign Policy: A New Way Forward?' *Australian Feminist Foreign Policy Coalition*, available at: https://iwda.org.au/assets/files/AFFPC-issues-paper-Indigenous-Foreign-Policy-Blackwell-Ballangarry-FINAL.pdf.

Bleiker, Roland. 2015. 'Pluralist Methods for Visual Global Politics', *Millennium: Journal of International Studies* 43(3): 872–90.

Bleiker, Roland. 2018. 'Mapping Visual Global Politics', in *Visual Global Politics*, ed. Roland Bleiker, 1–29. London: Routledge.

Bomford, Janette. 2001. *Soldiers of the Queen: Women in the Australian Army*. Oxford: Oxford University Press.

Bongiorno, Frank. 2014. 'Anzac and the Politics of Inclusion', in *Nation, Memory and Great War Commemoration*, eds Shanti Sumartojo and Ben Wellings, 81–97. Oxford: Peter Lang.

Bongiorno, Frank. 2017. 'A Century of Bipartisan Commemoration: Is Anzac Politically Inevitable?' in *The Honest History Book*, eds David H. Stephens and Alison Broinowski, 106–19. Sydney: New-South Publishing.

Booth, Ken. 1991. 'Security and Emancipation', *Review of International Studies* 17: 313–26.

Brandon, Laura. 2007. *Art and War*. London: I. B. Tauris.

Brennan, Anne. 2011. 'Lest We Forget: Military Myths, Memory, and Canberra's Aboriginal and Torres Strait Islander Memorial', *Memory Connection* 1(1): 35–44.

Brigg, Morgan, Mary Graham and Lyndon Murphy. 2019. 'Toward the Dialogical Study of Politics: Hunting at the Fringes of Australian Political Science', *Australian Journal of Political Science* 54(3): 423–37.

Brigg, Morgan, Mary Graham and Martin Weber. 2021. 'Relational Indigenous Systems: Aboriginal Australian Political Ordering and Reconfiguring IR', *Review of International Studies*, 48(5): 1–19.

Bromfield, Nicholas. 2017. 'Welcome Home: Reconciliation, Vietnam Veterans, and Anzac during the Hawke Government', *Australian Journal of Political Science* 52(2): 288–302.

Broome, Richard. 1988. 'The Struggle for Australia: Aboriginal–European Warfare 1770–1930', in *Australia: Two Centuries of War and Peace*, eds M. McKernan and M. Browne, 92–120. Canberra: Australian War Memorial.

Broome, Richard. 2010. *Aboriginal Australians: A History Since 1788*, 4th edn. Crows Nest: Allen & Unwin.

Bulmer, Sarah. 2013. 'Patriarchal Confusion?' *International Feminist Journal of Politics* 15(2): 137–56.

Burke, Kelly. 2023. 'Australian War Memorial Funding Dwarfed that of Other Cultural Institutions in Coalition's Final Years', *The Guardian*, 30 March, available at: https://www.theguardian.com/culture/2023/mar/30/australian-war-memorial-funding-dwarfed-that-of-other-cultural-institutions-in-coalitions-final-years?CMP=Share_iOSApp_Other.

Butler, Rex. 2017. 'Ben Quilty: The Fog of War', *Intellectual History Review* 27(3): 433–51.

Buzan, Barry, Ole Wæver and Jaap de Wilde. 1998. *Security: A Framework for Analysis*. Boulder, CO: Lynne Rienner.

Cadzow, Allison. 2019. 'Servicewomen', in *Serving Our Country: Indigenous Australians, War, Defence and Citizenship*, eds Joan Beaumont and Allison Cadzow, 239–60. Sydney: NewSouth Publishing

Cadzow, Allison and Mary Anne Jebb, eds. 2019. *Our Mob Served: Aboriginal and Torres Strait Islander Histories of War and Defending Australia*. Canberra: Aboriginal Studies Press.

Callahan, William A. 2020. *Sensible Politics: Visualizing International Relations*. Oxford: Oxford University Press.

Camacho, Keith L. ed. 2011. *Cultures of Commemoration: The Politics of War, Memory, and History in the Mariana Islands*. Honolulu: University of Hawai'i Press.

Carey, Jane. 2009. '"Women's Objective – A Perfect Race": Whiteness, Eugenics, and the Articulation of Race', in *Re-Orienting Whiteness: Transnational Perspectives on the History of an Identity*, eds L. Boucher, J. Carey and K. Ellinghaus, 183–98. New York: Palgrave Macmillan

Carey, Jane. 2011. '"Wanted! A Real White Australia": The Women's Movement, Whiteness and the Settler Colonial Project, 1900–1940', in *Studies in Settler Colonialism: Politics, Identity and Culture*, eds F. Bateman and L. Pilkington, 122–39. London: Palgrave Macmillan.

Carey, Jane and Claire McLisky. 2009. *Creating White Australia*, eds Jane Carey and Claire McLisky. Sydney: Sydney University Press

Carey, Jane and Ben Silverstein. 2020. 'Thinking With and Beyond Settler Colonial Studies: New Histories after the Postcolonial', *Postcolonial Studies* 23(1): 1–20.

Carruthers, Susan L. 2011. *The Media at War*, 2nd edn. Houndmills: Palgrave Macmillan.

Carter, Paul. 1987. *The Road to Botany Bay: An Exploration of Landscape and History*. London: Faber & Faber.

Caso, Federica. 2020. 'The Political Aesthetics of the Body of the Soldier in Pain', in *Making War on Bodies: Militarisation, Aesthetics and Embodiment in International Politics*, ed. Catherine Baker. Edinburgh: Edinburgh University Press.

Caso, Federica. 2021. 'Settler Military Politics: On the Inclusion and Recognition of Indigenous People in the Military', *International Political Sociology* 16(1): 1–20.

Caso, Federica. 2023. 'Indigenous Military Inclusion: A Settler Colonial Critique of the Regional Force Surveillance Units', *Australian Journal of Politics and History* 69(3): 542–60.

Chisholm, Amanda. 2022. *The Gendered and Colonial Lives of Gurkhas in Private Security: From Military to Market*. Edinburgh: Edinburgh University Press.

Chisholm, Amanda and Hanna Ketola. 2020. 'The Cruel Optimism of Militarism: Feminist Curiosity, Affect, and Global Security', *International Political Sociology* 14(3): 270–85.

Clark, Chris. 2019. 'Protecting Country: Indigenous Australians in the Defence of the North', *ASPI: The Strategist*, 29 March, available at: https://www.aspistrategist.org.au/protecting-country-indigenous-australians-in-the-defence-of-the-north.

Cochrane, Kathie. 1994. *Oodgeroo*. Brisbane: University of Queensland Press.

Cochrane, Peter. 2018. *Best We Forget: The War for White Australia, 1914–18*. Melbourne: Text Publishing.

Collins, Carolyn. 2021. *Save Our Sons: Women, Dissent and Conscription during the Vietnam War*. Melbourne: Monash University Publishing.

Connell, R. W. 2005. *Masculinities*, 2nd edn. London: Routledge.

Connor, John. 2016. 'Anzac Day and National Identity', in *Anzac Day: Then & Now*, ed. Tom Frame, 112–23. Sydney: University of New South Wales Press.

Connor, John. 2002. *The Australian Frontier Wars 1788–1838*. 2nd edn. Sydney: University of New South Wales Press.

Conversi, Daniele. 2008. '"We Are All Equals!" Militarism, Homogenization and "Egalitarianism" in Nationalist State-Building (1789–1945)', *Ethnic & Racial Studies* 31(7): 1286–314.

Coulthard, Glen Sean. 2014. *Red Skin, White Masks: Rejecting the Colonial Politics of Recognition*. Minneapolis: University of Minnesota.

Cowen, Deborah E. and Emily Gilbert. 2008. 'Citizenship in the "Homeland": Families at War', in *War, Citizenship, Territory*, eds Deborah E. Cowen and Emily Gilbert. New York: Routledge.

Crenshaw, Kimberle. 1991. 'Mapping the Margins: Intersectionality, Identity Politics, and Violence against Women of Color', *Stanford Law Review* 43(6): 1241.

Curran, James and Stuart Ward. 2010. *The Unknown Nation: Australia after Empire*. Melbourne: Melbourne University Press.

Curthoys, Ann. 1995. '"Shut Up, You Bourgeois Bitch": Sexual Identity and Political Action in the Anti-Vietnam War Movement', in *Gender and War: Australians at War in the Twentieth Century*, eds Joy Damousi and Marilyn Lake, 311–41. Cambridge: Cambridge University Press.

Curthoys, Ann. 1999. 'Expulsion, Exodus and Exile in White Australian Historical Mythology', *Journal of Australian Studies* 23: 1–19.

Curthoys, Ann. 2009. 'White, British, and European: Historicising Identity in Settler Societies', in *Creating White Australia*, eds Jane Carey and Claire McLisky, 3–24. Sydney: Sydney University Press.

Damousi, Joy. 1995. 'Socialist Women and Gendered Space: Anti-Conscription and Anti-War Campaigns 1914–1918', in *Gender and War: Australians at War in the Twentieth Century*, eds Joy Damousi and Marilyn Lake, 254–73. Cambridge: Cambridge University Press.

Damousi, Joy. 2008. 'War and Commemoration: "The Responsibility of Empire"', in *Australia's Empire*, eds Deryck Schreuder and Stuart Ward, 288–311. Oxford: Oxford University Press.

Dauphinee, Elizabeth. 2007. 'The Politics of the Body in Pain: Reading the Ethics of Imagery', *Security Dialogue* 38(2): 139–55.

Davies, Susanne. 1996. 'Women, War, and the Violence of History: An Australian Perspective', *Violence Against Women* 2(4): 359–77.

Davis, Alexander E. 2021. 'Making a Settler Colonial IR: Imagining the "International" in Early Australian International Relations', *Review of International Studies* 47(5): 637–55.

Davis, Megan. 2015. 'Closing the Gap in Indigenous Disadvantage: Trajectory of Indigenous Inequity in Australia', *Journal of International Affairs* 16(1): 34–44

Davis, Megan. 2016. 'Scant Recognition: Have Aboriginal and Torres Strait Islander Peoples Any Reason to Hope?' *ABC Religion & Ethics*, available at: https://www.abc.net.au/religion/scant-recognition-have-aboriginal-and-torres-strait-islander-peo/10096670.

Davis, Megan and Marcia Langton. 2016. 'Introduction', *It's Our Country: Indigenous Arguments for Meaningful Constitutional Recognition and Reform*, eds Megan Davies and Marcia Langton. Melbourne: Melbourne University Press.

Defence News. 2022. '80th Anniversary of Indigenous Unit Commemorated', available at: https://news.defence.gov.au/media/media-releases/80th-anniversary-indigenous-unit-commemorated.

Dennis, Peter, Jeffrey Grey, Ewan Morris, Robin Prior and Jean Bou. 2009. *The Oxford Companion to Australian Military History*, 2nd edn. Melbourne: Oxford University Press.

Department of Defence. 2020. 'Defence Census Workforce Compositional Change: 1991–2019', available at: https://www.defence.gov.au/about/information-disclosures/census.

Department of Veterans Affairs (DVA). 2019. 'The Fairlea Five'. *DVA, Anzac Portal*, available at: https://anzacportal.dva.gov.au/wars-and-missions/vietnam-war-1962-1975/events/conscription/save-our-sons/fairlea-five.

Department of Veterans Affairs (DVA). 2022. 'Female Veterans & Veterans' Families: Policy Forum'. Canberra.

Der Derian, James. 2009. *Virtuous War: Mapping the Military–Industrial–Media–Entertainment Network*, 2nd edn. Abingdon: Routledge.

Dodson, Patrick. 2007. 'Whatever Happened to Reconciliation?' *Coercive Reconciliation: Stabilise, Normalise, Exit Aboriginal Australia*, eds Jon Altman and Melinda Hinkson, 21–30. North Carlton: Arena Publications Association.

Donoghue, Jed and Bruce Tranter. 2015. 'The Anzacs: Military Influences on Australian Identity', *Journal of Sociology* 51(3): 449–63.

Dowler, Lorraine. 2012. 'Gender, Militarization and Sovereignty', *Geography Compass* 6(8): 490–9.

Drake, Michael S. 2002. *The Problematic of Military Power: Government, Discipline and the Subject of Violence*. Ilford: Frank Class.

Drozdzewski, Danielle. 2016. 'Does Anzac Sit Comfortably within Australia's Multiculturalism?' *Australian Geographer* 47(1): 3–10.

Du Bois, W. E. B. 1925. 'Worlds of Color', *Foreign Affairs* 3(3): 423–44.

Due, Clemence. 2008. '"Lest We Forget": Creating an Australian National Identity from Memories of War', *Melbourne Historical Journal* 4(1): 23–39.

Eastwood, James. 2018. 'Rethinking Militarism as Ideology: The Critique of Violence after Security', *Security Dialogue* 49(1/2): 44–56.

Edkins, Jenny. 2003. *Trauma and the Memory of Politics*. Cambridge: Cambridge University Press.

Eichler, Maya. 2013. 'Women and Combat in Canada: Continuing Tensions between "Difference" and "Equality"', *Critical Studies on Security* 1(2): 257–9.

Elder, Catriona. 2005. '"I Spit on Your Stone": National Identity, Women Against Rape and the Cult of Anzac in Australia', in *Women, Activism and Social Change*, ed. Maja Mikula, 71–81. London: Routledge.

Elder, Catriona, Cath Ellis and Angela Pratt. 2004. 'Whiteness in Constructions of Australian Nationhood: Indigenes, Immigrants and Governmentality', in *Whitening Race: Essays in Social and Cultural Criticism*, ed. Aileen Moreton-Robinson, 208–21. Canberra: Aboriginal Studies Press/University of Canberra E-Reserve.

Elshtain, Jean Bethke. 1987. *Women and War*. New York: Basic Books.

Enloe, Cynthia. 1983. *Does Khaki Become You? The Militarisation of Women's Lives*. London: South End Press.

Enloe, Cynthia. 1993. *The Morning After: Sexual Politics at the End of the Cold War*. Berkeley: University of California Press.

Enloe, Cynthia. 2000. *Manoeuvres: The International Politics of Militarizing Women's Lives*. Berkeley: University of California Press.

Enloe, Cynthia. 2004. *The Curious Feminist: Searching for Women in a New Age of Empire*. Berkeley: University of California Press.

Enloe, Cynthia. 2007. *Globalization and Militarism: Feminists Make the Link*. Lanham, MD: Rowman & Littlefield.

Eriksson Baaz, Maria and Judith Verweijen. 2018. 'Confronting the Colonial: The (Re)production of "African" Exceptionalism in Critical Security and Military Studies', *Security Dialogue* 49(1/2): 57–69.

Evans, Julie. 2009. 'Where Lawlessness is Law: The Settler-Colonial Frontier as a Legal Space of Violence', *Australian Feminist Law Journal* 30(1): 3–22.

Evans, Raymond and Bill Thorpe. 1998. 'Commanding Men: Masculinities and the Convict System', in *Australian Masculinities: Men and Their Histories*, eds Clive Moore and Kay Saunders, 17–34. Brisbane: University of Queensland Press.

Eveline, Joan. 2001. 'Feminism, Racism and Citizenship in the Twentieth-Century Australia', in *Women as Australian Citizens: Underlying Histories*, eds Patricia Crawford and Philippa Madden, 141–77. Carlton South: Melbourne University Press.

Farrell, Rita. 2001. 'Women and Citizenship in Colonial Australia', in *Women as Australian Citizens: Underlying Histories*, eds Patricia Crawford and Philippa Maddern, 115–40. Carlton South: Melbourne University Press.

Fassin, Didier and Richard Rechtman. 2009. *The Empire of Trauma: An Inquiry into the Condition of Victimhood*, trans. Rachel Gomme. Princeton: Princeton University Press.

Fewster, Kevin. 1982. 'Ellis Ashmead Bartlett and the Making of the Anzac Legend', *Journal of Australian Studies* 6(10): 17–30.

Finch, Lyn. 1995. 'Consuming Passion: Romance and Consumerism during World War II', in *Gender and War: Australians at War in the Twentieth Century*, eds Joy Damousi and Marilyn Lake, 105–16. Cambridge: Cambridge University Press.

Foley, Gary, Andrew Schaap and Edwina Howell. eds. 2014. *The Aboriginal Tent Embassy: Sovereignty, Black Power, Land Rights and the State*. Abingdon: Routledge.

Ford, Ruth. 1995. '"Lesbians and Loose Women": Female Sexuality and the Women's Services during World War II', in *Gender and War: Australians at War in the Twentieth Century*, eds Joy Damousi and Marilyn Lake, 81–104. Cambridge: Cambridge University Press.

Foucault, Michel. 1975. *Discipline and Punish*, trans. Alan Sheridan. New York: Penguin.

Foucault, Michel. 1991. 'Governamentality', in *The Foucault Effect: Studies in Governamentality*, eds Graham Burchell, Colin Gordon and Peter Miller. Chicago: University of Chicago Press.

Frame, Tom. ed. 2016a. *Anzac Day: Then & Now*. Sydney: University of New South Wales Press.

Frame, Tom. 2016b. 'Anzac Day: Controversy and Criticism', in *Anzac Day: Then and Now*, 1–14, ed. Tom Frame. Sydney: University of New South Wales Press.

Frame, Tom. 2016c. 'Anzac Hymns: Ancient or Modern?' in *Anzac Day: Then and Now*, 97–104, ed. Tom Frame. Sydney: University of New South Wales Press.

Fraser, Nancy and Axel Honneth. 2003. *Redistribution or Recognition? A Political Philosophical Exchange*, trans. Joel Golb, James Ingram and Christiane Wilke. London: Verso.

Fry, Gavin. 2003. "Ivor Hele (1912–1993)', in *Artists in Action: From the Collection of the Australian War Memorial*, ed. Lola Wilkins, 122–3. Portside Business Park: Australian War Memorial.

Fullenwieder, Lara. 2017. 'Framing Indigenous Self-Recognition: The Visual and Cultural Work of the Politics of Recognition', *Postcolonial Studies* 20(1): 34–50.

Furniss, Elizabeth. 2001. 'Timeline History and the Anzac Myth: Settler Narratives of Local History in a North Australian Town', *Oceania* 71(4): 279–97.

Furphy, Samuel. 2018. 'The Home Front in the First World War', in *Serving Our Country: Indigenous Australians, War, Defence and Citizenship*, eds Joan Beaumont and Allison Cadzow, 94–112. Sydney: NewSouth Publishing.

Gammage, Bill. 2016. 'Anzac Day's Early Rituals', in *Beyond Gallipoli, New Perspectives on Anzac*, eds Raelene Frances and Bruce Scates, 244–260. Clayton: Monash University Press.

Gani, Jasmine K. 2021. 'Racial Militarism and Civilizational Anxiety at the Imperial Encounter: From Metropole to the Postcolonial State', *Security Dialogue* 52(6): 546–66.

Garton, Stephen. 2008. '"Fit Only for the Scrap Heap": Rebuilding Returned Soldier Manhood in Australia after 1945', *Gender and History* 20(1): 48–67.

Geyer, Michael. 1989. 'The Militarization of Europe, 1914–1945', in *The Militarization of the Western World*, ed. John Gillis, 65–103. New Brunswick, NJ: Rutgers University Press.

Gilfedder, Deirdre. 2021. '"A Strange, New Race": Eugenics and the Australian Soldier in the First World War;, in *Commemorating Race and Empire in the First World War Centenary*, eds Ben Wellings and Shanti Sumartojo, 93–106. Liverpool: Liverpool University Press.

Gillis, John (ed.). 1989. *The Militarization of the Western World*. New Brunswick, NJ: Rutgers University Press.

Ginio, Ruth. 2017. *The French Army and Its African Soldiers: The Years of Decolonization*. Lincoln: University of Nebraska Press.

Goldstein, Joshua S. 2001. *War and Gender: How Gender Shapes the War System and Vice Versa*. Cambridge: Cambridge University Press.

González, Roberto J., Hugh Gusterson and Gustaaf Houtman. eds. 2019. *Militarization: A Reader*. Durham, NC: Duke University Press.

Gonzalez, Vernadette Vicuña. 2013. *Securing Paradise: Tourism and Militarism in Hawai'i and the Philippines*. Durham, NC: Duke University Press.

Gower, Steve. 2019. *The Australian War Memorial: A Century from the Vision*. Mile End: Wakefield Press.

Graham, Mary. 1999. 'Some Thoughts about the Philosophical Underpinnings of Aboriginal Worldviews', *Worldviews: Environment, Culture, Religion 3* 3(2): 105–18.

Grant, Lachlan and Michael Bell. 2018. *For Country, For Nation: An Illustrated History of Aboriginal and Torres Strait Islander Military Service*, eds Lachlan Grant and Michael Bell, 11–20. Canberra: Australian War Memorial.

Gray, Geoffrey. 2018. 'Labour and Surveillance in Northern Australia, 1939–45', in *Serving Our Country: Indigenous Australians, War, Defence and Citizenship*, eds Allison Cadzow and Joan Beaumont, 106–17. Sydney: NewSouth Publishing.

Grayzel, Susan. 2002. *Women and the First World War*. London: Longman Pearson Education.

Green, Charles, Lyndell Brown and Jon Cattapan. 2015. 'The Obscure Dimensions of Conflict: Three Contemporary War Artists Speak', *Journal of War & Culture Studies* 8(2): 158–74.

Hall, Robert A. 1997. *The Black Diggers: Aborigines and Torres Strait Islanders in the Second World War*, 2nd edn. Canberra: Aboriginal Studies Press.

Hansen, Lene. 2011. 'Theorizing the Image for Security Studies: Visual Securitization and the Muhammad Cartoon Crisis', *European Journal of International Relations* 17(1): 51–74.

Hansen, Lene. 2015. 'How Images Make World Politics: International Icons and the Case of Abu Ghraib', *Review of International Studies* 41(2): 263–88.

Haskins, Victoria. 2017. 'The Girl Who Wanted to Go to War: Female Patriotism and Gender Construction in Australia's Great War', *History Australia* 14(2): 169–86.

Hellyer, Marcus and Ben Stevens. 2022. 'The Cost of Defence: ASPI Defence Budget Brief 2022–23', *ASPI*, available at: https://www.aspi.org.au/report/cost-defence-aspi-defence-budget-brief-2022-2023#:~:text=This year%2C the consolidated defence,substantial nominal growth of 7.4%25.

Henry, Marsha. 2017. 'Problematizing Military Masculinity, Intersectionality and Male Vulnerability in Feminist Critical Military Studies', *Critical Military Studies* 3(2): 182–99.

Higate, Paul. 2012. 'Martial Races and Enforcement Masculinities of the Global South: Weaponising Fijian, Chilean, and Salvadoran Postcoloniality in the Mercenary Sector', *Globalizations* 9(1): 35–52.

Hobsbawn, Eric. 1983. 'Introduction: Inventing Traditions', in *The Invention of Tradition*, eds Eric Hobsbawn and Terence Ranger, 1–14. Cambridge: Cambridge University Press.

Hobson, John M. 2012. *The Eurocentric Conception of World Politics: Western International Theory, 1760–2010*. Cambridge: Cambridge University Press.

Holbrook, Carolyn. 2014. *Anzac: The Unauthorised Biography*. Sydney: NewSouth Publishing.

Holbrook, Carolyn. 2016. 'Commemorators-in-Chief', in *Anzac Day Then and Now*, ed. Tom R. Frame, 214–31. Sydney: University of New South Wales Press.

Holbrook, Carolyn. 2018. 'Adaptable Anzac: Past, Present and Future', in *The Honest History Book*, eds David H. Stephens and Alison Broinowski, 40–7. Sydney: NewSouth Publishing.

Holmes, Katie. 1995. 'Day Mothers Night Sisters: World War I Nurses and Sexuality', in *Gender and War: Australians at War in the Twentieth Century*, eds Joy Damousi and Marilyn Lake, 43–59. Cambridge: Cambridge University Press.

Honneth, Axel. 1995. *The Struggle for Recognition: The Moral Grammar of Social Conflicts*, trans. Joel Anderson. Cambridge, MA: MIT Press.

Horton, Patrick. 2022. 'Carceral Spectres: Hyperincarceration and the Haunting of Aboriginal Life', *Australian Journal of Anthropology* 33(S1): 35–45.

Hoskins, Andrew and Ben O'Loughlin. 2010. *War and Media: The Emergence of Diffused War*. Cambridge: Polity Press.

Howard, Ann. 1990. *You'll Be Sorry: How World War II Changed Women's Lives*. Newport, NSW: Big Sky Publishing.

Howe, Adrian. 1995. 'Anzac Mythology and the Feminist Challenge', in *Gender and War: Australians at War in the Twentieth Century*, eds Joy Damousi and Marilyn Lake, 302–10. Cambridge: Cambridge University Press.

Howell, Alison. 2012. "The Demise of PTSD: From Governing through Trauma to Governing Resilience', *Alternatives: Global, Local, Political* 37(3): 214–26.

Howell, Alison. 2018. 'Forget "Militarization": Race, Disability and the "Martial Politics" of the Police and of the University', *International Feminist Journal of Politics* 20(2): 117–36.

Huggins, Jackie. 1994. 'A Contemporary View of Aboriginal Women's Relationship to the White Feminist Movement', in *Australian Women: Contemporary Feminist Thought*, eds Norma Grieve and Ailsa Burns, 70–9. Melbourne: Oxford University Press.

Hughes, Karen. 2017. 'Mobilising across Colour Lines: Intimate Encounters between Aboriginal Women and African American and Other Allied Servicemen on the World War II Australian Home Front', *Aboriginal History Journal* 41: 47–70.

Hutchison, Emma. 2016. *Affective Communities in World Politics: Collective Emotions After Trauma*. Cambridge: Cambridge University Press.

Hutchison, Margaret 2015. '"Accurate to the Point of Mania": Eyewitness Testimony and Memory Making in Australia's Official Paintings of the First World War', *Australian Historical Studies* 46(1): 27–44.

Hutchison, Margaret. 2018. *Painting War: A History of Australia's First World War Art Scheme*. Cambridge: Cambridge University Press.

Inglis, Ken S. 1979. 'Bean, Charles Edwin (1879–1968)', *Australian Dictionary of Biography*. Melbourne: Melbourne University Press, available at:https://adb.anu.edu.au/biography/bean-charles-edwin-5166.

Inglis, Ken S. 1985. 'A Sacred Place: The Making of the Australian War Memorial', *War and Society* 3(2): 99–126.

Inglis, Ken. 1987. 'Men, Women, and War Memorials: Anzac Australia', *Daedalus* 116(4): 35–59.

Inglis, Ken S. 1998. *Sacred Places: War Memorials in the Australian Landscape*. Melbourne: Melbourne University Press.

Inglis, Ken S. 2016. 'Reflecting on a Retrospective', in *Anzac Day Then and Now*, ed. Tom Frame, 17–30. Sydney: University of New South Wales Press.

Jester, Natalie. 2023. 'Making Martial Politics Palatable: Constructing Neoliberal Feminist Subjects in Arms Manufacturers' Social Media Feeds Making Martial Politics Palatable: Constructing', *International Feminist Journal of Politics* 25(2): 310–33.

Kaempf, Sebastian. 2013. 'The Mediatisation of War in a Transforming Global Media Landscape', *Australian Journal of International Affairs* 67(5): 1–19.

Kent, David A. 1985. 'The Anzac Book and the Anzac Legend: C. E. W. Bean as Editor and Image-Maker', *Australian Historical Studies* 21(84): 376–90.

Killingray, David. 1999. 'Guardians of Empire', in *Guardians of Empire: The Armed Forces of the Colonial Powers c. 1700–1964*, eds David Killingray and David E. Omissi, 1–24. Manchester: Manchester University Press.

Killingray, David and David Omissi. eds. 1999. *Guardians of Empire: The Armed Forces of the Colonial Powers c. 1700–1964*. Manchester: Manchester University Press.

Knapman, Gareth. 2016. 'Anzac: Celebration or Commemoration?' in *Anzac Day Then and Now*, ed. Tom Frame, 31–52. Sydney: University of New South Wales Press.

Lake, Marilyn. 1992. 'Mission Impossible: How Men Gave Birth to the Australian Nation –Nationalism, Gender and Other Seminal Acts', *Gender & History* 4(3): 305–22.

Lake, Marilyn. 1993. 'Colonised and Colonising: The White Australian Feminist Subject', *Women's History Review* 2(3): 377–86.

Lake, Marilyn. 1995. 'Female Desire: The Meaning of World War II', in *Gender and War: Australians at War in the Twentieth Century*, eds Joy Damousi and Marilyn Lake, 60–80. Cambridge: Cambridge University Press.

Lake, Marilyn. 1998a. 'Australian Frontier Feminism and the Marauding White Man', in *Gender and Imperialism*, ed, Clare Midgley, 123–36. Manchester: Manchester University Press.

Lake, Marilyn. 1998b. 'Feminism and the Gendered Politics of Antiracism, Australia 1927–1957: From Maternal Protectionism to Leftist Assimilationism', *Australian Historical Studies* 29(110): 91–108.

Lake, Marilyn. 1999. *Getting Equal: The History of Australian Feminism*. St Leonards: Allen & Unwin.

Lake, Marilyn. 1999a. 'Child Bearers as Rights-Bearers: Feminist Discourse on the Rights of Aboriginal and Non-Aboriginal Mothers in Australia, 1920–50', *Women's History Review* 8(2): 347–63.

Lake, Marilyn. 2003. 'On Being a White Man, Australian, circa 1900', in *Cultural History in Australia*, eds Teo Hsu-Ming and Richard White, 98–112. Sydney: University of New South Wales Press.

Lake, Marilyn. 2010a. 'How Do Schoolchildren Learn about the Spirit of Anazc?' in *What's Wrong with Anzac? The Militarisation of Australian History*, eds Marilyn Lake, Henry Reynolds, Mark

McKenna and Joy Damousi, 135–56. Sydney: University of New South Wales Press.

Lake, Marilyn. 2010b. 'What Have You Done for Your Country?' in *What's Wrong with Anzac? 2*, eds Marilyn Lake, Henry Reynolds, Mark McKenna and Joy Damousi, 1–23. Sydney: University of New South Wales Press.

Lake, Marilyn. 2020. 'The "White Man", Race, and Imperial War during the Long Nineteenth Century', in *The Oxford Handbook of Gender, War, and the Western World since 1600*, eds Karen Hagemann, Stefan Dudink and Sonya O. Rose, 328–46. Oxford: Oxford University Press.

Lake, Marilyn and Joy Damousi. 1995. 'Introduction: Warfare, History and Gender', in *Gender and War: Australians at War in the Twentieth Century*, eds Joy Damousi and Marilyn Lake, 1–20. Cambridge: Cambridge University Press.

Lake, Marilyn and Carina Donaldson. 2010. 'Whatever Happened to the Anti-War Movement?' in *What's Wrong with Anzac? The Militarisation of Australian History*, eds Marilyn Lake, Henry Reynolds, Joy Damousi and Mark McKenna, 85–108. Sydney: University of New South Wales Press.

Lake, Marilyn and Henry Reynolds. 2008. *Drawing the Global Colour Line*. Melbourne: Melbourne University Press.

Lake, Marilyn, Henry Reynolds, Mark McKenna and Joy Damousi (eds). 2010. *What's Wrong with ANZAC? The Militarisation of Australian History*. Sydney: University of New South Wales Press.

Lorde, Audre. 1983. 'The Master's Tools Will Never Dismantle the Master's House', in *This Bridge Called My Back: Writings by Radical Women of Color*, eds Cherrie Moraga and Gloria Anzaldua, 98–101, 2nd edn. Boston, MA: Persephone Press.

Lowe, David. 1995. 'Australia in the World', in *Australia's War 1914–18*, ed. Joan Beaumont, 162–86. London: Routledge.

Luckham, Robin. 1984. 'Of Arms and Culture', *Current Research on Peace and Violence* 7(1): 1–64.

Lugones, Maria. 2008. 'The Coloniality of Gender', *Worlds & Knowledges Otherwise* Spring: 1–17.

Luttwak, Edward N. 1995. 'Toward Post-Heroic Warfare', *Foreign Affairs* 74(3): 109–22.

Lutz, Catherine. 2002. 'Making War at Home in the United States: Militarization and the Current Crisis', *American Anthropologist* 104(3): 723–35.

Lydon, Jane. 2018. 'Colonial "Blind Spots": Images of Australian Frontier Conflict', *Journal of Australian Studies* 42(4): 409–27.

MacKenzie, Megan, Thomas Gregory, Nisha Shah, Tarak Barkawi, Toni Haastrup, Maya Eichler, Nicole Wegner and Alison Howell. 2019. 'Can We Really 'Forget' Militarization? A Conversation on Alison Howell's Martial Politics', *International Feminist Journal of Politics* 21(5): 816–36.

Maclean, Pam. 1995. 'War and Australian Society', in *Australia's War 1914–18*, ed. Joan Beaumont, 54–81. London: Routledge.

Macoun, Alissa. 2011. 'Aboriginality and the Northern Territory Intervention', *Australian Journal of Political Science* 46(3): 519–34.

Maddison, Sarah. 2017. 'Recognise What? The Limitations of Settler Colonial Constitutional Reform', *Australian Journal of Political Science* 52(1): 3–18.

Maddison, Sarah. 2019a. *The Colonial Fantasy: Why White Australia Can't Solve Black Problems*. Sydney: Allen & Unwin.

Maddison, Sarah. 2019b. 'The Limits of the Administration of Memory in Settler Colonial Societies: The Australian Case', *International Journal of Politics, Culture and Society* 32(2): 181–94

Maddison, Sarah and Sana Nakata. 2020. *Questioning Indigenous–Settler Relations: Interdisciplinary Perspectives*. Berlin: Springer.

Manchanda, Nivi. 2022. 'The Janus-Faced Nature of Militarization', *Critical Military Studies* 1–5. DOI: https://doi.org/10.1080/23337486.2021.2022852.

Mangan, J. A. 2012. *Manufactured Masculinity: Making Imperial Manliness, Morality and Militarism*. London: Routledge.

Mann, Michael. 1987. 'The Roots and Contradictions of Modem Militarism', *New Left Review* 162: 35–50.

Mann, Michael. 1993. *The Sources of Social Power, Vol. II: The Rise of Classes and Nation-States 1760–1914*. Cambridge: Cambridge University Press.

Marti, Steve. 2018. '"The Symbol of Our Nation": The Slouch Hat, the First World War, and Australian Identity', *Journal of Australian Studies* 42(1): 3–18.

Maynard, John. 2007. *Fight for Liberty and Freedom: The Origins of Australian Aboriginal Activism*. Canberra: Aboriginal Studies Press.

Maynard, John. 2018. 'The Rise of the Modern Aboriginal Political Movement, 1924–39', in *Serving Our Country: Indigenous Australians, War, Defence and Citizenship*, eds Joan Beaumont and Allison Cadzow, 113–34. Sydney: NewSouth Publishing.

Mcdonald, Matt. 2010. '"Lest We Forget": The Politics of Memory and Australian Military Intervention', *International Political Sociology* 4(3): 287–302.

McDonnell, Siobhan and Mick Dodson. 2018. 'Race, Citizenship, and Military Service', in *Serving Our Country: Indigenous Australians, War, Defence and Citizenship*, eds Joan Beaumont and Allison Cadzow, 23–52. Sydney: NewSouth Publishing.

McHugh, Siobhan. 1993. *Minefields and Miniskirts: Australian Women and the Vietnam War*. Sydney: Doubleday.

McKenna, Mark. 2010. 'Anzac Day: How Did It Become Australia's National Day', in *What's Wrong With Anzac?* eds Marilyn Lake, Henry Reynolds, Mark McKenna and Joy Damousi, 110–34. Sydney: University of New South Wales Press.

McKenna, Mark and Stuart Ward. 2007. '"It Was Really Moving, Mate": The Gallipoli Pilgrimage and Sentimental Nationalism in Australia', *Australian Historical Studies* 38(129): 141–51. https://doi.org/10.1080/10314610708601236.

McQuire, Amy. 2019. 'Black and White Witness', *Meanjin Quarterly*. 2019, available at: https://meanjin.com.au/essays/black-and-white-witness.

McWatters, Anthony. 2005. 'Australian Women and War', *Australian Defence Force Journal* 166: 34–48.

Medcalf, Rory. 2022. 'Why the Anzac Legend is not Enough for the 21st Century', *Financial Review*, 23 April, available at: https://www.afr.com/politics/federal/why-the-anzac-legend-is-not-enough-for-the-21st-century-20220421-p5af4n.

Midgley, Clare. 1998. *Gender and Imperialism*. Manchester: Manchester University Press

Midgley, Clare. 2007. *Feminism and Empire: Women Activists in Imperial Britain, 1790–1865*. Oxford: Routledge.

Millar, Katharine M. 2019. 'The Plural of Soldier is Not Troops: The Politics of Groups in Legitimating Militaristic Violence', *Security Dialogue* 50(3): 201–19.

Millar, Katharine M. 2021. 'What Makes Violence Martial? Adopt a Sniper and Normative Imaginaries of Violence in the Contemporary United States', *Security Dialogue* 52(6): 493–511.

Millar, Katharine M. 2022. *Support the Troops: Military Obligation, Gender, and the Making of Political Community*. Oxford: Oxford University Press.

Moon, Seungsook. 1997. *Sex Among Allies: Military Prostitution in US–Korea Relations*. New York: Columbia University Press.

Moore, Clive. 1998. 'Colonial Manhood and Masculinity', in *Australian Masculinities: Men and Their Histories*, eds Clive Moore and Kay Saunders, 35–50. Brisbane: University of Queensland Press.

Moreton-Robinson, Aileen. 2004. *Whitening Race: Essays in Social and Cultural Criticism*, ed. Aileen Moreton-Robinson. Canberra: Aboriginal Studies Press.

Moreton-Robinson, Aileen. 2007. *Sovereign Subjects: Indigenous Sovereignty Matters*, ed. Aileen Moreton-Robinson. Crows Nest: Allen & Unwin.

Moreton-Robinson, Aileen. 2015. *The White Possessive: Property, Power, and Indigenous Sovereignty*. Minneapolis: University of Minnesota.

Moreton-Robinson, Aileen. 2020. *Talkin' Up to the White Woman: Indigenous Women and Feminism*, ed. Aileen Moreton-Robinson. 2nd edn. Brisbane: University of Queensland Press.

Moses, John A. 2016. 'The Nation's Secular Requiem', in *Anzac Day: Then and Now*, ed. Tom Frame. 54–65. Sydney: University of New South Wales Press.

Mosse, George L. 1990. *Fallen Soldiers: Reshaping the Memory of the World Wars*. New York: Oxford University Press.

Murrie, Linzi. 1998. 'The Australian Legend: Writing Australian Masculinity/writing "Australian" Masculine', *Journal of Australian Studies* 22(56): 68–77.

Na'puti, Tiara R. and Sylvia C. Frain. 2023. 'Indigenous Environmental Perspectives: Challenging the Oceanic Security State', *Security Dialogue* 54(2): 115–36.

Nelson, Brendan. 2013. 'National Press Club Address 2013', *Australian War Memorial*, available at: https://www.awm.gov.au/commemoration/speeches/national-press-club-address.

Nettelbeck, Amanda and Lyndall Ryan. 2018. 'Salutary Lessons: Native Police and the "Civilising" Role of Legalised Violence in Colonial Australia', *Journal of Imperial and Commonwealth History* 46(1): 47–68.

Nettelbeck, Amanda and Russell Smandych. 2010. 'Policing Indigenous Peoples on Two Colonial Frontiers: Australia's Mounted Police and Canada's North-West Mounted Police', *Australian and New Zealand Journal of Criminology* 43(2): 356–75.

Nicoll, Fiona. 2001. *From Diggers to Drag Queens: Configurations of Australian National Identity*. Annandale: Pluto Press.

Nicoll, Fiona. 2014. 'War by Other Means: The Australian War Memorial and the Aboriginal Tent Embassy in National Space and Time', in *The Aboriginal Tent Embassy: Sovereignty, Black Power, Land Rights and the State*, eds Gary Foley, Andrew Schaap and Edwina Howell, 267–83. Abingdon: Routledge.

Oppenheimer, Melanie. 2010. 'The "Imperial" Girl: Lady Helen Munro Ferguson, the Imperial Woman and Her Imperial Childhood', *Journal of Australian Studies* 34(4): 513–25.

Oppenheimer, Melanie. 2016. 'Red Crossing for War: Responses of Imperial Feminism and the Australian Red Cross during the Great War', in *Australia and the Great War: Identity, Memory and Mythology*, eds Michael Jk Walsh and Andrekos Varnava, 26–35. Melbourne: Melbourne University Press.

Parashar, Swati. 2018a. 'Discursive (In)securities and Postcolonial Anxiety: Enabling Excessive Militarism in India', *Security Dialogue* 49(1/2): 123–35.

Parashar, Swati. 2018b. 'The WPS Agenda: A Postcolonial Critique', *The Oxford Handbook of Women, Peace, and Security* June: 829–39.

Pastor-Elsegood, Jaya. 2021. 'The Two-Way Benefits of the Regional Force Surveillance Group: Building National Resilience from the Ground Up', available at: https://www.nisr.org.au/article/the-two-way-benefits-of-the-regional-force-surveillance-group-building-national-resilience-from-the-ground-up, last accessed 18 October 2022.

Pedersen, Peter. 2014. *ANZAC Treasures: The Gallipoli Collection of the Australian War Memorial*. Crows Nest: Murdoch Books.

Percy, Sarah A. 2007. *Mercenaries: The History of a Norm in International Relations*. Oxford: Oxford University Press.

Peterson, V. Spike. 1992. *Gendered States: Feminist (Re)Visions of International Relations Theory*. Boulder, CO: Lynne Rienner.

Posen, Barry R. 1993. 'Nationalism, the Mass Army, and Military Power', *International Security* 18(2): 80–124.

Povinelli, Elizabeth A. 2002. *The Cunning of Recognition: Indigenous Alterities and the Making of Australian Multiculturalism*. Durham, NC: Duke University Press.

Poyer, Lin. 2022. *War at the Margins: Indigenous Experiences in World War II*. Honolulu: University of Hawai'i Press.

Price, Megan. 2021. 'Australia is Building a Billion-Dollar Arms Export Industry: This is How Weapons Can Fall in the Wrong Hands', *The Conversation*, available at: https://theconversation.com/australia-is-building-a-billion-dollar-arms-export-industry-this-is-how-weapons-can-fall-in-the-wrong-hands-159817.

Puar, Jasbir K. 2017. *Terrorist Assemblages: Homonationalism in Queer Times*, 2nd edn. Durham, NC: Duke University Press.

Radford, Gail. 2019. 'Women Against Rape', *Canberra Museum and Gallery*, available at: http://www.cmag.com.au/blog/women-against-rape-in-war#_ftnref16.

Rancière, Jacques. 2004. *The Politics of Aesthetics: The Distribution of the Sensible*. New York: Continuum.

Rashid, Maria. 2020. *Dying to Serve. Militarism Affect and the Politics of Sacrifice in the Pakistan Army*. Stanford: Stanford University Press.

Reynolds, Henry. 1981. *The Other Side of the Frontier: Aboriginal Resistance to the European Invasion of Australia*. Sydney: University of New South Wales Press.

Reynolds, Henry. 2000. *Why Weren't We Told? A Personal Search for the Truth about Our History*. London: Penguin.

Reynolds, Henry. 2010. 'Are Nations Really Made in War?' in *What's Wrong With Anzac?* eds Marilyn Lake, Henry Reynolds, Mark McKenna and Joy Damousi, 36–57. Sydney: University of New South Wales Press.

Reynolds, Henry. 2013. *Forgotten Wars*. Sydney: NewSouth Publishing.

Richards, Jonathan. 2008. *The Secret War: The True Story of Queensland's Native Police*. St Lucia: Queensland University Press.

Rickard, John. 1998. 'Lovable Larrikins and the Awful Ockers', in *Australian Masculinities: Men and Their Histories*, eds Clive Moore and Kay Saunders, 78–85. Brisbane: University of Queensland Press.

Rickard, Jolene. 2011. 'Visualizing Sovereignty in the Time of Biometric Sensors', *South Atlantic Quarterly* 110(2): 465–86.

Riseman, Noah. 2007. 'Defending Whose Country? Yolngu and the Northern Territory Special Reconnaissance Unit in the Second World War', *LIMINA: A Journal of Historical and Cultural Studies* 13: 80–91.

Riseman, Noah. 2012. *Defending Whose Country? Indigenous Soldiers in the Pacific War*. Lincoln: University of Nebraska Press.

Riseman, Noah. 2014. 'Aboriginal Military Service and Assimilation', *Aboriginal History* 38: 155–78.

Riseman, Noah. 2015. 'Escaping Assimilation's Grasp: Aboriginal Women in the Australian Women's Military Services', *Women's History Review* 24(5): 757–75.

Riseman, Noah. 2017. 'Evolving Commemorations of Aboriginal and Torres Strait Islander Military Service', *Wicazo Sa Review* 32(1): 80–101.

Riseman, Noah. 2018a. 'Ex-Service Activism after 1945', in *Serving Our Country: Indigenous Australians, War, Defence and Citizenship*, eds Joan Beaumont and Allison Cadzow, 161–81. Sydney: NewSouth Publishing.

Riseman, Noah. 2018b. 'Opening the Military Door, 1945–65', in *Serving Our Country: Indigenous Australians, War, Defence and Citizenship*, eds Joan Beaumont and Allison Cadzow, 196–214. Sydney: NewSouth Publishing.

Riseman, Noah and Richard Trembath. 2016. *Defending Country: Aboriginal and Torres Strait Islander Military Service since 1945*. Brisbane: University of Queensland Press.

Robbins, Jane. 2007. 'The Howard Government and Indigenous Rights: An Imposed National Unity?' *Australian Journal of Political Science* 42(2): 315–28.

Robson, Lloyd. 1988. 'The Australian Soldier: Formation of a Stereotype', in *Australia: Two Centuries of War and Peace*, eds Michael Mckenna and M. Browne, 313–37. Canberra: Australian War Memorial.

Rogers, Thomas James. 2018. 'From the Frontier to the Veldt: Indigenous Australia Service (1788–1901)', in *For Country, For Nation*, eds Lachlan Grant and Michael Bell, 29–40. Canberra: Australian War Memorial.

Rose, Gillian. 2012. *Visual Methodologies: An Introduction to Researching With Visual Materials*, 3rd edn. Thousand Oaks, CA: SAGE.

Ross, Andrew L. 1987. 'Dimensions of Militarization in the Third World', *Armed Forces & Society* 13(4): 561–78.

Rossdale, Chris. 2019. *Resisting Militarism: Direct Action and the Politics of Subversion*. Edinburgh: Edinburgh University Press.

Rutherford, Dianne. 2014. 'The Australian Imperial Force (AIF): Headwear 1914–1918', *AWM*, available at: https://www.awm.gov.au/articles/blog/australian-imperial-force-aif-headwear-1914-1918.

Ryan, Lyndall. 2013. 'Untangling Aboriginal Resistance and the Settler Punitive Expedition: The Hawkesbury River Frontier in New South Wales, 1794–1810', *Journal of Genocide Research* 15(2): 219–32

Sabaratnam, Meera. 2023. 'Bring up the Bodies: International Order, Empire, and Re-Thinking the Great War (1914–1918) from Below', *European Journal of International Relations* 59(11): 1–23.

Said, Edward W. 1995. *Orientalism: Western Conceptions of the Orient*. London: Penguin.

Scarlett, Philippa. 2011. *Aboriginal and Torres Strait Islander Volunteers for the AIF: The Indigenous Response to World War One*. Macquarie: Indigenous Histories.

Scarlett, Philippa. 2015. 'Aboriginal Service in the First World War: Identity, Recognition and the Problem of Mateship', *Aboriginal History Journal* 39: 163–82.

Scates, Bruce. 2001. 'The Unknown Sock Knitter: Voluntary Work, Emotional Labour, Bereavement and the Great War', *Labour History* 81: 29–49.

Scates, Bruce. 2006. *Return to Gallipoli: Walking the Battlefields of the Great War*. Cambridge: Cambridge University Press.

Schneid, Frederick C. 2009. 'Introduction', in *Conscription in the Napoleonic Era: A Revolution in Military Affairs?* eds Donald Stoker, Frederick C. Schneid and Harold D. Blanton, 1–5. Abingdon: Routledge.

Seal, Graham. 2004. *Inventing Anzac: The Digger and National Mythology.* St. Lucia: University of Queensland Press.

Shaw, Martin. 1988. *Dialectics of War: An Essay in the Social Theory of Total War and Peace.* London: Pluto Press.

Sheffield, R. Scott. 2017. 'Indigenous Exceptionalism Under Fire: Assessing Indigenous Soldiers in Combat with the Australian, Canadian, New Zealand and American Armies During the Second World War', *Journal of Imperial and Commonwealth History* 45(3): 506–24.

Sheffield, R. Scott and Noah Riseman. 2019. *Indigenous Peoples and the Second World War: The Politics, Experiences and Legacies of War in the US, Canada, Australia and New Zealand.* Cambridge: Cambridge University Press.

Shepherd, Laura J. 2006. 'Veiled References: Constructions of Gender in the Bush Administration Discourse on the Attacks on Afghanistan Post-9/11', *International Feminist Journal of Politics* 8(1): 19–41.

Sheridan, Susan. 2002. *Who Was That Woman? The Australian Women's Weekly in the Post-war Years.* Sydney: University of New South Wales Press.

Shigematsu, Setsu and Keith L. Camacho. eds, 2010. *Militarized Currents: Towards a Decolonized Future in Asia and the Pacific.* Minneapolis: University of Minnesota.

Short, Damien. 2008. *Reconciliation and Colonial Power: Indigenous Rights in Australia.* Aldershot: Ashgate.

Shute, Carmel. 1995. 'Heroines and Heroes: Sexual Mythology in Australia 1914–18', in *Gender and War: Australians at War in the Twentieth Century*, eds Joy Damousi and Marilyn Lake, 23–42. Cambridge: Cambridge University Press.

Simpson, Audra. 2014. *Mohawk Interruptus: Political Life Across the Borders of Settler States.* Durham, NC: Duke University Press.

Sjoberg, Laura and Sandra Via (eds). 2010. *Gender, War, and Militarism: Feminist Perspectives.* Santa Barbara, CA: Praeger.

Smart, Judith. 2000. 'Modernity and Mother-Heartedness: Spirituality and Religious Meaning in Australian Women's Suffrage and Citizenship Movements, 1890s–1920s', in *Women's Suffrage in the British Empire: Citizenship, Nation and Race*, eds Ian Christopher Fletcher, Philippa Levine and Laura E. Nym, 51–67. London: Taylor & Francis.

Snyder, Claire R. 2003. 'The Citizen-Soldier Tradition and Gender Integration of the U.S. Military', *Armed Forces & Society* 29(2): 185–204.

Sontag, Susan. 2004. *Regarding the Pain of Others*. London: Penguin.

Spearim, Boe. 2020. 'Frontier War Stories', available at: https://boespearim.podbean.com.

Speck, Catherine. 2004. *Painting Ghosts: Australian Women Artists in Wartime*. Melbourne: Craftsman House.

Speck, Catherine. 2009. 'The Australian War Museum, Women Artists and the National Memory of the First World War', in *When the Soldiers Return: November 2007 Conference Proceedings*, ed. Martin Crotty, 277–90. Brisbane: School of History, Philosophy, Religion and Classics, University of Queensland.

Speck, Catherine. 2019. 'Women, Art and Wartime Industries: A Feminist Inter/Modern Analysis', *Australian Feminist Studies* 34(101): 295–308.

Stahl, Roger. 2009. 'Why We "Support the Troops": Rhetorical Evolutions', *Rhetoric and Public Affairs* 12(4): 533–70.

Stanley, Peter. 1988. 'Soldiers and Fellow-Countrymen in Colonial Australia', in *Australia: Two Centuries of War and Peace*, 65–91. Canberra: Australian War Memorial.

Stanley, Peter. 2017. *Charles Bean: Man, Myth, Legacy*. Sydney: University of New South Wales Press.

Stanner, W. E. H. 2009. *The Dreaming and Other Essays*. Collingwood, VIC: Black Inc.

Stasiulis, Daiva and Nira Yuval-Davis. 1995. 'Introduction: Beyond Dichotomies – Gender, Race, Ethnicity and Class in Settler Societies', in *Unsettling Settler Societies: Articulations of Gender, Race, Ethnicity and Class*, eds Daiva Stasiulis and Nira Yuval-Davis, 1–38. London: Sage.

Stavrianakis, Anna and Jan Selby. 2013. 'Militarism and International Relations in the Twenty-First Century', in *Militarism and International Relations: Political Economy, Security, Theory*, eds Anna Stavrianakis and Jan Selby, 21–36. Oxford: Routledge.

Steering Committee for the Review of Government Service Provisions (SCRGSP). (2020). *Overcoming Indigenous Disadvantage 2020*, available at: https://apo.org.au/sites/default/files/resource-files/2020-12/apo-nid309865.pdf.

Strakosch, Elizabeth. 2015. *Neoliberal Indigenous Policy: Settler Colonialism and the 'Post-Welfare' State*. New York: Palgrave Macmillan.

Strakosch, Elizabeth. 2019. 'The Technical is Political: Settler Colonialism and the Australian Indigenous Policy System', *Australian Journal of Political Science* 54(1): 114–30.

Strakosch, Elizabeth and Alissa Macoun. 2012. 'The Vanishing End-point of Settler Colonialism', *Arena Journal* 29(37/38): 40–85.

Streets, Heather. 2017. *Martial Races: The Military, Race and Masculinity in British Imperial Culture, 1857–1914*, 2nd edn. Manchester: Manchester University Press.

Sumartojo, Shanti and Ben Wellings. eds. 2014. *Nation, Memory and Great War Commemoration: Mobilizing the Past in Europe, Australia and New Zealand*. Oxford: Peter Lang.

Sumartojo, Shanti and Ben Wellings. 2021. 'Anzac, Race and Empire Memorialising Soldiers and Warriors in Australia', in *Commemorating Race and Empire in the First World War Centenary*, eds Shanti Sumartojo and Ben Wellings, 168–86. Liverpool: Liverpool University Press

Swain, Shurlee, Patricia Grimshaw and Ellen Warne. 2009. 'Whiteness, Maternal Feminism and the Working Mother, 1900–1960', in *Creating White Australia*, eds Jane Carey and Claire McLisky, 214–29. Sydney: Sydney University Press.

Syron, Liza-Mare. 2015. '"Addressing a Great Silence": Black Diggers and the Aboriginal Experience of War', *New Theatre Quarterly* 31(3): 223–31.

Taylor, Charles. 1994. *The Politics of Recognition*, ed. Amy Gutmann. Princeton, NJ: Princeton University Press.

Teaiwa, Teresia K. 2008a. 'Globalizing and Gendered Forces: The Contemporary Militarization of Pacific/Oceania', in *Gender and Globalization in Asian and the Pacific: Method, Practice, Theory*, eds Monique Mironesco and Kathy E. Ferguson, 318–32. Honolulu: Hawai'i Press.

Teaiwa, Teresia. 2008b. 'Security Disarmed On Women and "Indians": The Politics of Inclusion and Exclusion in Militarized Fij', in *Security Disarmed: Critical Perspectives on Gender, Race, and Militarization*, eds Sandra Morgen, Barbara Sutton and Julie Novkov, 111–35. New Brunswick, NJ: Rutgers University Press.

Tello, Verónica. 2019. 'Counter-Memory and And–and: Aesthetics and Temporalities for Living Together', *Memory Studies* 1–12.

Thomson, Janice E. 1990. 'State Practices, International Norms, and the Decline of Mercenarism', *International Studies Quarterly* 34(1): 23–47.

Tilly, Charles. 1992. *Coercion, Capital, and European States, AD 990–1992*. Oxford: Blackwell.

Tong, Karen. 2023. 'What are Aboriginal People Saying about the Voice to Parliament?' *ABC News*, 1 February, available at: https://www.abc.net.au/news/2023-02-01/what-are-aboriginal-people-saying-about-the-voice-to-parliament/101912918.

Travers, Richard. 2017. *To Paint a War: The Lives of the Australian Artists Who Painted the Great War, 1914–18*. Melbourne: Thames & Hudson.

Tuck, Eve and K Wayne Yang. 2012. 'Decolonization is Not a Metaphor', *Decolonization: Indigeneity, Education & Society* 1(1): 1–40.

Tuhiwai Smith, Linda. 2012. *Decolonizing Methodologies: Research and Indigenous Peoples*. London: Zed Books.

Twomey, Christina. 2013. 'Trauma and the Reinvigoration of Anzac: An Argument', *History Australia* 10(3): 85–108.

UN Human Rights Council. 2023. *Impact of Militarization on the Rights of Indigenous Peoples*, draft study by the Expert Mechanism on the Rights of Indigenous Peoples, available at: https://undocs.org/Home/Mobile?FinalSymbol=A%2FHRC%2FEMRIP%2F2023%2F2&Language=E&DeviceType=Desktop&LangRequested=False.

Ure, Michael and Mervyn Frost. 2014. 'Introduction', in *The Politics of Compassion*, eds Michael Ure and Mervyn Frost, 1–18. Abingdon Routledge.

Veracini, Lorenzo. 2015. *The Settler Colonial Present*. London: Palgrave

Walsh, Gerald. 1988. 'The Military and the Development of the Australian Colonies 1788–1888', in *Australia: Two Centuries of War and Peace*, eds M. McKernan and M. Browne, 43–64. Canberra: Australian War Memorial.

Ward, Stuart. 2008. 'Security: Defending Australia's Empire', in *Australia's Empire*, eds Deryck Schreuder and Stuart Ward, 232–58. Oxford: Oxford University Press.

Watego, Chelsea. 2021. *Another Day in the Colony*. Brisbane: University of Queensland Press.

Watson, Irene. 2007. 'Settled and Unsettled Spaces: Are We Free to Roam?' in *Sovereign Subjects: Indigenous Sovereignty Matters*, ed. Aileen Moreton-Robinson, 15–32. Crows Nest: Allen & Unwin.

Welland, Julia. 2015. 'Compassionate Soldiering and Comfort', in *Emotions, Politics and War*, eds Linda Åhäll and Thomas Gregory. London: Routledge.

Wellings, Ben and Shanti Sumartojo. eds. 2021. *Commemorating Race and Empire in the First World War Centenary*. Liverpool: Liverpool University Press.

West, Brad. ed. 2017. *War Memory and Commemoration*. Abingdon: Routledge.

White, Richard. 1981. *Inventing Australia: Images and Identity 1688–1980*. Sydney: Allen & Unwin.

White, Richard. 1988. 'War and Australian Society', in *Australia: Two Centuries of War and Peace*, eds M. McKernan and M. Browne, 391–7. Canberra: Australian War Memorial.

Wibben, Annick T. R. 2011. *Feminist Security Studies : A Narrative Approach*. New York: Routledge.

WILPF. 2021. 'Militarisation in Australia: Normalisation and Mythology', available at: https://doi.org/10.1007/978-3-030-11795-5_103-1.

Wilson, Kathleen. 2004. 'Empire, Gender, and Modernity in the Eighteenth Century', in *Gender and Empire*, ed. Philippa Levine, 14–45. Oxford: Oxford University Press.

Winter, Jay. 2006. *Remembering War: The Great War between Memory and History in the Twentieth Century*. New Haven, CT: Yale University Press.

Winter, Jay. 2017. *War beyond Words: Languages of Remembrance from the Great War to the Present*. Cambridge: Cambridge University Press.

Winter, Jay and Emmanuel Sivan. 1999. 'Setting the Framework', in *War and Remembrance in the Twentieth Century*, eds Jay Murray Winter and Emmanuel Sivan, 6–39. Cambridge: Cambridge University Press.

Wolfe, Patrick. 1994. 'Nation and MiscegeNation: Discursive Continuity in the Post-Mabo Era', *Social Analysis: International Journal of Anthropology* 36(36): 93–152.

Wolfe, Patrick. 1998. *Settler Colonialism: The Politics and Poetics of an Ethnographic Event*. London: Cassell.

Wolfe, Patrick. 2006. 'Settler Colonialism and the Elimination of the Native', *Journal of Genocide Research* 8(4): 387–409.

Wolpin, Miles D. 1981. *Militarism and Social Evolution in the Third World*. Totowa, NJ: Allanheld, Osmun.

Wool, Zoë H. 2015. 'Critical Military Studies, Queer Theory, and the Possibilities of Critique: The Case of Suicide and Family Caregiving in the US Military', *Critical Military Studies* 1(1): 23–37.

Woollacott, Angela. 2000. 'Australian Women's Metropolitan Activism from Suffrage, to Imperial Vanguard, to Commonwealth Feminism', in *Women's Suffrage in the British Empire: Citizenship, Nation and Race*, eds Ian Christopher Fletcher, Philippa Levine and Laura E. Nym, 207–23. Abingdon: Routledge.

Woollacott, Angela. 2006. *Gender and Empire*. New York: Palgrave Macmillan.

Woollacott, Angela. 2009. 'Frontier Violence and Settler Manhood', *History Australia* 6(1): 11.1–15.

Woollacott, Angela. 2010. 'Gender and Sexuality', in *Australia's Empire*, eds Deryck Schreuder and Stuart Ward, 312–35. Oxford: Oxford University Press.

Woollacott, Angela. 2013. 'Manly Authority, Employing Non-White Labour, and Frontier Violence 1830s–1860s, *Journal of Australian Colonial History* 15: 23–42.

Woollacott, Angela. 2015. *Settler Society in the Australian Colonies: Self-Government and Imperial Culture.* Oxford: Oxford University Press.

Wright, Christine. 2011. *Wellington's Men in Australia: Peninsular War Veterans and the Making of Empire c. 1820–40.* London: Palgrave Macmillan.

Yuval-Davis, Nira. 1997. *Gender and Nation.* London: Sage.

INDEX

EU representative:
Easy Access System Europe
Mustamäe tee 50, 10621 Tallinn, Estonia
Gpsr.requests@easproject.com

www.ingramcontent.com/pod-product-compliance
Lightning Source LLC
Chambersburg PA
CBHW050648270326
41927CB00012B/2924